Bluestockings

The Remarkable Story of the
First Women to Fight for an Education

JANE ROBINSON

PENGUIN BOOKS

PENGUIN BOOKS

Published by the Penguin Group
Penguin Books Ltd, 80 Strand, London WC2R ORL, England
Penguin Group (USA) Inc., 375 Hudson Street, New York, New York 10014, USA
Penguin Group (Canada), 90 Eglinton Avenue East, Suite 700, Toronto, Ontario, Canada M4P 2Y3
(a division of Pearson Penguin Canada Inc.)
Penguin Ireland, 25 St Stephen's Green, Dublin 2, Ireland (a division of Penguin Books Ltd)
Penguin Group (Australia), 250 Camberwell Road,
Camberwell, Victoria 3124, Australia (a division of Pearson Australia Group Pty Ltd)
Penguin Books India Pvt Ltd, 11 Community Centre, Panchsheel Park, New Delhi – 110 017, India
Penguin Group (NZ), 67 Apollo Drive, Rosedale, North Shore 0632, New Zealand
(a division of Pearson New Zealand Ltd)
Penguin Books (South Africa) (Pty) Ltd, 24 Sturdee Avenue, Rosebank, Johannesburg 2196, South Africa

Penguin Books Ltd, Registered Offices: 80 Strand, London WC2R ORL, England

www.penguin.com

First published by Viking 2009
Published in Penguin Books 2010

3

Copyright © Jane Robinson, 2009
All rights reserved

The moral right of the author has been asserted

Typeset by Palimpsest Book Production Limited, Grangemouth, Stirlingshire
Printed in England by Clays Ltd, St Ives plc

ISBN: 978-0-141-02971-9

www.greenpenguin.co.uk

Penguin Books is committed to a sustainable future
for our business, our readers and our planet.
The book in your hands is made from paper
certified by the Forest Stewardship Council.

For Mollie Haigh,
an inspirational lady

Contents

List of Illustrations

Illustrations in the Text

Chronology

Landmark Dates in the History of Higher Education for Women in England

1096 The earliest record of Oxford as a centre of teaching and learning. It is the first university in the English-speaking world.

1209 The University of Cambridge is (one could argue) indirectly founded by an Oxford woman, when scholars are banished from Oxford for her manslaughter, and decide to settle by the Cam.

1673 Bathsua Makin publishes *An Essay to Revive the Antient Education of Gentlewomen.*

1694/7 Mary Astell's *A Serious Proposal to the Ladies* appears, suggesting a type of university education for women.

1750s–70s The heyday of the original Bluestockings, led by Elizabeth Montagu: mostly women, meeting in one another's houses to discuss literature, philosophy, art, and intellectual discourse.

1792 Mary Wollstonecraft's *Vindication of the Rights of Woman* is published.

1826 The founding of University College, London (originally known as London University).

1829 The Governesses' Mutual Assurance Society is established.

1830 Birkbeck College (then known as the London Mechanics' Institute) admits women to lectures.

1832 Durham University is founded.

1841 Whitelands (teacher-training) College opens in London.

1847 London 'Lectures to Ladies' are instituted by Professor F. D. Maurice (whose sister is a governess).

1848 Queen's College, London, is founded by Professor Maurice.

1849 Bedford College opens, later to become part of the University of London.

1850 North London Collegiate School opens.

1854 The Cheltenham Ladies' College opens.

1854 The Oxford University Act removes the requirement for religious tests for BA students, thus widening access; the Act for Cambridge is passed in 1856.

1858 The *English Woman's Journal* is first published, by the Ladies of Langham Place.

1863 Girls are allowed to attempt Cambridge 'Junior Local' examinations.

1864 The North of England Council for Promoting the Higher Education of Women is established by Josephine Butler and Anne Jemima Clough.

1865 Cambridge 'Local' examinations are formally opened to girls.

1867 The University Extension Scheme administers lectures in Liverpool and Manchester, to which women are admitted.

1868 The Taunton Commission reports damningly on the education of girls in England.

1869 Cambridge 'Higher Local' examinations come into being, for both sexes.

Emily Davies sets up an academic community at Benslow House, Hitchin, later to become Girton College, Cambridge (1873).

1871 Teaching Fellows at Oxford and Cambridge are

allowed to marry, so the higher reaches of academia cease to be male preserves.

A community of five women students is founded by Henry Sidgwick and Anne Clough in Cambridge; it develops into Newnham College.

1872 The Girls' Public Day School Trust is founded.

1874 London School of Medicine for Women opens.

1875 Oxford 'Higher Local' examinations come into being.

1876 The Enabling Act technically allows the admission of women to universities.

1878 London University is the first to admit women undergraduates on the same terms as men. The first degrees are awarded in the summer of 1880.

The Association for the Education of Women in Oxford is founded, and is responsible for the administration of 'Home Students' (local women) from 1879. (In 1952, the Society of Home Students coalesces into St Anne's College.)

1879 Somerville Hall (later College) and Lady Margaret Hall open in Oxford.

1881 Women are allowed to sit Cambridge Tripos (but not officially to graduate).

Victoria University incorporates colleges at Manchester, Liverpool, and Leeds, and admits women undergraduates.

1881 Nottingham becomes a co-educational university college.

1882 Westfield College, London, opens.

1883 Bristol becomes a co-educational university college.

1884 Oxford degree examinations are opened to women (but no certificate is awarded to those who pass).

1886 St Hugh's College, Oxford, is founded.

Royal Holloway College, London, opens.

1892 Reading awards London University degrees to women.

1893 St Hilda's College opens in Oxford.

1895 Durham allows women degrees.

1895 The London School of Economics opens.

1897 Sheffield awards London University degrees to men and women.

1901 Exeter becomes a co-educational university college. Birmingham University awards men and women degrees.

1902 The 'Ladies' Department' at King's College, London, awards degrees.

Southampton University College is founded.

1907 Imperial College, London, opens.

1908 Edith Morley of Reading becomes the first woman university professor in England.

1915 Queen Mary College becomes part of the University of London.

1919 The Sex Disqualification Removal Act.

1920 Women are awarded degrees at Oxford.

1921 Leicester University College founded.

1923 Women students at Cambridge are admitted to university lectures by right, rather than by privilege.

1927 Hull University College founded.

1948 Women students at Cambridge are officially allowed to graduate.

1959 The five women's 'societies' at Oxford (Somerville, Lady Margaret Hall, St Hugh's, St Hilda's, and St Anne's) finally become full members of the university.

Acknowledgements

The best thing about writing this book has been the opportunity to meet so many inspiring people. I have corresponded with or interviewed some 120 erstwhile bluestockings, all of whom welcomed my questions and gave generously of their time and memories. None was younger than her mid-eighties; the eldest were proud centenarians. Without exception I found their courtesy and spirit hugely uplifting, and I must thank them all.

I am also grateful to the friends and families of women who graduated before the Second World War for responding so readily to requests for information and reminiscences. I make no apology for the length of these lists, and hope those named will forgive the lack of titles or letters showing academic achievement. It might look a bit impersonal, but shouldn't imply any want of respect or gratitude. This book is more theirs, after all, than mine.

So: for all their help, and for permission to quote from correspondence and interviews, I should like to thank: Diana Allen (née Wimberly); Mary Applebey; Joan Bayes (for Miriam, Elsie, Rose, and Dolly Morris); Gordon Bebb (for Gwyneth Bebb); Ruth Beesley (née Ridehalgh); Martha Camfield (née Kempner); Michael Crump; Clare Currey (for Ruth Wilson); Barbara, Lady Dainton; Lucy de Burgh (née Addey); Katherine Duncan-Jones (for Elsie Phare); Kathleen Edwards; Hugh Epstein (for Mary Noake); Robin Fabel (for Mariana Beer); Barbara Fletcher; Patrick Frazer (for Cynthia Stenhouse); Grace and Julie

Fredericks; Norah Frost (for Sarah Beswick); Hilda Gaskell; Edith Gersay (née Wood); Dilys Glynne (for Dilys Lloyd Davies); Carolyn Greet (for Nora Wilde); Mary Grice (née Plant); Barbara Groombridge (for Marjorie Collet-Brown); Beryl Harding; Constance Hayball (née Houghton); Daphne Hope Brink (née Harvey); Barbara Hutton (née Britton); Leta Jones; John Killick (for Emma Mason); Tom Lester (for Sarah Mason); Daphne Levens (née Hanschell); Ceridwen Lloyd-Morgan (for Joan); Hazel Lowery (née Bray); Frederick Macdonald (for Louisa and Isabella Macdonald); Anne Milner (for Christine Burrows); Helen Nicholson (for Ivy Beatrice Jenkins); Angela Nosley (née Allen); Audrey Orr; Rosalind Page; Christina Roaf (née Drake); Dominica Roberts; Jane Robson (for Honoria Ford); Geoff Seale (for Stella Pigrome); Mary Tyndall; Myles Varcoe (for Rachel Footman); Harlan Walker (for Katie Rathbone, née Dixon); the Walsh family (for Trixie Pearson); Pippa Warren (for Kathleen Proud); Rosalind Willatts (for Edna Green); the late Hannah Winegarten (née Cohen) and her family; Beatrice Worthing; Diana Young (née Murray); Rosina Mary Young (née Stevens); and Marie-Luise Ziegler (née Haardt).

For colouring in the background, I am indebted to: Mary Abraham; Prudence Addison; Alex Aldrich-Blake; Bob Anderson; Jane Anderson; Hilary Arnold; Charles Arthur; Joan Aubrey Jones; Phyllis Austin; Ian Aveson; Simon Baguley; Mary Berry; Cindi Birkle; Joan Blyth; Vivian Bone; Helen Boon; Irene Boss; Elaine Bound; Sibyl Boyes; Gaynor Bramhall; Winifred Brancker; Anne Brew; Christine Bridgen; Barbara Briggs; Tony Bron; Margaret Bruce; Joan Carter; Dorothy Chadburn; Clemency Chapman; Violet Chell; Robyn Christie; Joyce Clifton; Penny Cloutte; Joan Coates; Mary Corran; Margaret Cosgrave; Hester Crombie; Valerie Crowson; Sarah Curtis; John Dainton;

Brian Davis; Jacqueline de Trafford; Elizabeth Dimmock; Caroline Essame; Yvonne Fox; Anne Francis; Eileen Fraser; Phyllis Firth; Jean Glover; Helen Goodliffe; Joanna Gordon; Robin Gordon-Walker; Helen Gray; Christopher Grimaldi; Isobel Grundy; Celia Haddon; Anne Haward; Jocelyn Hemming; Sylvia Hiller; Barbara Horsfield; William Horwood; Sr Anna Howley; Noel Ing; Paul Jeffery; Barbara Jones; Sally King; Mary Kirkman; Janet Lambley; David Le Tocq; Jenny Lister; Cindi Lockett; Esther Lucas; Margaret Macdonald; Margaret Macpherson; Deborah Manley; Annette Marshall; Christine Martin; Margaret Matthews; Sarah McCabe; Mary Midgley; Anne Mille; Margaret Morgan; Jane Morris-Jones; Helen Mortimer; Lionel Munby; Nina Nathan; Frederick Nicolle; Joyce Openshaw; Clare Passingham; Anthony Peabody; Jonathan Peacock; Barbara Pease; Lucy Pollard; Helena Port; Cora Portillo; Rosemary Pountney; Dorothy Price; Barbara Raban; Margaret Ralphs; Elizabeth Rattenbury; Joyce Reynolds; Edith Rhodes; Jean Ross; Timothy Scott; Frances Sellers; Mother Serafima; Alison Sims; Gilia Slocock; Sally Smith; Eileen Steel; Nell Steele; Diana Stephens; Olivia Stevenson; Elizabeth Strevens; Joan Stubbings; Noel Sumner; Angela Swetenham; Celia Tate; Charlotte Tester; John Theakstone; Sir Crispin Tickell; Michael Toothill; Barbara Twigg; Kathleen Ward; Sheila Ward; John Warren; Selby Whittingham; Joan Wilson; Olive Withycombe; Dorothy Wood; Joe Woolwich; Maisie 'Pip' Wray; and M. Yates.

Various institutions have kindly given me permission to quote from printed and manuscript material in their care. Extracts detailed in my notes and references are reproduced by courtesy of: Ashburne Hall, Manchester; Special Collections, University of Birmingham; by permission of Durham University Library; the Mistress and Fellows, Girton College, Cambridge; Hull University; King's College

London; by kind permission of the Principal and Fellows of Lady Margaret Hall, Oxford; the University of Leeds; the University of Liverpool; the University Librarian and Director, the John Rylands University Library, the University of Manchester; Newnham College, Cambridge; Queen Mary, University of London Archives (including Westfield College material); Royal Holloway, University of London (including Bedford College material); St Anne's College, Oxford; the Principal and Fellows of St Hilda's College, Oxford; by kind permission of the Principal and Fellows of St Hugh's College, Oxford; St Mary's College, Durham; the Governing Body of Somerville College, Oxford; College Collections, UCL Library Services, Special Collections; and the Women's Library, London Metropolitan University. I also acknowledge with thanks the support and efficiency of the curatorial staff at all these institutions, as well as at the universities of Bristol, Exeter, Leicester, Nottingham, Reading, Sheffield, and Southampton.

I have quoted from Vera Brittain's *Chronicle of Youth* and *Testament of Youth* by kind permission of Mark Bostridge and Timothy Brittain-Catlin, Literary Executors for the Estate of Vera Brittain 1970; extracts from *Miss Weeton: Journal of a Governess*, edited by Edward Hall (1936), are published by permission of Oxford University Press; the Society of Authors as the Literary Representative of the Estate of Virginia Woolf granted permission to quote from *A Room of One's Own*.

Finally, I should like to thank the following people for services above and beyond the call of scholarly duty: Pauline Adams; Adrian Allen; Elizabeth Boardman; Mark Bostridge; Elizabeth Boyd; Val Clark; Liz Cooke; Angela Evans; Liza Giffen; Eddie Glynn; Sheila Griffiths; Ele Hunter; Anne Keene; Kate Perry; Deborah Quare; and Anne Thomson. Alison and Rusty listened to two years' commentary on the book's progress with humour and forbearance. My sister Hannah Mortimer did sterling work transcribing records, which I much appreciate. My former agent Caroline Dawnay lent expertise and encouragement (both invaluable assets), and my editor Eleo Gordon has been – as any undergraduette worth her salt would put it – a brick. Richard and Edward tolerated my EFV with remarkable kindliness, while Bruce was – and continues – peerless.

While every effort has been made to contact copyright holders, the publishers would be pleased to hear from any not here acknowledged.

Introduction

In mixed company, always keep at least one foot on the ground.[1]

Alison Hingston was a student at Newnham College, Cambridge, from 1899 to 1902. There are three stout cardboard boxes in the college archives, containing her scrapbooks. It takes two hands to heave out the volume inside each box; as you do so, bits of apparent rubbish escape from uneven gaps between the wavy pages. The covers bulge under the strain of their contents. Most Victorian scrapbooks are dainty little albums with pasted drawings, poems, and paper decorations. Miss Hingston's are monsters.

They were almost my first discoveries when I began researching this book. Newnham was high on the list of places to visit, being among the earliest women's colleges in England. And even though *Bluestockings* covers every university extant in England before 1939, Cambridge – the first to host women students, and the last to give them a degree – seemed the obvious starting point.

I did not have particularly high hopes of Miss Hingston's college souvenirs. Words, I thought, reveal far more than things. But even after a full two years' research, happily exploring letters and diaries in scores of libraries, archives, and private collections, those scrapbooks still loom large.

Intensely personal (and slightly weird), Alison's *objets trouvés* include a few pale wisps of moss from the college grounds; chips of bark from a tree by the hockey field; a poke of paper with some sweets still inside; a half-smoked cigarette (which, despite the impossibly early date, I have reason to believe was hers); two twigs with their evergreen leaves in shards; a small tooth of unknown provenance; the printed results of university exams; a cryptic note in a strange hand. Yet, eclectic as it is, this collection seems to me to articulate everything *Bluestockings* seeks to convey about the pioneering women within its pages: enthusiasm, adventure, self-discovery, and the importance of cherishing whatever is most precious.

Newnham College was less than thirty years old when Alison arrived at the close of the nineteenth century. By that time, some 15 per cent of undergraduates in England were women. The proportion had grown to about 22 per cent by 1939.[2] Seventy years earlier, when the first women's college was founded, the total of female university students in the country was a lonely five. Then, a female was politically classed with infants, idiots, and lunatics, as 'naturally incapacitated . . . and therefore . . . so much under the influence of others that [she] cannot have a will of her own'.[3] That is why there were such strict regulations governing her behaviour at university (and beyond), not only to protect her moral and physical welfare, but to defend good men, such as undergraduates and lecturers, from temptation and involuntary folly.

No more was asked of a virtuous Victorian daughter than domestic duty. In its first issue, on 3 March 1880, the popular *Girl's Own Paper* urged its middle-class readership: 'amiable ever, but weak-minded never, brave in your duty be, rather than clever'. Intellectually, a young lady was close to non-existent. Her brain was considered small and dilute compared with a man's, and her understanding generically shallow. Her constitution was not thought to have the physical, mental, or emotional resources to withstand reproduction *and* academic study. A fertile womb and a barren brain, or vice versa: the choice, *pro bono*, was clear.

Therefore, for the first few decades of their admission to university, women were treated with little more confidence than those infants and idiots. When Manchester allowed female undergraduates in the 1880s, it put them in a small room in the attic, sternly guarded by a stuffed gorilla and some moth-eaten lions and tigers from the university museum. Chaperones were required for social and academic occasions, everywhere, until the First World War. Lecturers could refuse to teach or even acknowledge women. For a long time no males – including fathers and brothers – were allowed in women's rooms; after dispensation was granted to family members and (at a push) fiancés, it was still the rule that the bed should first be removed from the room, and the door propped open.

You might argue the situation was not much better by 1939, the end of the period covered by this book: Cambridge refused to award women degrees before 1948, and it was not until 1959 that the women's 'halls' at Oxford became fully incorporated into the university. Less than a quarter of the country's undergraduates were women, and when they graduated, they were still encouraged to choose between a profession and marriage.

To focus on these negatives, however, would be unfair. Nothing should distract us from the achievements of ordinary, extraordinary women like Alison Hingston, on whom this book is based. Quietly (or occasionally with some hullabaloo) they cleared the path that hundreds of thousands of women have since followed; most of us without a backward glance.

A word or two about terminology: an undergraduate is taken to be a student at any university, even though women were not allowed officially to graduate from Oxbridge until comparatively late, and were therefore not strictly *under-graduates* at all. I know Dorothy L. Sayers was not alone in abhorring the term 'undergraduette', finding it intolerably patronizing. But in the context of its era (principally the 1920s) it was also used with affection and even pride, both by students themselves, and by their observers. Bluestockings with a capital 'B' are those luminous intellectuals who graced the literary and artistic salons of fashionable eighteenth-century society; stripped of the pejorative gloss the label has acquired since then, it is here reclaimed – with a small 'b' – for all the undergraduates who give this book its voice.[4]

1. Ingenious and Learned Ladies

A Learned Woman is thought to be a Comet, that bodes Mischief, when ever it appears. To offer to the World the Liberal Education of Women is to deface the Image of God in Man, it will make Women so high, and men so low, like Fire in the House-top, it will set the whole world in a Flame . . .[1]

Life had not been kind to Ruth Pearson. She grew up around the turn of the twentieth century, when the second generation of women students was enjoying a university education. She might have gone to college herself, but brains and ambition in those days were not enough. She lacked the necessary background and money. Now, in the early 1930s, she found herself impoverished, living in a tiny house in south London, with an unemployed husband in his seventies, their children, and no reliable income. Keeping the family together, fed, and sheltered during the Depression was a struggle to which Ruth, in her darker moments, felt unequal.

One person kept her going: a daughter, Beatrix, in whom she recognized her younger self. Beatrix – known to everyone as Trixie – was indomitably cheerful. She was also extraordinarily bright. Somehow, Ruth managed to keep Trixie at school beyond the minimum leaving age of fourteen (even though she could have been earning a wage and off her mother's hands), and when the girl was encouraged to apply for a scholarship to university in 1932, the whole family was overjoyed. A teacher suggested St Hilda's

College, Oxford. It would have been far cheaper to send Trixie to one of the women's colleges in London; then she could have lived at home, and walked to her lectures each day. But if she was good enough to try for Oxford, declared Ruth, then Oxford it must be.

Everyone rallied round. As soon as the incredible news came through that Trixie had been accepted by St Hilda's, work parties sprang into action to create what her mother proudly called her Oxford trousseau. Convinced (wrongly) that all Trixie's peers would have their family crests lavishly embroidered on silken underclothes, and engraved on silver knives and forks and napkin rings, an aunt doggedly stitched Trixie's initials on her clothes and linen, as the next best thing. Fashion magazines were borrowed and scoured, material cadged and bartered for, with the mortifying result that Trixie attended her first 'cocoa party' at college clad not in homely winceyette, like everyone else, but in a gloriously sophisticated one-piece 'lounging pyjama' in glancing black satin, straight from the pages of *Vogue*.

One of the most difficult things for Trixie to get used to at St Hilda's was the silence. On the banks of the River Cherwell, opposite Christchurch Meadows, it was surreally still at night. She had never before had a room of her own, privacy, carpets, so many books at her disposal, and all the food and heat she needed. There was butter at teatime, *and* jam. She felt guilty. They could afford only a scrape of putty-coloured margarine at home. Never mind, she told herself; her being at Oxford would mean butter for them all in the end.

While Trixie was away, the Pearson family slumped even deeper into poverty. The obvious economy was for Trixie to leave Oxford and find a job. But Ruth Pearson was adamant that her daughter should not even be told about their difficulties and, despite ill-health, went for an interview for a full-time job as a charwoman. She failed to get it: she could hardly bend.

Soon the financial situation became so desperate at home that Trixie had to know. She was distraught, and promptly lined up a post as a bank clerk at £2 per week. Her mother was furious: it was madness for Trixie to mortgage her university career and the whole family's future for little more than £100 a year. As an Oxford graduate, teaching, she would earn more than twice that, and have a pension. She would be able to climb out of all this, insisted Ruth, and the family would climb out too, on her coat-tails.

So Trixie stayed at Oxford. The Pearsons went on to poor relief, and discreetly, with infinite sensitivity, the college invented grants and bursaries to help, some of which − Trixie discovered later − came straight from the pockets of her tutors.

Trixie adored university life, and was one of the most popular, shining girls of her college generation. Occasionally, members of her family would come to visit. They had to take turns, once enough money had been scrimped for someone's train fare, and none of them seem to have resented her being there. Ruth Pearson hardly ever came, so that others could, but when Trixie graduated, she insisted her mother be present. The Dean of St Hilda's spotted Ruth in the Sheldonian Theatre, where the ceremony took place, quietly making for the high balcony with the parents of other students. They were supposed to sit well away from the ranks of academic dignitaries below, but the Dean fished Ruth out, leading her down to the reserved VIP seats right at the front. 'This ceremony means more to Mrs Pearson,' explained the Dean, 'than to anyone else here today. Of *course* she must have a good view.' Trixie, waiting behind the scenes, knew nothing of all this until

she emerged to receive her degree. Then came the proudest moment of her life:

As Bachelors we naturally came last, of interest only to ourselves
and our families. When the Proctor called upon our Dean to read
out her candidates' names and present us, we had to go forward
and stand in a group around her. In that position we were face to
face with and only two or three yards from the Vice-Chancellor,
the Proctors – and my mother.[2]

I wish those who fought so hard for the right of women to
attend university and be awarded degrees could have known
about Trixie Pearson. Everything about her story vindicates
what they were trying to do. Despite her social background,
her academic abilities were recognized and nurtured; she was
encouraged to aim for the best, and supported financially,
emotionally, and academically to do so; doors opened for her
as she approached, and nothing was allowed to stand in the
way of her undergraduate career, until she stepped confidently
out into the working world as a professional woman. The
family *did* climb out of poverty on her coat-tails, just as Ruth
Pearson promised, and through her own teaching Trixie passed
on the excitement of learning and the concept – very new to
young women at the time – that nothing is impossible.

Trixie graduated in 1936, nearly sixty years after the first
degree courses were opened to women at an English university. The image of the 'bluestocking' had been a familiar concept throughout those years. It still is, to a certain extent. I
remember being thrilled when my English teacher called me
a bluestocking the day I won my place at Oxford. Like Trixie,
I was not expected to get in, since no girls from my school
had been before, and the college to which I had blithely

applied was renowned for its clever women. I naturally assumed blue stockings were part of their uniform and that on special academic occasions, with gown, cap, and a sober suit, I should wear them too. One of the first things I did on hearing the news was visit Mr Beckwith, the local draper, to buy a couple of pairs of navy tights (a daring take on tradition). Someone put me right before I embarrassed myself too much, but achieving bluestocking status remained a slightly exotic badge of intellectual honour in my imagination.

The very first bluestocking was not a woman at all, but the naturalist and writer Benjamin Stillingfleet (1702–71). He belonged to a group of fashionably learned friends who met together during the latter half of the eighteenth century in various London salons to cultivate the art of intellectual conversation. The novelty of Stillingfleet's group was that most of its members were female. Elizabeth Montagu (1720–1800), its 'Queen', was a wealthy woman passionately interested in English literature; a patron and an author, she counted the celebrities of the day – writer Samuel Johnson, actor David Garrick, painter Joshua Reynolds – as fellow scholars as well as friends. At first they humoured her because of her income of £10,000 a year, one suspects; later, however, they appear genuinely to have admired her critical flair. Partly thanks to her, being an overtly intelligent woman acquired (fleetingly) the gloss of high culture and became fashionable.

One evening in 1756, Stillingfleet presented himself at Elizabeth Montagu's Mayfair house for one of the company's regular meetings, bizarrely clad not in customary white silken hose, but in workaday knitted blue stockings. Woad-blue wool was cheap and common; Mrs Montagu and her friends thought it hilarious that Stillingfleet was eccentric enough not only to have countenanced possessing such stuff in the first place, but wearing it in public.

Stillingfleet's solecism was gossiped about throughout literary London, and soon Mrs Montagu's clique became
known collectively as the 'blue stocking philosophers'. Especially the women. Her house was dubbed 'Blue Stocking
Lodge' or 'the Colledge' and considered an urbane sort of
private university over which she and her scholarly lady
friends presided as unofficial Doctors of Letters.

*Dr Syntax woos a 'Blue Stocking Beauty' in one of Thomas
Rowlandson's cartoons illustrating a popular satirical poem,* The Third
Tour of Dr Syntax in Search of a Wife, *by William Combe (1821).*

Stillingfleet's tendency to eccentricity was shared by other
members of the group. The very idea of a female's opinion
actually mattering to the intelligentsia was unconventional, for
a start. The historian Catherine Macaulay (1731–91) was one
of the highest-profile members of the coterie (or 'petticoterie',
as one wit put it); she was definitely strange, inviting Samuel

Johnson's footman to dine with her, and marrying a man nearly half her age. But she was famous, well connected, and indisputably clever; her idiosyncrasies spiced the image of the whole circle. At least she *did* marry: a reputation for ostensible moral virtue was still a *sine qua non* in English high society, and the true Bluestockings always held that dear. Polymath writer Elizabeth Carter (1717–1806) was another member of the group, with essayists Catherine Talbot and Hester Chapone; later the playwright Hannah More joined, novelist Fanny Burney, and – a little jealously on the periphery – poet and diarist Hester Thrale.[3]

Macaulay and More were largely responsible for allying the Bluestockings' image to applied education. Though neither woman experienced extensive schooling herself, both strongly advocated reforms in the teaching of girls, and the establishment of more and better schools. Supported by the 'Colledge' tag, the implication that Mrs Montagu's Mayfair mansion had become an exclusive, if rather perverse, academic institution quickly took root.

A correspondence emerged in the literary press about how far this university idea should go. In March 1773, a new Vice-Chancellor was installed at Oxford (the Prime Minister, Lord North), and as part of the celebrations honorary degrees were awarded to Sir Joshua Reynolds and Hester Thrale's first husband, Henry. It was reported that a saboteur had also been present during the ceremony: a *woman*, dressed as a man, had outrageously got herself awarded a degree. This apocryphal incident caused much merriment in the papers, but also sparked off a serious debate about whether or not 'Academical Ladies' like the Bluestockings should formally be recognized. 'Learning is not confined to Sex,' decided one commentator in the *Westminster Magazine*, 'nor have the men, in my opinion, any exclusive right to those honorary distinctions in Literature, which they so insolently arrogate to themselves.' The writer went on to urge Oxford and Cambridge – the only English universities at the time – to 'make an innovation in their academical Laws in favour of . . . ingenious and learned Ladies, whom custom excludes from a College education', and to make them 'Mistresses of Arts'.[4]

These 'ingenious and learned Ladies' ('ingenious' meaning witty) certainly worked hard enough; harder than most real undergraduates at the time. Elizabeth Carter's studies, for example, sound like some ghastly never-ending essay crisis. She was a Kentish girl, the daughter of a clergyman with a love of languages. He passed this on to Elizabeth, and though she was eager to learn, and teach her younger siblings, she never found it easy. But learning was her sacred vocation, she insisted. She would work obsessively to overcome what she perceived to be her slowness, to achieve God's bizarre purpose for her. In her anxiety to acquire French, German, Spanish, Italian, Latin, Greek, Hebrew, and an understanding of mathematics, music, and natural science, she drove herself dangerously hard on a few hours' sleep a night. This gave her sickening migraines, which she would feverishly try to soothe by binding wet cloths around her head and stomach. She chewed green tea leaves and sucked raw coffee beans to avoid drifting off when the headaches subsided. She even began snorting powdered tobacco, or snuff, on which she quickly became dependent (to her father's horror), not only to work, but to function at all.

The journalist Dilys Powell talked of wrapping her head in a wet towel to keep awake for work while an undergraduate at Oxford in the 1920s; caffeine is still a student's staple, and it is every parent's nightmare that their son or daughter should sink under academic pressure into addiction. The pressure Elizabeth Carter faced was entirely self-inflicted. Yet it bore fruit and she did become a famous intellectual, her career crowned by the publication in 1758 of Epictetus' *Complete Works* in translation. She wrote poetry, too, and – significantly – a version of Francesco Algarotti's Italian edition of Sir Isaac Newton's *Philosophy Explain'd for the Use of the Ladies* (1739). All her life it mattered overwhelmingly that she should fulfil her own academic potential – but sadly, it only mattered to her. By the time she died in 1806, she was publicly remembered as 'very learned, very excellent, and very tiresome'.[5]

There may have been solidarity among Bluestockings, but once the novelty of listening to clever female celebrities had worn off by the beginning of the nineteenth century, public respect turned to ridicule. The suggestion that they be awarded honorary degrees was a step too far. Performing intellectual tricks was fine, but infiltrating the Establishment was not acceptable. Regency frothiness began to suffuse polite society, and revolution first in America and then France bred distrust of anything too radical at home. Jane Austen tried a gentle voice in educating her readership about intelligent women, but few noticed the message.

Mary Wollstonecraft (1759–97) was more strident. In her *Vindication of the Rights of Woman*, published in 1792, she wrote passionately about the state of political, cultural, and moral degradation to which her sex had been reduced. According to her, women were wilfully imbued by society with a warped, ignorant sense of duty designed to corrupt their emotional and intellectual potential. They were more like cats than sentient beings, trained to purr at men in return for the odd stroke and a saucer of cream. Give them *education*, she pleaded. Let them learn for themselves what is true and good. Emancipate them. Real wisdom and virtue are rooted in intellectual liberty (since God is good); when women's minds are properly developed, their souls will flourish too. So will men's, 'for the improvement must be mutual, or the injustice which one-half of the human race are obliged to submit to retorting on their oppressors, the virtue of man will be worm-eaten by the insect whom he keeps under his feet'.[6]

Perhaps, had Wollstonecraft been more subtle, her arguments might have carried more clout. They were certainly well founded. In fact, the main objection to her theories stemmed not from her politics, but from her probity. Piety in a woman excused much, as the Bluestockings realized. Everyone knew (since she hardly bothered to hide it) that Mistress Wollstonecraft was living with a man not her husband and had a bastard daughter. What is more, she had once tried to commit suicide: the ultimate sin. And witty ladies were fine as long as they limited themselves to cultural pursuits. A clever woman with a cause was dangerous. What could the *Vindication* be but the meretricious rantings of a fallen woman? In retrospect, Wollstonecraft's brave book appears a feminist masterpiece, well ahead of its time. She was regarded by her contemporary audience, however, as a dangerous iconoclast apt, if taken seriously, to set the world aflame.

Despite the indulgence given to the Bluestockings, and the lone voices of their intellectual predecessors, it seems that by the beginning of the nineteenth century while learning and ingenuity in a man were popularly taken to be assets, in a true woman, or 'lady', they were seen as flaws. The author Lady Mary Wortley Montagu (Elizabeth Montagu's cousin by marriage), famous for her almost freakish intelligence, had said as much in the 1750s when offering bitter advice on the education of a daughter. Under no circumstances, she warned, should the girl ever admit to intellectual curiosity. Instead, she must conceal whatever learning she attains, with as much solicitude as she would hide crookedness or lameness: the parade of it can only serve to draw on her the envy, and consequently the most inveterate hatred, of all he and she fools, which will certainly be at least three parts in four of her acquaintance.[7]

So what was the ideal, the goal of a girl's so-called education? Almost the same in 1800, depressingly, as it had been for centuries. According to the Bible's blueprint, in Proverbs 31, the true, womanly woman was principally an instrument of influence, a conduit of modesty and simplicity of heart for her husband and children. She readily aroused her husband, but no one else; spun and cooked, day and night, to save money; was meek yet strong, silent yet wise, utterly submissive, yet the cornerstone of the household.

Not surprisingly, a woman like this was rarer than rare; her price 'far above rubies'. It made sense to commentators on religion and teaching before the Renaissance for men not to waste energy searching for the gems, but concentrate on avoiding the dross: the toxic majority of womankind.

After the first creation of man the first wife of the first Adam sated the first hunger by the first sin, against God's command. The sin was the child of Disobedience, which will never cease before the end of the world to drive women tirelessly to pass on to the future what they learned from their mother. My friend, a disobedient wife is dishonour to a man: beware.[8]

There was no discussion of formally educating women. Why bother? It would be like pouring God's precious gift of knowledge into a cracked vessel. That is not to say that no women *were* educated. Certain local heroines were excused Eve's inheritance. Abbess Egeria produced the earliest piece of autobiography by a woman in a series of letters home to her Pyrenean convent from the Holy Land in the 380s: her writing is witty, well informed, and beautifully descriptive. The Christian convert Fabiola opened a hospital in Ostia in 390, where she practised surgery. Hypatia of Alexandria (*c.*355–415) lectured on maths and astronomy at the university there. There are several outstanding scholars like these, remembered now for their wisdom as well as their learning, and allowed then to shine in small worlds still free from the inky stain of misogyny that grew – ironically – with the spread of (male) literacy.

In England, the leading light was Hild (614–80). Still considered the unofficial patron saint of women's education, Hild, deeply eligible and of royal descent, was baptized in 627, and preferred to become a nun than to marry. This was not an unusual choice, since convents were rich in young ladies deposited by wealthy families as moral investments. It was a convenient arrangement. Perhaps there were too many daughters in the family and the local marriage market was flooded, or maybe some were less obviously attractive or more wayward than others and so unlikely to make an advantageous match. Convents benefited from the dowries such girls brought with them; their families secured a constant stream of prayers on their behalf, and the girls themselves acquired (if they were lucky) an education.

Even so, it took some strength of character for a king's niece to opt out of the world. Hild had a genuine vocation; her religious conviction together with a graceful intellectualism and political awareness brought her to the attention of Bishop Aidan, who commissioned her to run a convent and adjoining monastery in Hartlepool in Northumbria. Thus, remarkably, Hild was in charge of the minds and souls of men as well as women. After her transfer to Whitby, at the request of King Oswy she hosted the first ever synod of English bishops. She was responsible for the education of five future bishops at the school attached to her convent, and for the education of hundreds of nuns, too, in arts as well as sciences.

It was people like Hild, quietly working away in religious houses throughout Europe, who inspired those calling for women's education so eloquently during the Renaissance. In a Europe-wide literary debate, the *Querelle des Femmes* (the 'Woman Question'), which spanned several decades of the fourteenth and fifteenth centuries, men of letters (and the odd lady) fired arguments at each other about the nature of woman. Did she have a soul? Any sort of intellect? The Latin for woman is *mulieris*, which means soft-minded, and the old guard – scholars like Jean de Meun and Giovanni Boccaccio – followed the teachings of Aristotle and Ovid on the matter, assuming women feeble and treacherous, biologically deformed and morally corrupt. An idealized lady might be an interesting literary or artistic device, but apart from procreation, she had no worthwhile purpose.

The new Humanists, on the other hand, allowed women more potential. Erasmus and his sympathizers were more Platonic; they saw in women a chance to improve mankind as a whole, and argued that the first teachers of men's sons – their mothers – should be better equipped for the job.

Real-life role models of feminine scholarship began to emerge during the Renaissance, celebrated for their virtue and dignity as well as their intelligence. Novella d'Andrea (d. 1333) lectured in law at her father's university in Bologna (while meekly sitting behind a screen so as not to distract the students). Her compatriot Christine de Pizan (*c.*1364– *c.*1430) is acknowledged as the first professional woman writer in Europe, and was an ardent, sensitive feminist. She took part in the *Querelle* herself in *The Book of the City of Ladies*

(1405), a long allegorical argument for women's freedom, and *The Book of Three Virtues* (also 1405), about how a woman should behave in order to do herself and others justice. Intelligence, in women as well as men, merited careful husbandry, she advised, and should be cherished.

Sometimes it was. The medieval and early Tudor period in England was rife with businesswomen, tradeswomen, and female estate managers. They were taught (or picked up) literacy, numeracy, and the habit of independent thought, usually within the family. There was no system of formal education for girls outside convent walls until the late sixteenth century. By then, personal tutors were occasionally engaged by wealthy and progressive fathers for their daughters. Thomas More's girls were famously 'ingenious' and learned; so was Queen Elizabeth in her youth. The princess remained fond of her tutor, Roger Ascham, all his life. 'I would rather have cast ten thousand pounds into the sea than be parted from my Ascham,' she wrote on his death in 1568, and he genuinely admired her princely talent for improvement, marvelling at her masculine 'constitution of mind' and capacity for languages, including French, Italian, Latin, and Greek.

Other girls, less exalted, were now able to go to school without joining a religious community first. Some convents ran boarding schools for the (lay) daughters of the rich, where the curriculum might include embroidery, herbal medicine, and sacred singing, as well as reading. Yorkshire-woman Mary Ward (1585–1645) founded a teaching order of women missionaries, nicknamed 'the Galloping Girls', which still flourishes today as the Institute of the Blessed Virgin Mary. Her first 'Institute of English Ladies', a boarding school in Munich, was opened in 1609; she never managed to establish one in her own country. In England the first private school for girls, 'Ladies Hall', appeared in Deptford in 1617. Others

opened at Hackney, Chelsea, and Putney, and eventually in
the provinces. A few grammar schools offered places to girls,
with women teachers as well as men, as did the odd charity
school (the first being Red Maids, Bristol, in 1634). Dame
schools – so called because they were run by women – operated as child-minding services for working parents; there,
boys were sketchily taught to read and write, and girls to sew
and be good. In all these institutions the girls' curriculum
was limited, even for quick-witted pupils, and rarely matched
what was offered to boys.

Pioneers in the fight for educational equality were quick
to point this out. Bathsua Makin (*c.*1600–*c.*1676), 'the greatest scholler, I thinke, of a woman in England',[9] grew up in
her father's school; produced a volume of Greek and Latin
verse at sixteen; went on to found schools of her own for
boys and girls; and during the 1640s was appointed Royal
Tutor to Princess Elizabeth, daughter of Charles I. She had
about a dozen children of her own, too. In 1673, her *Essay
to Revive the Antient Education of Gentlewomen* was published:
a brilliantly logical apologia for a new kind of academy. In it
she explains why girls have not been offered a sound education before, and – like her devotee Wollstonecraft – she pulls
no punches. What is to blame is a mixture of habit and an
inherent male predilection for bestiality:

Custom, when it is inveterate, has a mighty influence: it has the
force of Nature itself. The Barbarous custom to breed Women
low is grown general amongst us, and has prevailed so far, that it
is verily believed (especially amongst a sort of debauched sots)
that Women are not endued with such Reason, as Men; nor
capable of improvement by Education, as they are . . .

Had God intended Women only as a finer sort of Cattle, he
would not have made them reasonable . . . Monkies, (which the

Indians use to do many Offices) might have better fitted some men's Lust, Pride, and Pleasure; especially those that desire to keep them ignorant to be tyrannized over . . .[10]

She acknowledges that some girls are dispatched to schools, but what pitiful schools they are, where the pupils are only expected to 'trifle away so many precious minutes meerly to polish their Hands and Feet, to curl their Locks, to dress and trim their Bodies; and in the meantime to neglect their Souls'.[11] It is intriguing that, throughout the book, Mrs Makin equates a woman's soul with her intellect. She does not deny that the odd accomplishment is an asset, such as needlework or looking 'comely and decent', but spending time and money on teaching females to frisk about on the dance floor with painted faces and fussy clothes is profligate. Why not invest in the mind? 'Seeing Nature produces Women of such excellent Parts, that they do often equalize, some-times excel men, in what ever they attempt; what reason can be given why they should not be improved?'

Mrs Makin knows very well what reason. In fact, there are several, which she proceeds to enumerate. *No one will want to marry an educated woman, because she will mock her husband's ignorance and make a fool of him.* That is a clear case of double standards, retorts the forthright Mrs Makin. Just as a man likes to sleep around, then marry a virgin, he wants education for himself but not his wife. But throughout history wise women have been a good influence on all around them, and surely it is sensible to make an informed teacher of your children's mother?

Education will make women vain. Why? Just because a woman gains knowledge, it does not mean she will automatically lose some other quality. Education is not a question of balancing credits and debits. Women, like men, can be clever *and* humble, wise *and* virtuous. In fact the deeper their knowledge, the less likely they are to be 'puffed up and proud'.

Why bother educating women if they cannot hold public office? Let them learn, and then influence society through their husbands. *Women will forget the housework if their heads are full of knowledge.* Men get their work done, don't they? And they are positively stuffed with egregious facts. *Who will have the time to teach women?* It will not take long. Boys are at school between the ages of seven and sixteen, yet only a quarter of them learn enough, even then, to get to university (for what it's worth). Girls are quicker-witted, and the novelty of a sound education makes them eager to learn. A better method of teaching both boys and girls is what is needed – and Mrs Makin has developed just that. One last question: *What if girls don't want to learn?* Well, show me a schoolboy who does . . .

The *Essay* closes cannily with an advertisement for Mrs Makin's own school in Tottenham High Cross, London. It costs £20 a year (more for advanced students) and goes well beyond anything offered to girls before. The basics are attended to: the principles of religion, needlework, a little dancing and musical appreciation, learning how to write clearly, and enough arithmetic to keep accounts; these take up half the school week. The other half is spent more imaginatively in studying not only Latin and French, but Italian, Spanish, Greek, and even Hebrew. A 'repository for visibles', a superior sort of primary-school nature table, teaches them the names, properties, and uses of flowers and herbs, shrubs, trees, minerals, metals, and stones. As well as such culinary skills as pastry-making and preserving, girls can take astronomy, geography, and philosophy.

Here is a worthy forerunner of the great headmistresses of the Victorian era – Miss Buss and Miss Beale and their ilk (see

Chapter 2) – who believed passionately in a girl's right to learn *important* things, to be useful to herself and others; who knew the allure (to parents) of choice and a mixture of tradition and innovation, and who inspired by example. When King James I was given a copy of the virtuosic Latin and Greek verses Bathsua Makin published in 1616, he was mildly impressed. 'But can she spin?' he inquired. No doubt she could.

A contemporary of Bathsua Makin's, Hannah Woolley (*c.*1623–*c.*1678), was another pioneer of educational equality. In her innocently titled conduct-book *The Gentlewomen's Companion* (1675), she was just as damning as Makin about the custom of 'breeding women low', or keeping them ignorant, and filling the vacuum with vanity and silliness:

I cannot but . . . condemn the great negligence of Parents, in letting the fertile ground of their Daughters lie fallow, yet send the barren Noddles of their sons to the University, where they stay for no other purpose than to fill their empty Sconces and make a noise . . . Vain man is apt to think we were merely intended for the World's propagation, and to keep its humane inhabitants sweet and clean; but . . . had we the same Literature [or learning], they would find our brains as fruitful as our bodies.[12]

This last comment was recalled in a poem, 'Elegy', for Margaret, Duchess of Newcastle, published the following year. The duchess had herself been an advocate of female 'ingenuity', or intellectualism, but a little too eccentric in behaviour and unguarded in expression to convince anyone. On the contrary: she was dubbed 'Mad Madge', and considered an embarrassment by her aristocratic peers. This poem, full of rhetorical frills and furbelows, reminds its readers that Madge was not like most wives. She had no children. Instead she left a prodigious collection of writings – 'the best Remains'. But she might have been better admired (the poet implies) had she conformed to the rest of her sex, who complacently enjoyed their allotment of 'Fruitful Wombs but Barren Brains'.[13]

The mention of university in *The Gentlewoman's Companion* is significant. It reveals the common perception during the seventeenth and eighteenth centuries that many young men at Oxford and Cambridge wasted both time and money by going there. Mrs Woolley cannot seriously have imagined that women would benefit from going themselves. But the idea may have sewn a rogue seed in the fertile mind of another contemporary agitator, Mary Astell.

Miss Astell (1666–1731) was the first writer to blame her sex for their own ignorance. No wonder the world thinks women weak, she complains in *A Serious Proposal to the Ladies* (1694/7), when they settle so easily for silliness. 'How can you be content to be in the World like Tulips in a Garden, to make a fine shew and be good for nothing; have all your Glories set in the Grave, or perhaps much sooner?' she demands. 'The Soul is rich and would, if well cultivated, produce a noble Harvest.'[14] All that is needed is application, and a little peace and quiet.

Astell proposes a safe, isolated place where women can gather together and be taught to understand, criticize, and perhaps even change the world in which they live. Not like the Bluestockings' 'Colledge', which was too preoccupied with wittiness and fashion, and too public; more like a convent for lay sisters, where the mind is as important as the soul.

Daniel Defoe took up the idea, after reading the *Serious Proposal*. His contribution to the debate on women's education has rather slipped through the net, hidden as it is in an early, obscure work, *An Essay Upon Projects* (1697), but it is well worth notice. Defoe's *Essay* is a little like Mrs Makin's, in that it bewails contemporary attitudes to women's moral and mental capacity. He, too, thinks it pitiful that women are denied the advantages of learning, yet blamed for their ignorance. What does it say about a nation's leaders, he asks, that they deny God's grace of education to the mothers of their sons? And what right has the clergy to encourage brutishness in the souls of half their congregation? Besides, he continues (somewhat lubriciously), a well–educated woman is 'all Softness and Sweetness, Peace, Love, Wit, and Delight'.

On the other hand, Suppose her to be the very same Woman, and rob her of the Benefit of Education, and it follows thus . . .

Her Wit, for want of Teaching, makes her Impertinent and Talkative.

Her Knowledge, for want of Judgement and Experience, makes her Fanciful and Whimsical . . . And from these she degenerates to be Turbulent, Clamorous, Noisy, Nasty, and the Devil.[15]

To avoid such domestic disaster, which has been recurring each generation since Eve, Defoe proposes the establishment of an 'Academy for Women'. Like Astell's, it would be isolated, carefully structured both architecturally and educationally, with a wide curriculum, and its own rules and regulations. But there would be nothing of the nunnery about it: no vows of celibacy would be required, and no guards at the doors; no spies. The students would be free to come and go, free to *learn*. An Act of Parliament would be passed, that whenever they chose to attend, no man would be allowed to enter – not even their husbands – so they could study in privacy and undisturbed (shades of Virginia Woolf's *A Room of One's Own*).

After implying that Eve was not evil after all, just uneducated, Defoe closes the work with the following paragraph:

I need not enlarge on the Loss the Defect of Education is to the Sex, nor argue the Benefit of the contrary Practice; 'tis a thing will be more easily granted than remedied: this Chapter is but an Essay at the thing, and I refer the Practice to those Happy Days, if ever they shall be, when men shall be wise enough to mend it.[16]

Surprisingly, those Happy Days were not so far ahead.

2. Working in Hope

I want girls educated to match their brothers. We work in hope.[1]

In 1872, two generations before Trixie Pearson went to Oxford, a young woman from a very different background prepared to make history. Constance Louisa Maynard was a pioneer of Girton College, and the first woman to read philosophy (or 'moral science') at Cambridge. No women actually *graduated* from Cambridge until 1948; they just passed through the university as more or less welcome guests, sitting the requisite exams (if they chose to) without the right to formal recognition. At this stage, that hardly mattered. To Constance and her peers, unable to imagine being awarded a degree, it was the work that counted; the means rather than the end.

Despite her independent spirit, and the fact that she was twenty-three when she planned to go to college, Constance still needed her parents' permission. The omens were not good: she was considered whimsical and rhapsodic, and was rarely taken seriously by her family. She had little formal schooling behind her and no need to make a living; why (argued Mr and Mrs Maynard) should she suddenly resolve to join some dubious establishment purporting to offer a university education to ladies? Reputation was more valuable an asset in life than learning.

At worst, the college was described as an 'infidel place';[2] at best it sounded more like something out of Tennyson's *Princess*, with a comic cast of 'sweet girl graduates', 'prudes for proctors' and 'dowagers for deans',[3] clamouring uselessly after learning like dainty little moths at a lamp. It was hardly the sort of place a respectable man would commit his daughter.

Constance, however, was determined. Her father was the easier parent to manage, so choosing her time carefully, and wearing her prettiest smile, she asked him – 'because learning is a beautiful thing' – if she might go to Girton. His initial response was not promising. He laughed. 'I say, Conse, this is something new . . . But what's the use? What's it for?' Constance then embarked on a treatise about the soul-enhancing properties of Greek, philosophy, and science. Papa murmured something about staying at home and being like her sisters, before pulling out a trump card by offering to buy her a new pony if she would abandon altogether the idea of Cambridge.

At last, Constance managed to bring him round. He was prepared to allow her to leave home, he wearily agreed, and to pay her fees – but only if Mother concurred. Mother did, but on strict conditions. Constance was to be on her guard at all times at Girton: it was likely to be a 'worldly' place, and its inhabitants 'not at all our sort'. She must not degrade herself by taking university exams, nor stay longer than a single year. When she returned home, she must never entertain the idea of becoming a teacher or entering some other equally wretched employment. She must treat the whole enterprise as a long visit to slightly unsuitable friends, and when it was over, do her best to forget all about it. 'And I promised anything,' remembered Constance, 'everything!'[4]

Why should someone like Constance have been so desperate to go to university? Florence Nightingale, like most intelligent young gentlewomen, knew the answer to that. Florence was bred to be passive in all things. She was shown how to read, and more, but never taught to learn independently, nor explore new ideas. She was even discouraged from choosing her own books, 'and what is it to be "read aloud to"? The most miserable exercise of the human intellect. Or rather, is it any exercise at all? It is like lying on one's back, with one's hands tied and having liquid poured down one's throat.' She was force-fed received wisdom, and it choked her. 'Why have women passion, intellect, moral activity – these three – and a place in society where no one of the three can be exercised?' Why are they denied the 'brilliant, sharp radiance of intellect', suppressed in darkness?[5] She knew how desperate a life lived in the shallows could be, and how soul-destroying it was to be condemned to triviality.

Florence Nightingale found a different way to fulfil her potential, but had a university education been available, she would have been the perfect candidate. She became one of the first reputable Englishwomen to enjoy a career. She was a formidable statistician, a quick and sinewy thinker who deftly exposed the sclerotic blunderings of the British military machine. She was a philosopher, too, of startling insight. A woman's life is sketchy, she maintained. Someone needs to colour in the picture, give it depth. She had the bravery to do that herself; others, like Constance Maynard, needed help.

In fact, help was on its way. It dragged its feet, it's true, for the first half of the nineteenth century, but by the time Nightingale discovered her own vocation in the early 1850s, the political and cultural movement that was to result in university places for women was beginning to gather pace and a sense of purpose. Her argument was just one of many urging on the juggernaut.

The reason for the initial lack of progress is obvious. For all the practical efforts of reformers like Bathsua Makin and

Catherine Macaulay, and the theoretical proposals of Woll-stonecraft and Defoe, a vicious circle still swirled round the subject of educating girls. Until there were good schools in place to teach them the basics, there was no hope of girls' academic development. That called for good teachers, but without good schools in the first place, where were they to come from?

Home tutoring was available, of course, to those whose fathers could afford it, and happened to approve of spending money informing the mind of a mere wife-to-be. Childhood was a middle-class invention of the Victorian era; before that infant girls were dressed as miniature women, and expected to behave as such – with some allowances – until they could earn money either by manual work or marrying well. It must have seemed to traditionalists an extravagant caprice to con-sider investing in female intellect. But some middle-class sisters did share their brothers' tutors, and daughters could learn fast and well from amiable parents.

Constance Maynard, born in 1849, was one of them. Her early education, like that of so many of the other pioneers, was largely a matter of scavenging. Every Thursday after-noon, her mother would teach the four youngest Maynards an unconventional curriculum of 'exactly what we liked', which included printing, willow-plaiting, heraldry, drawing in perspective, and memorizing the Greek alphabet. Con-stance soon tired of this, and longed for her brother George to come home from boarding school and feed her real (if regurgitated) knowledge. One holiday, he brought her a map of the stars, and every clear night the two of them would steal outside and learn the constellations. 'Here was a sort of out-let into Eternity . . . George and I were left to ourselves, and we laboured away at the starry sky till we "got it right".'[6]

Constance's elder sisters had also been sent to school, and

Constance joined them for a couple of years, but it was her parents' whim that in her case this was a waste of time and money. Father failed to see why he should go on paying for an expensive school, when Constance could quite easily pick up her education at second hand from the older girls. The implication that she was not worth the investment hurt Constance deeply, but she never complained. She had been too well brought up.

A hand-me-down education might have had its attractions for Mr Maynard, but to Constance it was useless. The Maynards' money bought their daughters gentility, but very little learning. All those unimpeachable maiden ladies (often clusters of sisters) who ran nice, private schools for upper-middle-class daughters were more concerned with cultivation than education. If indeed they did that: the political activist Barbara Bodichon (Florence Nightingale's cousin) publicized a worrying rise during the mid-nineteenth century of academies, institutions, collegiate establishments for young ladies – call them what you will – offering nothing but a place to deposit your daughter for a while. Most of them were staffed by incompetent opportunists, charlatans, who had failed in other walks of life and fancied opening a school to make some money. Teaching hardly featured.

Bodichon herself was lucky: she was sent to a progressive Unitarian school in London which was co-educational (something Mary Wollstonecraft advocated in her *Vindication of the Rights of Woman*) and which welcomed a mix of children from different social backgrounds. But then Barbara was from an unconventional and slightly outrageous family. Her father, a Radical MP (in his forties when she was born), never married her mother (a milliner's apprentice in her teens), and Barbara was brought up to question received wisdom wherever it might rear its lazy head.

In an illustration from The Workwoman's Guide, by a Lady *(1840), a teacher and her assistant preside over a girls' schoolroom. Books lie discarded while the pupils sit and sew.*

Alternative schools included those run by the Quakers, or Anglican charities such as the Society for the Propagation of Christian Knowledge, the Home and Colonial Infant School

Society, or the National Society for the Promotion of Education for the Poor, which sprang up in parishes all over the country. Many of these new charity and government-aided schools were designed for the children of men and women working in the engine-room of the Industrial Revolution, yet even then only a fraction of 'the poor' sent their girls. It is estimated that during the 1830s three in ten children between the ages of six and fourteen went solely to Sunday school; two in ten went to a dame or a private school; one went to a National Society or parish school; and the remaining four went nowhere.[7] The sexes are not differentiated in these statistics, but it is safe to assume the minority was female.

In 1823, Casterton School was founded in west Yorkshire by the Church of England, expressly for daughters of the clergy. It was there – when it was Cowan Bridge School, the dismal pattern for Lowood in *Jane Eyre* – that the Brontë sisters went, and where their friends became pupil-teachers, ploughed back into stony ground before they had a chance to flourish in the world.

Being a pupil-teacher could be a haphazard, frustrating affair. Ellen Weeton, not so far from the Brontës, over the Yorkshire/Lancashire border, hated the position when forced into it by her indigent widowed mother in Wigan. Mrs Weeton ran her own school, and at first Ellen had been allowed to learn along with the paying pupils, soon outstripping them all. When her mother realized how precocious Ellen was, she panicked. What use to herself or anyone else was a strikingly clever girl? Rather than encouraging Ellen's fast-developing intellect, Mrs Weeton prohibited her from lessons, except to teach the basics to fellow pupils:

Oh! how I have burned to learn Latin, French, the Arts, the Sciences, anything rather than the dog-trot way of sewing, teaching,

writing copies, and washing dishes every day. Of my Arithmetic
I was very fond, and advanced rapidly. Mensuration [or how to
measure things] was quite delightful, [and] Fractions, Decimals, &
Book keeping. So would Geography and Grammar have been,
but . . . I could not get on as my mother would not help me.[8]

Like so many in her position, Ellen was being exploited, and
her eager mind trained more to shrink than to stretch.

There was a formal pupil-teacher system in place in well-
regulated schools, which offered the only (vaguely) official
training for women teachers in England. Grants were available to cover the apprentice's costs from the age of fourteen
until she graduated at eighteen into teaching full time. But
with more schools opening, even though compulsory education was not introduced until 1870, demand for teachers
was in danger of exceeding supply. The National Society
decided to keep that supply 'in house' by opening a London
training college, Whitelands, in 1841. Its aim was 'to produce a superior class of parochial schoolmistresses'; *their* aim
was to teach their girls to be good, 'and let who will be
clever'. Another five teacher-training colleges for women
appeared over the next four years, and by 1850, of 1,500
women teachers working in England, 500 were professionally trained.[9] To an extent, anyway: the curriculum was neither rigorous nor challenging, but it was a start. Indeed,
Whitelands was the first establishment to come anywhere
close to Astell's and Defoe's visions of the future. The colleges were not residential (at first), nor highfalutin in their
academic expectations, but they took women, young and not
so young, and educated them for a career, just as Nightingale's
school for nurses did later on. The next step, of course, was to
offer women *non*-vocational higher education.

★

Not all those registering for training at college were straight
from school. Many were governesses, with several years'
experience behind them, but not much expertise: a little
like Ellen Weeton. Constance Maynard had governesses
from time to time (in fact her family seems to have run the
gamut of educational opportunities). Their lessons were
dreadful. Constance was expected to read aloud page after
page of the dullest of history books (but never to take notes);
endlessly to repeat French verbs without necessarily knowing what they meant; learn useless facts such as 'which of
our four British Queens have given the greatest proofs of
courage and intrepidity', or what tapioca was, and why the
thunder did not precede the lightning. 'I do not think I
remember a spark of real interest being elicited . . . Of all
the arithmetic I learned, and there was a little every day for
several years, I can call to mind only one single rule, and it
ran thus: "Turn the fraction upside down, and proceed as
before."'[10]

One of Constance's fellow students at Cambridge in the
early 1870s, Mary Paley, had the same experience. All she
could remember of her governess's teaching was the date at
which black silk stockings were first worn in England, and
(following a theme, here) 'What to do in a thunderstorm at
night'. The pragmatic answer was to 'draw your bed into the
middle of the room, commend your soul to Almighty God
and go to sleep'.[11] There is no doubt both Constance and Mary
were taught by their governesses to draw, sing, probably dance,
and to make polite conversation. There was even a lugubrious
textbook available for the latter, with common examples of
mistakes – one should not, for example, say 'I have lost my
doll's pretty bonnet that I took so much trouble to make, and
I am quite miserable about it. I told the nurse she must find it
for me,' but 'I have met with a heavy loss. The doll's bonnet

you saw me making the other day: mama said it was pretty; and I am grieved lest she should be angry with me for not taking better care of my things. I have intreated [sic] nurse to assist me in seeking it.'[12] This was the tinselly stuff of a governess's education. Expectations were so low.

But it is unfair to blame the governess generically for this, nor for the pervasive frivolity of female education and its emphasis on accomplishment over understanding. After all, attempts to reform her meagre career were responsible, ultimately, for the foundation of sound secondary schooling for girls, which eventually led to university access.

These attempts first got off the ground with the foundation of the Governesses' Benevolent Institution (GBI) in 1843, two years after Whitelands College opened. There had been a Mutual Assurance Society for governesses for some time, but the GBI offered more to the estimated 25,000 of them working in England during the mid-nineteenth century. It gave annuities, operated a savings bank, and ran an employment registry, as well as providing accommodation for those temporarily 'disengaged', and a longer-term home, or asylum, for those described in popular literature as 'distressed' or, worse still, 'decayed'. The high profile of the GBI (Charles Dickens was an early supporter) ensured plenty of attention for the plight of the over-worked, under-trained, and poorly paid governess. *Jane Eyre* appeared in 1847, with its eponymous heroine, as did Becky Sharp in Thackeray's *Vanity Fair*, two of English fiction's most memorable governesses, and sketches emerged in comfortable periodicals of wan-looking damsels gazing over their charges' heads into a middle-distance of frustration, regret, and scarcely quelled emotion.

Behind the scenes, meanwhile, a dedicated group of agitators was working hard to make the governess extinct. The

Secretary of the GBI's Committee of Education was among them. Frederick Denison Maurice, himself the brother of a governess, was Professor of English History and Literature at King's College in London, and it was his radical idea in 1847 to institute a series of evening lectures for governesses to improve their teaching repertoire. They were to be called 'Lectures to Ladies', delivered by the professor himself, and were to include 'all branches of female knowledge'.

There had been open lectures before, to which women could go if so moved. The Mechanics' Institute in London, later Birkbeck College, was opened in 1823 to provide out-of-hours education to working men; in 1830, it admitted women (rather by default, when it was discovered that they weren't *not* allowed to go), and having got over the delicate matter of whether those females who did choose to attend should be allowed through the front door (it was decided that they were), it offered them an eclectic choice of electricity, optics, geology, chemistry, phrenology, political economy, and various arts courses. Not many went.

There is a record of two women attending lectures at University College in London in 1832. They were a Mrs Potter and a Miss Rogers, and they share the distinction of being the first women in England to be entered on to the student roll of a university. It is rather disappointing to find that their brief studies comprised attending the 'Juvenile Course in Natural Philosophy', along with Mrs Potter's fourteen-year-old son. Still, it was a precedent, and precedent is a great thing in progress.

The popularity of Professor Maurice's Lectures to Ladies tempted him to put into practice an idea he and his sympathizers had been pondering for some time. In the spring of 1848, he announced the opening of what he proudly called a 'College for the Education of Young Ladies' – Queen's College – in London. Its purpose was to produce a new generation of students: girls who enjoyed high academic achievement and who appreciated the value of high expectation, in themselves and of others in them. Many would inevitably go on to become teachers themselves, which was all part of Maurice's grand plan. He was one of the first academics to acknowledge school-teaching as a responsible and admirable vocation for women. Its practitioners should be properly prepared and worthy of intellectual respect.

While a good education was essential to an effective teacher, Maurice insisted, rather radically, that teaching should not be considered the only end of such an education. This was a crucial statement, sounding the death-knell of the traditional governess. Maurice suggested that it was the right of every intelligent thirteen-year-old (if her family could afford it) to be offered access to a professionally taught, wide-ranging curriculum. Queen's College was essentially the first serious secondary school for girls.

It duly opened its doors on Harley Street, London, with Maurice as its Principal. During the day it ran classes for 'ladies above the age of twelve', for which fees were payable; free evening lectures, subsidized by the GBI, were offered to working governesses in search of better things.[13] After all, as one supporter bitterly remarked, 'The wretchedness of an empty brain is perhaps as hard to bear as that of an empty purse.'[14] Women like Ellen Weeton, for whom Queen's was designed, suffered both.

The organization of the classes and curriculum at Queen's was ambitious. There was no social segregation: tradesmen's daughters were as welcome as gentlemen's, so long as they could pay. The timetable covered much the same subjects as Bathsua Makin's had, back in the 1670s, but explored them all to greater depth, and included specific sessions on pedagogy.

Two of Queen's College's earliest pupils were to become England's most famous headmistresses, Frances Mary Buss and Dorothea Beale. Miss Buss (1827–94) went along to the evening classes, six nights a week, after a day's work teaching in her mother's school. She had left school herself at fourteen, one of ten children in an artist's family; her upbringing was warm, good-humoured, chaotic, and usually impecunious. The course at Queen's was a business enterprise as much as anything: armed with the increasingly well-respected qualifications it offered, she would be an asset to her mother's school. The more certificates she had, the higher the fees they could demand for her teaching. But ideology was important too. Mrs Buss's establishment in Camden, north London, was progressive, teaching mixed infants using the gentle, intuitive methods pioneered in Switzerland by Johann Pestalozzi, and attracting girls over the age of twelve with an advanced curriculum and the respect for learning per se that Queen's had fostered in Frances. 'I want girls educated to match their brothers,' she declared, and the school developed into what remains one of the highest-calibre girls' schools in the country, the North London Collegiate, with Frances as headmistress.

Dorothea Beale (1831–1906) came from a similarly large household, but less disorganized than Frances's, and rather more earnest. There was both money and influence in the Beale family, but neither was invested in Dorothea's education. Like Constance Maynard, she endured a succession of governesses before briefly attending school, which she abandoned at thirteen. Then she was left to educate herself, with the help of hand-me-downs from her brothers' lessons, and copious reading. At the age of sixteen, in 1847, she was sent to a finishing school in Paris, which she considered 'of a nature to induce atrophy of the thinking powers'; luckily, when revolution broke out in France in 1848, she was dispatched home. Immediately Queen's opened that same year, she enrolled on courses for a wide variety of subjects and so excelled that she was invited, at eighteen, to become the first female member of its teaching staff. She stayed at Queen's until resigning in 1856. A short, unhappy spell at Casterton School followed; she resigned again, and for broadly the same reasons: that her authority as a senior member of staff was being undermined and her constructive suggestions for reform ignored, due to her gender.

In 1858, Dorothea was appointed Headmistress of the Cheltenham Ladies' College (founded in 1854), and there she stayed. She developed the school into an intellectual beacon, shining still. The school was her husband, she said, and she the alma mater to generations of academic young women. She educated them, equipped them for training colleges after school, sent them eventually to Oxford, Cambridge, and beyond, and then installed them as the wardens and principals of other influential schools and university colleges around the country, to pass the message on. Those pupils who chose not to practise a profession (and few of them from the Ladies' College would need to) were taught to do their duty to their husbands and children as intelligent, well-informed, God-fearing women.

The North London Collegiate School was less elite than the Ladies' College. Frances Buss was anxious, if possible, to take any girl she felt could learn to her own and society's advantage. Nor did pupils need to be of the Anglican faith. Both establishments shared firm discipline, a sense of intellectual aspiration, and a forceful, charismatic personality at the helm.

Miss Buss and Miss Beale became famous, and were caricatured as admirable, slightly alarming but well-meaning bluestockings, whose femininity was inevitably flawed by strong-mindedness, as exemplified by this popular rhyme of the day:

> Miss Buss and Miss Beale
> Cupid's Darts do not feel,
> They leave that to us,
> Poor Beale and poor Buss.

Nevertheless, their schools became patterns for the best in modern education for girls and crucibles for progress, resulting in a system of public examinations that finally made university accessible for women.

That progress was astonishingly rapid between the founding of Queen's College in 1848 and the establishment of Girton a couple of decades later. Bedford College, founded by the abolitionist Elizabeth Jesser Reid in 1849, was a non-denominational equivalent of (Anglican) Queen's, and still exists, amalgamated with Royal Holloway College as part of the University of London (whose degrees it awarded from 1878 onwards). Barbara Bodichon went there, as, for a short time, did Mary Ann Evans (the novelist George Eliot) and medical pioneer Elizabeth Blackwell (1812–1910).

The campaign for high-quality secondary and tertiary education for girls gradually emerged into the public eye; articles were published discussing its advisability, and debates conducted in print to argue the pros and cons. Some of the sharpest opposition came from women. The novelist Charlotte Yonge was cynical when asked to contribute to the founding of Girton. She abhorred the prospect of 'bringing large numbers of girls together', and thought a home education, under the supervision of 'sensible' fathers, was invariably best.[15] The concept of paying for a young lady's education was something she found distasteful, and faintly vulgar.

Elizabeth Sewell, a teacher herself, and author of several popular books for children, agreed. She was a pragmatist (or defeatist?) rather than a reformer. Since the aim of education, she said, is to fit children for adult life, it seems foolish to encourage intellectual curiosity and thinking skills in girls. They should not need them. 'Girls are to dwell in quiet homes, among a few friends [just what Florence Nightingale detested]; to exercise a noiseless influence, to be submissive and retiring.' And no one likes 'strong-minded' or over-educated females. 'They might be useful in their generation; but we may well desire to be spared them as a race.'[16]

Queen Victoria granted a royal charter to Queen's College in 1853. She approved of a sound Christian education for girls, certainly, but the thought of that leading to any unladylike demands for political attention (as some said it might) was outrageous:

The Queen is most anxious to enlist everyone who can speak or write to join in checking this mad, wicked folly of 'Women's rights' with all its attendant horrors, on which her poor feeble sex is bent, forgetting every sense of womanly feeling and propriety . . . It is a subject which makes the Queen so furious she cannot contain herself.[17]

Despite such illustrious disapproval, individual role models for the campaign began to grow in confidence and promi-nence. The most vociferous of these tended to be members of a new, more business-like 'petticoterie' of bluestockings known as the Ladies of Langham Place. Intellectual, outspoken femi-nists, who argued in public for political and social reform, they ran a sort of clubhouse in Langham Place, London, a 'Ladies'

Institute', which provided a reading room, an employment
registry, a committee room available to philanthropic associations, and the office of their house publication, the *English
Woman's Journal*.[18] A glance at the first few numbers of the *Journal* gives a reasonable idea of the editors' wide-ranging concerns. There is an article on the profession of teaching, naturally
enough; the annual reports of the GBI are printed; a digest of
current affairs; thoughtful book reviews; an article on Elizabeth Blackwell's triumph in qualifying as a medical doctor in
New York; statistics from the 1851 census about women's
occupations; a notice on the opening of a public swimming
bath for ladies in Marylebone; and a long piece, 'Women's
Dress in Relation to Health', reporting that the average weight
of an eighteen-year-old's clothes – 'a lynsey [coarse linen]
dress, a thick cloth cloak, a scarlet flannel upper petticoat, a
steel skeleton skirt, a flannel under-petticoat, and all the rest
. . .' – was, staggeringly, just over fourteen pounds (about six
and a half kilos) in weight. There is also a discussion on wom-
en's intellectual capacity: 'Aristotle has remarked that the
female brain is absolutely smaller than the male, it is nevertheless not *relatively* smaller, compared with the body . . .'

Barbara Bodichon was one of the Langham Place circle,
editing the *Journal* and campaigning for higher education and
legal privilege; so were the philanthropist Bessie Rayner Parkes;
Adelaide Procter, who founded the Society for the Promotion
of Employment for Women; and Emily Faithfull, a lobbyist for
working women. What set these people apart from any of their
feminist predecessors (except, perhaps, Bathsua Makin) was
that they got things done. Bodichon petitioned vigorously for
the passing of the Married Women's Property Act in 1858.
Emily Faithfull was appointed Royal Printer to Queen Victoria. Elizabeth Garrett Anderson broke down the barriers to
women training as doctors in England. Emily Davies intro-

duced public examinations for schoolgirls, and then founded Girton College, Cambridge.

Meanwhile, away from the capital, a new, slightly gentler phenomenon was developing. In towns and cities across England, more Lectures to Ladies were being advertised, and from Exeter to Nottingham, Guernsey to Liverpool, little flocks of gentlewomen were emerging from the parlour, and scuttling their way to talks in public rooms by gentlemen academics. The cartoonists of the day adored them: ladies in search of learning were intrinsically rather ridiculous. But despite their apparent sciolism, there were some extremely strong-minded men and women behind this movement, and like the Langham Place circle, they achieved real results. Ladies' Educational Associations were formed, with local committees, to arrange and publicize courses; lists of prospective students were signed up, and if there were enough to subsidize a visiting lecturer, peripatetic professors were engaged from London, Oxford, Cambridge, and Durham, under the auspices of the University Extension Movement.[19]

One particularly enthusiastic young tutor from Cambridge, James Stuart, spent his vacation in 1867 touring Liverpool, Manchester, Leeds, Sheffield, Rotherham, and Crewe for the North of England Council for Promoting the Higher Education of Women, established by Josephine Butler and Anne Jemima Clough. He delivered an eight-week course on physical astronomy, was paid the handsome sum of £200, and attracted some 550 students. Such was the popularity of his lectures that the local circulating libraries had to ditch some of their novels in favour of scientific books, and the number of ladies hoping to attend further lectures threatened to reach unmanageable proportions.

Some of these women were vicariously academic: professors' wives, sisters or daughters, perhaps in middle age, desperate, like Florence Nightingale, to find a place for the 'passion, intellect, and moral activity' so inconveniently lodged

A cynical survey of the opportunities open to the educated woman in 1916, all of them useless, distasteful, or laughable.

in their breast. Others were girls in their late teens, who had finished with school but not with scholarship. They might hope to be teachers themselves, like the students of Queen's or Bedford; maybe, like George Eliot's heroines, they felt a moral – almost physical – compulsion to use their minds. Many, quite simply, had nothing else to do.

Constance Maynard and Mary Paley were in this latter category. Once Constance had done with her governesses and notional schooling, she found herself incarcerated by home life, shut up like an eagle in a cage, unable to summon the energy or courage to break free. She felt external events were passing her by. 'Out in the world, artisans received the franchise and the first Education Act foreshadowed changes even greater than those it enforced, and trade-unionism came into the open, and Gladstone succeeded Disraeli.'[20] Meanwhile, Constance festered. By 1872, aged twenty-three, she had had enough.

Mary Paley, who knew what to do in a thunderstorm at night, felt the same sense of ennui vegetating at home while her fiancé was posted to India for three years. Somewhat bolder than Constance, she announced to her family, rather than requested, that she intended to 'go in' for the new examination available to women in England, the Cambridge 'Higher Local'. It would, she said, be something harmless to occupy her mind.

At this point, it might be useful to draw a deep breath and try to explain the system of public exams at the time. For that we have to return to one of the Langham Place Ladies, Emily Davies (1830–1921). Influenced by the feminist philosophy of Barbara Bodichon and the dazzling effrontery of Elizabeth Garrett Anderson, who (unsuccessfully) demanded admission to London University as a medical student in 1862, Miss Davies and her sympathizers set out on a personal crusade. It is said that she first articulated it while sitting with Garrett Anderson by the fireside one evening in 1860. They were chatting about hopes and ambitions. 'Well, Elizabeth,' declared Emily at the end of the evening, 'it is clear what has to be done. I must devote myself to securing higher education while you open the medical profession for women. After these things are done, we must see about getting the vote.'[21] Come 1918, Emily was indeed one of the first women to vote in England, at the age of eighty-eight – but that is another story.

Emily remembered being wildly jealous of her brother when he went to Cambridge. Jealousy fermented into anger, and she determined to offer the sisters of the next generation of undergraduates all the educational opportunities denied to her. Having failed in her petition to London to make the matriculation or entrance examination available to women in the early 1860s, she turned her attention to Cambridge. Logically, she reckoned that if girls took the same exams at school as boys did, then it would be harder to refuse their progress to the next stage of education. So in 1863, with the support of Miss Buss and other pioneering headmistresses (but not the more cautious Miss Beale), Emily managed to persuade the authorities that girls should at least be allowed to attempt the Cambridge 'Junior Locals', the precursor of today's GCSEs, which had been available to boys of sixteen or so since 1858. The girls were required to sit them in seclusion, engage qualified people to mark them, and do without the results being published; it was also made clear that this was an experiment, likely to fail because girls would not be up to the task. Indeed, Emily was warned, the effort of taking them might well prove injurious to female health.

In fact, good schools welcomed the introduction of a benchmark qualification for girls, and the experiment was a success. In 1865, the Locals were permanently opened to girls. 'The idea almost takes one's breath away,' wrote one horrified critic, convinced that the Empire's mothers-to-be were being mentally and probably physically addled by spurious intellectual competition. Most people concerned with the general progress of education in England, however, were in favour. The corresponding Local exams administered by Oxford were opened two years later.

The next stage in Emily Davies's crusade was to institute more advanced exams – ultimately 'A' levels – which had not existed for boys before but, because of the demand for a plenary test at the end of a girl's career in education, soon became commonplace in schools for both sexes. The Cambridge 'Higher Locals' came into being in 1869 (and Oxford's in 1875). Constance Maynard took Cambridge Highers, as entrance exams to Girton.

She had to travel to London during the hot summer of 1872 to sit the exams. There were several papers, and after overcoming an initial conviction of 'bewildering incompetence', Constance relaxed. She was thrilled by the complete silence of the examination hall (but for the scratching of pens), the urgency of the occasion, the intense collective concentration of her fellow candidates. And when the morning exams were over, she loved the novelty of 'turning out alone into the streets of London, choosing a shop and ordering coffee for luncheon'.

The series of papers went on. The New Testament was quite obvious, the Euclid would have been perfect had I had more time, but my distinctly slow hand-writing was against me, and the dreaded Arithmetic let me do fully nine out of twelve questions. The Drawing was nothing, the Greek so hard I heartily wished I had taken German, the Grammar (English) I did badly as I

thought, but the Essay was charming . . . Counting all together it
was absurd to think I might have failed, but I did, and returned
home late on the 21st June, sometimes rejoicing in the new experience, and sometimes almost bent double with fear that my last
chance had gone . . .

On 27th came the splendid word 'Passed'.[22]

Constance was bound not for Girton village, where the
college now stands, but for Hitchin, an inoffensive market
town in the heart of middle England. In 1869, Emily Davies's
quest had led to her renting a building there, Benslow House,
for herself and five other women.[23] They were orphan Anna
Lloyd, aged thirty, whose sisters were so outraged at her self-
ishness in abandoning them that they forced her to leave college after a year; Louisa Lumsden, twenty-nine, later Dame
Louisa, who took Classics and became a lecturer at Girton
herself; Emily Gibson, a shipbuilder's daughter who had been
working as a pupil-teacher and was subsidized through college by her brother; Sarah Woodhead, a mathematician, who
at eighteen was the youngest student in residence; and Rachel
Cook, another Classicist, whose father was Professor of History at St Andrew's University in Scotland. With the support
of visiting professors from Cambridge, less than an hour away
by train, the five would live together, learn together, and
become the first women to study a degree course at any
English university.

Emily Davies had campaigned long and hard for this. She
depended on the headmistresses of girls' schools: if they did
not enter their most able pupils for the Junior Locals and
Highers, the cause was lost. And even though her college
had no official connection with the University of Cambridge, she relied on the authorities' goodwill and forbearance. High-profile members of the Langham Place Ladies

helped too, by publicizing the venture and arguing its advantages in print. Elizabeth Garrett Anderson, not surprisingly, did all she could to further her old friend Emily's enterprise, and Barbara Bodichon was a stalwart champion. Funds were raised, prejudices whittled away (just enough), and students recruited so that by October 1873, when Benslow House was forsaken for Girton College proper, there were fifteen women on the roll.

Constance Maynard was among them, and felt, for the first time, that she had found her spiritual home. '*That's* what you've been waiting for!' she told herself. At last.

3. Invading Academia

Gently, gently
Evidently
We are safe so far,
After scaling
Fence-paling
Here, at last, we are![1]

Meanwhile, a couple of miles down the road from Girton at 74 Regent Street, Cambridge, Mary Paley and four other women were settling in to a very similar community to Constance Maynard's. This little 'garden of flowers', as one of the kinder critics put it, blossomed into Newnham College, and was 'planted' in 1871 by Professor of Philosophy Henry Sidgwick (1838–1900). He was a gentle soul with a stammer and an impish sense of humour, and his dedication to the cause of university access for women was unstinting.

Sidgwick supported Emily Davies at Girton, but disagreed with aspects of her approach. With his wife, Eleanor, and a firebrand from the North of England Council for Promoting the Higher Education of Women, the Liverpudlian teacher Anne Jemima Clough (1820–92), Sidgwick planned 'a place of academic excellence' like Girton, to provide an edifying home-from-home for clever women attending Cambridge lectures.

Girtonians, once they were comfortably ensconced in their college, were expected to pass the dreaded 'Little-Go', a preliminary qualification usually taken during the first year of a degree course including compulsory elements – whatever one's subject – of Latin, Greek, and divinity. For the majority of girls, lacking the standard classical education trotted out in boys' schools, it was a tiresome hurdle and delayed engagement with the Tripos (honours degree) course they had chosen. But it was what undergraduates at Cambridge had always done; therefore, insisted Emily Davies, her girls must do it too. There must be no question of concession.

The Sidgwicks and Miss Clough were more circumspect at Newnham. They refused to prescribe the Little-Go, since it offered no intellectual advantages. The newly available Cambridge Higher was stringent enough, in their view, to test a student's abilities. Newnham girls were to be allowed to work for the Tripos from the beginning. There was nothing to stop them; the college (actually a small rented house at this stage) was not yet affiliated to the university, nor subject to its regulations. It relied like Girton on the goodwill – or reluctant chivalry – of visiting lecturers and accommodating examiners.

To Miss Davies the fight for university access was all about equality, and Girton was a public statement of her demands. For the Sidgwicks and Miss Clough, at Newnham, it was the individual's intellectual development that mattered, and appropriately, they chose a kinder, more secluded environment for their students.

In 1873, Girton moved to its startling new buildings, designed by the municipal architect Alfred Waterhouse to rear out of the Cambridgeshire cabbage fields with uncompromising trenchancy, like a dowager duchess at the WI. The grounds were, and are, lovely, but even now they hardly soften the maroon Gothic bulk of the college.

That same year, the more discreet Newnham relocated,

too. Regent Street was too noisy, and the house's inhabitants, whose rooms abutted the road, were being peered at.
Miss Clough chose Merton Hall, an old and picturesque
house in Northampton Street, principally because of its gar-
dens. Mature trees screened her students from impertinent
passers-by, and though the bedrooms were uncomfortable,
with several girls having to share, and water slithered down
the dining-room walls when it rained, the privacy and quiet
were welcome. Professor Sidgwick paid the first year's rent
himself, and bought extra furniture.

Two years later, the college moved again, this time to
Newnham Hall, the nucleus of Sir Basil Champney's
purpose-built accommodation in the gracious, domestic style
reminiscent of a Queen Anne country house.[2] Indeed, for all
the new women's colleges the suggestion of country-house
ambience was quite deliberate. It was supposed to lend an air
of well-ordered conviviality and social propriety to comfort
the students and confound those who thought you might as
well let cretins or criminals invade academia, as women.

In the early days, not all of those who came up to college
stayed the full three years. Options included living in while
attending one or two series of lectures, and then leaving;
working for a 'pass' or 'ordinary' degree (that is, a lower-
calibre course), or buckling down to full honours – including, at Girton, 'Little-Go'. It has been a feature of women
students' lives across the span of this book, however, that at
any time the call might come from home to abandon the
life of an intellectual sybarite and return to reality. As Anna
Lloyd from Girton knew (whose sisters' disapproval grew
too strident to ignore), for women domestic duty was too
often pitted against scholarship, and reputation against self-
fulfilment. Welsh girl Dilys Lloyd Davies was another reluctant drop-out: she had gone up to study natural sciences at

Newnham after a brief stint as pupil-teacher at her old school
– Miss Buss's North London Collegiate – in 1877.

Dilys wrote letters home every Sunday, like everyone else,
and hers shimmer with enthusiasm. She drew a careful plan of
her room for her family. It had three chairs, a chest of drawers,
a washstand, a curtained-off corner for hanging dresses, and
a dressing table under the window next to her bed 'with a
snowy quilt'; she used her tin trunk for a bedside cabinet.
Most of the college furniture was donated by well-wishers, or
found by the Sidgwicks in antique shops around Cambridge.
The wallpaper and curtains were riotously floral (mostly pas-
sionflowers), and clashed with the cheerful green and red carpet. At night, Dilys was kept awake by nightingales.

The other students were fascinating. One was a thin girl
whom Dilys was shocked to realize wore no petticoats.

She is given just a little to manly or rather masculine movements
of the lower limbs: sitting on tables now and then and spreading
her feet out a little but I dare say she is nice . . . One or two are
rather given that way.

She found the 'ladylike ones' a great comfort. They did not
gossip or use slang, and though they could be rather earnest
and drab, at least they were safely conventional. The young
men she saw at lectures looked equally fascinating; especially
one who asked if he could walk along beside her. 'That is
against the rules, I find, but I didn't know.' He asked her and
a chaperone to come on the river with him, but Miss Clough
said it was out of the question, 'so that', Dilys wrote regret-
fully, 'is the end of that'.[3]

Chaperones were an unavoidable feature of university life
for women right through to the 1920s, and even, in some
archaic cases, beyond.[4] They were married ladies or widows

engaged as guardians. Guardians against moral, perhaps physical, violation when students were out and about among undergraduates and university staff; and against moral, perhaps physical, turpitude if students were tempted to interact in any way with said risky gentlemen. In other words, they were paid to safeguard young women from themselves as much as others. Their presence was also a comfort to parents at home, worrying about their unprotected daughters at large in a man's world. Chaperones were issued with cheap tickets to lectures where, having corralled their charges into a corner of the hall, they sat and noisily knitted. If a woman student wished to go to a concert (only with her college Principal's permission, of course), to tea with family friends, to conduct an experiment in a laboratory, for a little stroll along the river, *anywhere* indeed, without a chaperone she could not do it.

Naturally enough, these duennas were resented as being staid, strict, interfering, and inconvenient. No doubt many were all of these things, but it could be a thankless task, and those who volunteered were doing the cause of higher education for women a considerable service. Eventually, women undergraduates were trusted enough to manage life by themselves, but it took a good half-century for that to happen.

No chaperones were required for life in college. There the staff and senior students took their place. As a 'fresher', or first-year, Dilys Lloyd Davies was forbidden to go to a college dance at Girton (an all-female affair), but she wrote home breathlessly describing those lovely creatures who were allowed, accompanied by Miss Clough:

Miss Bettany wore a very pale blue cashmere trimmed with silk, a fan, gold bracelet, snowdrops and heath[er] in her head and dress . . . Miss Gill, who is about 5 feet nothing wore a white lama [fine

woollen fabric] with snowdrops in a chain round the square body
and on the elbow sleeves and fan – and in her hair. She looked a
regular little doll. I wished I were a man to dance with her . . .
Miss Prideaux, a long and narrer [sic] lady wore a dark green velvet dress; Miss Harrison white silk and gold beads on neck, wrists
and head. She is very graceful. Miss Richmond wore pink silk
with white crocuses. Miss Clough wore grey slate silk, so pretty.[5]

No wonder Professor Sidgwick was worried that his college would not be taken seriously: the girls, he said, looked
far too lovely to be clever.

Dilys stayed only a year at Newnham. During her first
summer term, she was summoned by Miss Buss, who
needed a new member of staff at the North London Collegiate and thought Dilys would do. The young Welsh girl
was reluctantly forced to accept the post. It is ironic that
someone who did so much to promote the university
careers of such crowds of young women should be responsible for denying an individual student the same. But Miss
Buss was not renowned for her empathy.

In 1881, the University of Cambridge formally opened its
examinations to women, a move welcomed by Girton and
Newnham with slightly exasperated gratitude. (The next
step would be the granting of a degree to those candidates
who passed them.) This may have been a local triumph, but
by now Cambridge had relinquished its place at the vanguard of higher education for women, never to regain it.
The university itself had never been proactive: it just suffered pioneers like Miss Davies and Miss Clough to fuss
about in its shade for a while. London University had a tradition of dissent, however, and in 1878 radically announced
that, following the passing of the Enabling Act two years

previously, all scholarships, prizes, and degrees (except medicine) would henceforth be open to men and women equally. Soon a dedicated hall of residence was established for those women undergraduates attending University College; others went to Bedford College, now an official part of the university establishment; Constance Maynard set up Westfield College in Hampstead in 1882; Royal Holloway was opened on the outskirts of London in 1886, and was later presided over by Miss Tuke, who wore silver slippers and, naturally enough, azure blue silk stockings. Then there was King's College for Women in Kensington, with the following also opening their doors in due course to women as well as men: Imperial College (formerly the Royal College of Science), the London School of Economics and Queen Mary College in the East End.

The first two women's colleges in Oxford, Somerville and Lady Margaret Hall (LMH), were opened in 1879. As in the Other Place (Cambridge), they were originally homely hostels for ladies keen to attend university lectures, and then developed into what Dorothea Beale of the Cheltenham Ladies' College described as 'academic institutions in family form'. Somerville was rigorously non-denominational, while LMH embraced Anglican principles. St Hugh's followed in 1886, and St Hilda's, founded by Miss Beale, in 1893.[6] The local branch of the Association for the Education of Women administered a lodging-house system for local ladies, known as the Society of Home Students (later St Anne's), to allow those who could not afford full-blown college accommodation, or did not need it, the chance to attend lectures and (after 1884) take finals. Not that college accommodation was very grand. Jessie Emmerson was one of the first girls at St Hugh's, then housed in a semi-detached residence in Norham Road, and was bemused on her arrival in 1886 by its spartan lack of charm. There was hardly any furniture, and nowhere quiet to work, since next door's child seemed constantly to be practising the piano. Social interaction was awkward: there was only a handful of students, none of whom knew each other:

> We all felt rather shy . . . especially during the first meals in the little dining room which looked into a small back garden containing nothing in particular except grass. But next door there were some rabbits in a hutch, and they at once arrested our attention and naturally became a subject of conversation when other topics failed.

> One day someone's undergraduate brother came to visit, 'and looking out of the window exclaimed – "What a dull hole! I expect you have nothing to talk about except those rabbits".[7]

Things were much more exciting in the provinces. At the time of its momentous announcement in 1878, London University was solely an examining body; this meant that any teaching institution with staff and students of sufficient intellectual calibre could apply to award its external degrees. All around the country, colleges of higher education realized that they could class themselves as vicarious universities, and attract undergraduates of both sexes, by subscribing to London's matriculation and final exams. Thus Nottingham became a university college in 1881, Bristol in 1883, Reading in 1892, Sheffield in 1897, and Exeter in 1901. At several of them there were more women than men among the non-resident students.

Back in 1868, a commissioner reporting on the state of secondary education for girls in England had made a bitter observation:

Although the world has now existed for several thousand years, the notion that women have minds as cultivable and as well worth cultivating as men's minds is still regarded by the ordinary British parent as an offensive, not to say revolutionary paradox.[8]

Now, apparently quite suddenly, that revolution was well under way. It was happening in the north of the country, too. The vigorous Ladies' Educational Associations which had employed lecturers like James Stuart as part of the University Extension Scheme in Liverpool, Manchester, and Leeds in the 1870s helped galvanize the colleges already in place there to form their own collective degree-granting body in 1881. It was called Victoria University, refreshingly unencumbered by an arcane male provenance, and it declared itself proud to admit women as undergraduates on equal terms with men from the very beginning. Each of its constituent colleges admitted day-students, but also ran single-sex halls of residence which became the focus of undergraduate life, much like the colleges of London, Cambridge, and Oxford.

Durham University, founded in 1832, did not decide to award women degrees until 1895; once made, however, the decision was broadly welcomed, and there was obvious satisfaction at beating Oxbridge:

Durham has come to the rescue where Cambridge and Oxford have failed. The little University nestling under the shadow of that great Cathedral of St Cuthbert which looks so majestically down upon the Wear, is chivalrously coming forward to allow the young ladies of the day to write the magic letters 'BA' after her [sic] name . . . And when the ladies go to Durham, won't there be a large increase in the number of male Undergraduates? Fortunate Tutors! Lucky Dons! Happy Durham![9]

By about 1900, 16 per cent of university students in England were women.[10] The University of Birmingham was
granted its charter in 1900, Southampton University College (offering external London degrees) was founded in
1902, Leicester in 1921, and Hull (on the same lines as
Southampton) in 1927. All these admitted women as well as
men and awarded degrees to both. No more emerged before
the Second World War.[11]

As university places increased, so did the number of young
women eligible to take advantage of them. Encouragement
came from several quarters. The success of the Cheltenham
Ladies' College spawned other seriously academic boarding
schools for girls, including Roedean, Wycombe Abbey, and
Downe House. More schools were opened in the pattern of
the North London Collegiate, including Camden School
for Girls, founded by Miss Buss as a cheaper, more accessible
alternative for bright local girls. The Girls' Public Day School
Trust came into existence in 1872, responsible for so many
of the independent high schools still flourishing today. The
Woodard Trust established rigorous schools with a strong
Christian ethos, and state education profited hugely from
the Taunton Commission's findings – steered by Misses Buss,
Beale, and Emily Davies – in 1868.[12]

The examination system for girls grew far more robust after
the introduction of the Cambridge (and later the Oxford)
Higher Locals in 1869. They were soon acknowledged to be
so effective a measure of students' achievement and potential
that boys' schools used them, too. A typical paper, proudly
preserved by Edith Cass of Leeds (who read botany in 1909),
looks horribly challenging to modern eyes. It expects candidates to cope with a panoply of questions, from the nature of
sin, or Machiavellianism, to the American system of taxation;
to be able to draw a map of Queensland, Australia, labelling

its railways and rivers; and to compose essays on military training, spelling reform, or Florence Nightingale.[13]

Something else encouraging the university system towards
maturity in England was the progress of that system elsewhere in the world. In America, Oberlin College in Ohio
had been welcoming men and women (albeit with a very
limited curriculum) since 1833. The universities of Iowa,
Wisconsin, and Michigan were also co-educational; the
ladies' colleges of Vassar and Smith opened in 1865, and
Wellesley ten years later. How these institutions compared
to their English counterparts was open to argument, but
they existed: opportunity was there. For women wishing to
read medicine, only the universities of New York and Zurich
offered respectable degrees in the subject; in England, before
most medical faculties admitted women at the end of the
nineteenth century, there was only the London School of
Medicine for Women, opened in 1874. (The Irish and Scottish universities all accepted women by 1892, incidentally,
and the Welsh by the following year.) A German visitor to
the University of Birmingham in 1904 declared his country's
undergraduates far more advanced, in every way, than England's. The crippling social conventions so strictly observed
in England simply didn't exist there; the 'proprieties of the
drawing-room' were irrelevant. There were no 'women',
'ladies', or 'gentlemen scholars', just students and 'perfect
equality'.[14]

Such comparisons encouraged reform, and led to progress.
Everywhere, that is, but at Oxford and Cambridge. There,
degrees for women remained elusive and apparently un-
deserved.

Admission was one thing; assimilation quite another. The
German visitor's observations prove that. Publicly, this new

species must be seen to be coping well. Jessie Emmerson of St Hugh's was well aware of this: 'So greatly did the responsibility of keeping up the honour and dignity of my sex press upon me,' she confided, 'that I hardly dared address a word to anyone around me. One false step – and – for all I knew – they would never allow another woman student . . .'[15] Pioneers of LMH made the same point, reminding the first residents that 'nothing should happen in any way to make college authorities anxious, or to strengthen the very decided initial prejudice of the undergraduates against the supposed "bluestockings" . . . invading Oxford'.[16]

Society at large, and university communities in particular, needed persuading that this hazardous innovation was working well. So did the parents paying for it. It was therefore in students' interests to present as appealing a picture of their university life as possible in letters home. What appealed to Bessie Macleod's family was obviously flat-out activity. Bessie describes a typical day at Girton for them, during her first term in October 1881. It starts at 6.30, with the shriek of an alarm clock, and Bessie fumbling about in the dark, with chilblained fingers, for a candle. Once it's lit, she wraps up warmly and takes it through to her en-suite study to do an hour's Latin. She has to pick her way through the debris of last night's revels (she had a cocoa party, and her guests brought cake). The 'Gyp', or maid, will clear that up later, after she has delivered Bessie her daily ration of coal for the fire and a jug of hot water for washing.

At eight o'clock it's prayers. As a fresher, Bessie has to sit at the back, which means she is last to breakfast. By the time she gets to the dining hall, there is nothing left but an un-alluring cocktail of cold ham and treacle. She has a cup of tea instead, and making sure there are no tutors around to see, sprints straight back upstairs to continue her Latin prose, which she has until 10.00 a.m. to complete. Sprinting is not what Girtonians do.

She rushes her work to the post room (the ink still wet) just in time for it to be bundled up and dispatched to a tutor down the road in Cambridge. There are several postal collections and deliveries a day, and it is quicker to mail essays and assignments than physically to take them. The rest of the morning is spent on theology, Greek, and maths.

Lunch is at 1.00 p.m., and to signal that she is not in the mood for conversation, Bessie arms herself with a stern expression and a book. Neither works: with awful inevitability, Girton's dreariest daughter makes straight for her. The college population is encouraged to take a constitutional stroll around the grounds after lunch; at two o'clock Bessie has a lecture, and the rest of the afternoon evaporates in work.

The menu for dinner at six o'clock is unpromising: fish, mutton casserole, potatoes, turnips, and sago pudding. Feeling weary and weighed down by stodge, Bessie looks forward to a little free time – and then remembers tonight is fire drill night.

Every women's college in the country had its own fire brigade, unless it happened to be in a city centre (which very few were). In Bessie's era there was still candlelight; surprisingly soon, smoking was to be allowed in students' rooms, and open fires were everywhere right up to the Second World War. Girton especially relied on its brigade: it would be ages before the Cambridge fire fighters got there on their horse-drawn cart in an emergency. The brigade boasted buckets, hoses, and a portable chute for dramatic bedroom rescues. There are several photographs in university archives of young women beaming from top-floor windows, holding the cavernous mouth of a rickety-looking

The Captain grim with strong right arm
Peals forth the dreaful Bell's alarm.

Lieutenants sunk in slumber deep
List to that Voice that murders sleep

With "Sleep no more" in accents fell
My maledictions on that bell.

Then forth they rush in quaint attire
Bang on the doors, cry Fire! Fire!! FIRE!!!
Arousing protests, wrath, abuse,
Or grumpy grunts, yet these excuse.

*A student at Manchester University in 1905 depicts the frequent
ritual of the fire drill at her hall of residence, Ashburne Hall.*

canvas tube, down which they must plummet when the flames start pulling at their stay-laces. One of the maids at LMH was so plump that she was excused the chute, for fear of getting stuck. Death rather than indignity. Bessie describes the Girton fire drill:

Within three minutes all the corps are drawn up in their respective places. Each corps (there are three) has a captain and a sub-captain, who stand near, and overlooking all is the Head Captain. It is a bucket practice today, the one least liked by the Brigade, for there is not much incident in it, to say the least, especially in the winter when we have beans to weight the buckets instead of water . . . we go at a quick trot to the Middle Corridor. There we draw up in two long lines; one end joining the 'Gyps' Wing', where the taps of water are. From here the buckets are handed out full – passed down to the pump at the other end (at the supposed seat of the fire) and passed back empty along the other line . . . At last after a weary twenty minutes of Halt! Move on! Pass buckets! – the welcome order is heard . . . 'The fire is over' is said by the H.C., and instantly everyone falls out and begins talking hard to make up for twenty minutes' silence. Now what time is it? Five minutes to seven! . . .

Well now I must tackle my 'Prometheus Vinctus' [Aeschylus].[17]

Bessie works until just after 9.00 p.m. Then it's off to a dress rehearsal for the Drama Society play (Thackeray's *The Rose and the Ring*) and at last, when everyone else is tucked up asleep, she returns to her room. The fire has long since died down, so it is rapidly growing cold. Breath steaming, her last task of the day is to set the alarm for next morning: 6.30 again.

How this indefatigable chronicle was meant to encourage Bessie's family is unclear. Maybe they, like Florence Nightingale, could appreciate how gratifying it must be for an intelligent, energetic young woman like Bessie to fill her day like this, instead of sitting in the drawing room at home, measuring life out in coffee spoons and loops of crochet.

Not everyone lived a life of such breeziness. The fabric of daily existence at college, for the first few student generations at least, was slubbed with masses of little obstacles and inconveniences. It was unnerving, for example, to be laughed at so uproariously by locals when turning up for one's first (ever) hockey match, on a cowpat-splattered field in Durham, just because no one had told you how to hold a hockey stick and you assumed it was like a walking cane, curved end up.[18] When the first women arrived at Manchester University in the 1880s, they bravely signalled their intention to stay by installing an umbrella stand for their parasols in the original Owen's College building. But when they asked for a common room of their own, they were allotted a small storeroom in the attics of the University Museum, which they shared with several large stuffed fish, goggling at their temerity much as the old-school academics did. When female medical students were admitted to Manchester in 1899, they were required to keep well in the background, so as not to distract the 'real' doctors, and to eat their lunch in an unappetizing corner of the dissecting room.[19]

Most students had their meals provided for them in college or their hall of residence. Typical menus would render present-day undergraduates comatose, but the quantities and choice available were quite normal for the middle-class trencher-women of the age. At Newnham, for example, breakfast was usually porridge, eggs, ham, bacon, and smoked haddock; lunches included four or five meat or fish dishes – a roast, boiled leg of mutton, minced rabbit, giblet pie, salmon mayonnaise, stewed tongue – and sponge, milk, or fruit puddings;

for dinner there might be boiled cod, galantine of veal, curried eggs, macaroni cheese, and any amount of stewed prunes.
Afternoon tea involved heaps of bread and butter (cold suet
pudding being a Manchester alternative), sometimes cakes,
and after dinner there would be private 'revels', like Bessie
Macleod's cocoa party, to which everyone brought precious
biscuits or fruitcake sent from home. Sarah Mason, a former
North London Collegiate pupil at Girton in the late 1870s,
was outraged when Miss Buss turned up on a surprise visit
one teatime and proceeded to make a great 'hole' in her term's
supplies.

If a young lady was forced to cook for herself, over-
enthusiasm and lack of experience could result in chaos. Constance Watson of Somerville, in digs in Oxford in 1909, decided
to make her own broth for visiting friends. Its ingredients were
hair-raising: 'a ham bone, a mutton bone, macaroni, buttered
eggs, toast, two apples, herbs, almonds, sultanas, peas, a date,
pepper, salt, milk, mushroom ketchup, and essence of lemon'.
She declared it tasted 'grand'.[20]

Etiquette at mealtimes was bewildering. There were
unwritten rules about who could talk to whom, in terms of
seniority, and the rituals of processing into Hall, or dining at
High Table, were fraught with danger – even if, as in the
early days at Girton, High Table only sat two people. You
had to change for dinner – nothing too gaudy – and, either
on an ad hoc or rota basis, accompany the Principal into
Hall every so often, and sit at her right hand making polite
and erudite conversation. These occasions were completely
terrifying (the Principal was often as shy as you were), and
usually happened when there were undercooked peas or
overcooked meringue on the menu, liable to shoot off your
plate at the merest touch of a fork.

Often university would be the first place young women

mixed relatively freely with others outside their own social circle. A glimpse at the variety of entries in the space for 'father's occupation' on student registration forms suggests what a melting pot colleges and halls of residence were. At King's College, London, among those matriculating in the first few years of its existence were a shopkeeper's daughter laden with prizes and scholarships in Classics; a hatter's daughter from Crystal Palace ('the best student in her year'); a builder's labourer's daughter who had to cope with her course being frequently 'interrupted by home anxieties'; and an Indian girl – whose father was listed somewhat starkly as a dead doctor – struggling with work, health, and homesickness, and eventually achieving a BA in history.[21] But there were professors' daughters there too, and those of MPs and diplomats, all studying together in what one of them called a scholarly sisterhood. In Durham, a mine-owner's daughter might be reading for the same degree as a collier's; lawyers' children mixed with commercial travellers', bishops' with boiler-makers', and civil engineers' with fishmongers'.[22] In a country still stratified by social distinctions, this was a quiet revolution.

There were different age groups, too: gauche eighteen-year-olds straight from boarding school, well-read debutantes bored at home, women who worked to finance their courses (one, at Manchester, was a charlady), young widows, or – very occasionally – mothers with children at home. Pitched into the mixture were lonely, self-conscious students from Europe, America, and the British colonies around the globe, forging a strange new world in which most early women undergraduates flourished, but some inevitably failed and fled.

To all the early women students, this unprecedented way of life was a challenge. It could be coped with using common sense and open-mindedness (qualities not fostered much in late-Victorian England), or by adopting defensive strategies. Some women shut themselves away, working eleven or twelve hours a day and emerging only to eat and take the odd stroll round the grounds or in town. There is a cautionary tale about one of these, from Leeds:

> In a college, in a city, in a building large and fine,
> There is many, there is many, there is many-a Clementine.
> One there was among the others, like the college, very fine,
> Sweet she was and very pretty, such a darling Clementine.
>
> She delighted all Professors, and they said 'Would she were
>   mine!
> She's so clever, more than ever I did see a Clementine!'
> She went in for Honours Classics, and her brain was
>   like a mine,
> Full of knowledge and of college, such a marvellous
>   Clementine . . .

She refused to join societies or go out with friends – too busy working:

> As Exam time was approaching, thinner got poor Clementine,
> Then a white and pale and withered, beauty-faded
>   Clementine.
> But she still worked hard at Classics, poor demented
>   Clementine,
> And she took the examination, classic, classic Clementine.
>
> On the day results were issued, to the coll. crept Clementine;
> From the list her name was missing; thunder-stricken
>   Clementine . . .

When she asked her professor why, he explained:

> 'For I hear you've ne'er attempted in your life to merry be,
> So the Senate have decided not to give you a degree!'
> She departed from the college, left the University,
> Soon she wearied of existence, and she laid her down to dee.[23]

Poor Clementine: the archetypal bluestocking swot.

One way to accommodate the pressures of university life was to retreat – or blossom – into eccentricity. Somerville College in Oxford seems to have had more than its fair share of the weird and wonderful. Portia Hobbs went everywhere with roses threaded into her hair and a flowing silk gown made from sample squares from the draper's.[24] Agneta Ruck had a white rat called Martin, which she took to lectures: 'I think she was one of the first to exhibit an open neck . . . and obvious lack of corsets,' remembered a wary contemporary.[25] Martin obviously had free range of her clothes. Another 'original' girl cleared out all the furniture in her college room, and remodelled it. The walls were stripped bare, but for a portrait of Edward Carpenter (a radical socialist of rather beautiful aspect); she arranged a cluster of green balloons in one corner of the room and a bunch of dried honesty in the other. Two lonely daffodils sprouted from a tub, and cushions littered the floor, with a blowsy design of delphiniums on them exactly matching the queer cretonne frock she always wore. She festooned her bookcase with a wizened garland of rosehips, and the effect, all together, was 'most sinister'.[26]

To preserve the decorum and reputation of these undergraduate pioneers, university authorities, as well as issuing them with chaperones, resorted to exhaustive lists of rules, regulating *everything*. They stated exactly whom one could meet, in what circumstances, when, where, wearing what, and for how long. Most students, like Katie Dixon, at Newnham from 1879 to 1882, took them in good part, accepting them as a condition of their admittance to academia:

[College] was bound really in those days to be prim and respectable, the reason being that we needed the support, financial and moral, of the prim and respectable, a mistake in that way would have put us back a lot. We weren't going to 'give occasion', a perfectly reasonable point of view, and I for one wasn't going to do any mischief that way. But it makes me laugh rather to think of hedging in all those extraordinarily serious and hard-working young women, as they were, who would hardly have known how to kick over the traces, even if they had been given the chance . . .[27]

Feistier individuals were not so submissive. Sarah Mason, whose biscuits had been demolished by Miss Buss, did kick at the traces. She was constantly being hauled up before her college Mistress, or Principal, for minor misdemeanours such as refusing to wear a hat in public ('"If any undergraduates saw you, they might think you villagers!" . . . at which I grinned, but maintained a rigorous silence'). When she and her friends were asked to make less noise in the corridors and their rooms, they pinned up sarcastic notices around college wanting to know: 1) at what pitch to raise their voices; 2) what precise thickness the soles of their shoes should be; and 3) how they could have fires that required no poking.

Worst of all, Sarah and her closest friend, Charlie (Charlotte), brazenly walked around Cambridge without a chaperone, and were witnessed one Sunday being escorted into King's College Chapel by some 'wicked' male undergraduates. 'I'm afraid our behaviour was not quite *comme il faut* throughout the service.'[28]

It is a credit to the college authorities that they managed Sarah's rebellious behaviour without sending her down (expelling her). The resultant fuss would have been desperately damaging at this early stage in the history of women students, and there were plenty of greedy Jeremiahs both within and without the university system ready to pounce on mistakes. They hoped to prove the university experiment a joke – just as Gilbert and Sullivan tried to do in *Princess Ida* (1884):

> They intend to send a wire
>> To the moon – to the moon;
> And they'll set the Thames on fire
>> Very soon – very soon;
> Then they'll learn to make silk purses
>> With their rigs – with their rigs,
> From the ears of Lady Circe's
>> Piggy-wigs – piggy-wigs.
> And weasels at their slumbers
>> They trepan – they trepan;
> To get sunbeams from cucumbers,
>> They've a plan – they've a plan;
> They've a firmly rooted notion
> They can cross the Polar Ocean,
> And they'll find Perpetual Motion,
>> If they can – if they can . . .
>
> As for fashion they forswear it,
>> So they say – so they say,
> And the circle they will square it
>> Some fine day – some fine day,
> Then the little pigs they're teaching
>> For to fly – for to fly,

And they'll practise what they're preaching
> By and by – by and by,
Each newly joined aspirant
> To the clan – to the clan,
Must repudiate the tyrant
> Known as Man – known as Man.
They mock at him and flout him,
For they do not care about him,
And they're 'going to do without him'
> If they can – if they can.

These are the phenomena
That ev'ry pretty domina
Is hoping at her Universitee we shall see.[29]

Sending women to university was a travesty of common sense, scoffed the critics, a wanton waste of time and money, which upset the natural order of things, and made monsters of England's daughters. Women undergraduates should be content to go home and remain 'the soft and milky rabble' God designed.[30] Then gentlemen scholars could reclaim their seats of learning, and all would be well again. 'Woman was created as an helpmeet for man, not as his equal or rival,' explained an article called 'The Disadvantages of Higher Education', from 1882, 'and woman nowadays is apt to forget that fact.' It advised the wise young lady to concentrate on life's 'little things', such as soothing a baby or mending a shirt, since

> Little things
> On little wings
> Bear little souls to heaven.[31]

4. Most Abhorred of All Types

A Cambridge professor who is in the habit of addressing his students most pointedly as 'Gentlemen!' proceeded to his lecture room on Ash Wednesday, to find only the ladies present. With head erect and eyes riveted on the opposite wall, he announced, 'As there is nobody here, I shall not lecture today,' and with stately dignity made his departure.[1]

Invisibility was the least of their problems. The ignorance, distrust, derision, and abuse the Establishment displayed (like a respectable-looking flasher) to women undergraduates throughout the period covered by this book were shocking. There is little wonder the vanguard was so anxious its students should keep their heads below the parapet, behave impeccably, work hard, and keep quiet. 'Never argue with your opponents,' advised one lady tutor, 'it only helps to clear their minds.'[2]

Opposition came from all sides, but although vociferous, it never was very clear-minded. The medical fraternity shouted loudest, watching their backs for a similar invasion of 'petticoat pioneers'; peevish academics and male undergraduates joined them, with commentators on the moral and cultural welfare of the country. All of them tried to weaken young women's resolve to become scholars, and shame their friends and families into keeping them at home and out of trouble. From the 1890s onwards, there emerged in literature discussing the advisability of university education for women the sense of society having a moral choice. A suitable school, supported by a well-disciplined family

life, would produce young women of gentility and firm
principle. Send them to university, and they would either
mutate into bluestockings – creatures with deviant minds
and corrupt femininity – or become nervous wrecks. One
of the few women students brave enough publicly to dispute
this wrote in the *Durham University Journal* of 1899 how
hurtful that assumption was to ordinary, hard-working
women students like her: 'This was, indeed, the most
unkindest cut of all – to assert that because a woman uses the
brain which nature has bestowed upon her, even as a man
does, she is therefore a blue-stocking – most abhorred of all
types.' She resented being thought to belong to a 'shrieking
sisterhood' of freaks, dressed in 'green spectacles and a classic
frown', just because she enjoyed scholarship. It was as though
women could not cope with learning, as though assimilating
too much knowledge choked their minds to poetry, romance,
humour, and integrity. This was so unfair.[3]

The 'shrieking sisterhood' was a favourite term for the collective voice of Britain's suffragette movement, with whom
Emily Davies of Girton was so careful not to be identified, for
all her support of its ambitions. People assumed the stridency
of those agitating for 'the vote' to be shared by those working
for wider university access for women; hence the gentler
campaign suffered. This lone voice from Durham recognized
that those quietly encouraging equal opportunities at university in terms of degrees, prizes, scholarships, and employment
were hindered by what was in most cases spurious association
with violent political activists. She also realized that some
influential physicians considered it arguable whether nature
had bestowed upon woman a brain worth using. One of the
most prominent was Dr Henry Maudsley, after whom the
Maudsley Psychiatric Hospital in London is named.

It is neither surprising nor wholly their fault that doctrinaire medics considered women physiologically incapable of scholarship. There might be circumstantial evidence to the contrary, they admitted, but no proof, and proof – like reputation – was all. What could be proven was that women's brains were on average five ounces (nearly 150 grams) lighter than men's. And that menstruation sapped the body of life-blood. The inference was that a smaller brain meant a weaker one, and that loss of blood meant a periodic loss of vigour, bodily and mental. It was a woman's duty as national child-bearer to take care of her body, keep it free from stress. Her mind must be pure, too: if a woman was clever she should not squander that cleverness, but hold it pristine in trust for her children, especially her sons.[4] Use her brain too much and she would wear it out, compromising her physical and moral femininity. 'When nature spends in one direction,' warned Dr Maudsley, 'she must economise in another.'

It is not that girls have not ambition, nor that they fail generally to run the intellectual race which is set before them, but it is asserted that they do it at a cost to their strength and health which entails lifelong suffering, and even incapacitates them for the adequate performance of the natural functions of their sex . . . For it would be an ill thing, if it should so happen, that we got the advantages of a quantity of female intellectual work at the price of a puny, enfeebled, and sickly race.[5]

Another commentator was even more blunt, insisting that no woman 'could follow a course of higher education without running some risk of becoming sterile'.[6] Even Miss Buss was inclined to agree that protecting what were called one's 'muscles of motherhood' was more important (in some cases) than academic striving. She was apt to give her pupils' parents homely advice: 'I hope your daughter wears woollen

combinations in winter. That is of more importance to her
than passing matriculation.'[7]

The author of the 1882 article urging girls to concentrate
on 'little things' implied it was not just the physical organization of the female body that prevented intellectual achievement, but her temperament. Much might be heard nowadays
about the advantages of producing 'girl graduates', the writer
allowed, but had anyone thought through whether it was psychologically safe for women to exert themselves mentally?
Brain power depends on bodily strength, and as women's
bodies are demonstrably weaker than men's, so must their
minds be. Is it wise to tease women with the promise of intellectual equality? Would it not be kinder to lower expectation,
and (revisiting an age-old theme) make home her sphere of
accomplishment, rather than university? In any test of nature
versus nurture in womankind, nature would always win.

The author of that article, acknowledged only as 'M.P.S.',
was not some gravy-stained male academic, but a woman, and
though it may be convenient to label the anti-bluestockings as
chauvinists or even misogynists, that would be too simplistic.
It is true, for instance, that careers for women graduates
remained frustratingly limited well after professional qualifications in the form of degrees became available. University
broadened the mind (granted women had one), but what
for? Did it not dangle possibilities in front of them which, as
soon as they left, were whipped away by society? Did it not
open tantalizing doors and allow women to peep through,
even though everyone knew they would be slammed shut in
their faces? Surely, then, university bred discontent?

There was particular concern among the more bigoted
branches of the medical profession that if this movement to
make scholars of schoolgirls were allowed to develop, the
Englishwoman might end up in the same dire straits as the

The pioneers:
1. Frances Buss of North London Collegiate School (*top left*).
2. Constance Louisa Maynard of Girton and Westfield Colleges (*top right*).
3. Emily Davies, founder of Girton College, Cambridge (*bottom left*).
4. Anne Jemima Clough, the first Principal of Newnham College, Cambridge (*bottom right*).

5. Dorothea Beale, founder of the Cheltenham Ladies' College, in her study, *c.*1885.

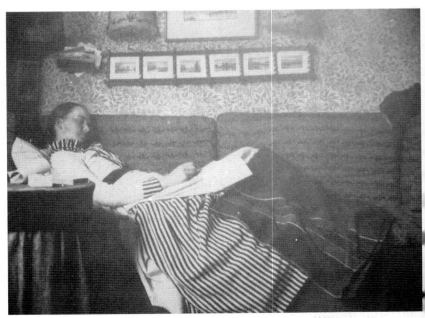

6. Eleanor (Nora) Sidgwick, maths tutor and later Principal of Newnham.

7. Miss Buss, surrounded by staff and sixth-form students at
North London Collegiate School, 1877.

8. 'The Ladies'
College', Somerville
Hall (later Somerville
College), 1880.

9. Students at Cambridge in 1897 protest at the preposterous idea of degrees for women.

10. A proud graduate, probably of Birmingham University, *c.*1890.

11. Chinese student Pao Swen Tseng on her graduation from Queen Mary College, London, 1916.

12. Sarah Mason (Mrs Tebbutt) and her children. Sarah was at Girton from 1878 to 1882.

13. A student cocoa party at Royal Holloway College, London, *c.*1890.

14. Oxford 'Home Students' (whose college became St Anne's in 1952) take a break from tennis, cycling, rowing and reading, 1899.

15. Durham University's first female graduates, 1898.

16. The Principal and students of St Hilda's, Oxford, 1907. Note the college kitten.

17. Girton's 'College Five': its very first students, photographed at Hitchin, 1869.

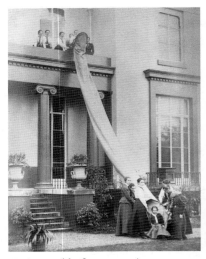

18. A portable fire-escape in use during a fire drill at Westfield College, London, c.1890.

19. The Girton student fire brigade, formed because of the college's remoteness from Cambridge.

American, who was – with staggering overgeneralization – acknowledged 'physically unfit for her duties'.[8] Doctors noted what Edward Clarke of Boston had to say in a well-publicized lecture, 'Sex in Education', delivered at Harvard in the 1870s. His research into the sexual health of women graduates had produced shocking results. So hard had their brains been worked that their wombs had atrophied, to conserve energy. Occasionally a muffled maternal voice might call a child into existence, but college-educated mothers were unlikely to be able to breastfeed. Brain work was not the only risk: American women students sat down, all slumped, for hours on end, ate too much, and rarely exercised. They indulged themselves in what Clarke called 'the zone of perpetual pie and dough-nut' and neglected to cultivate the judicious activity, rest, and mental serenity so necessary to bountiful mothers. This resulted in a ghastly merry-go-round of leucorrhoea, amen-orrhoea, dysmenorrhoea, chronic and acute ovaritis, prolap-sus uteri, hysteria, and neuralgia, from which, if she emerged

Mens sana in corpore sano: *Regular callisthenics were a feature of the university routine for all Victorian and Edwardian women students.*

at all, the learned lady emerged infertile and – probably – insane. No good to anyone.

Suddenly, we are back in the realms of the fruitful womb and barren brain.

Emily Davies's friend Elizabeth Garrett Anderson read Dr Clarke's lecture, and was furious. On his own terms, as a professional medical practitioner, Garrett Anderson published a riposte.[9] Women need not be incapacitated by their periods, either in the short or in the long term, she stated. Manual workers manage perfectly well, and domestic servants are not allowed to rest for a week each month. Exercise is an integral part of the curriculum at most girls' schools and colleges, which refreshes both mind and body. In fact, she argued, *not* going to university is far more perilous than going. To keep a bright young mind at school for long enough to grasp at new ideas and then to cast her into an exile of dull domesticity is dangerous. Boredom and restlessness breed unhappiness, and unhappy people are vulnerable. Their health tends to falter, their moral fibre frays. They become self-absorbed, depressed, hysterical, perhaps anorexic – or so 'languid and feeble' in feeding themselves, as Garrett Anderson puts it, that their menstrual cycle shuts down.

If they had upon leaving school some solid intellectual work which demanded real thought and excited genuine interest, and if this interest had been helped by the stimulus of an examination, in which distinction would have been a legitimate source of pride, the number of such cases would probably be indefinitely smaller than it is now.[10]

Medical opposition to women undergraduates eventually petered out, as credible evidence failed to materialize, but a certain amount of academic prejudice persisted, stemming from low intellectual expectation. That was rooted in all sorts of things: universities' suspicion of women's motives in coming, fear of change, lack of precedent, cronyism, professional jealousy, a genuine apprehension that degrees would be devalued or the academic integrity and reputation of English universities be compromised, and good old-fashioned institutional chauvinism. A male undergraduate at Durham was succinct in his estimation of any bluestocking's potential: 'her proudest achievements, her loftiest thoughts, when compared with the quantity and quality of her brother's work, are, and always must be, "blinder motions bounded in a shallower brain".'[11] Dean Burgon of Chichester Cathedral was even more brutal, informing the women of Oxford in a sermon in 1884: 'Inferior to us God made you: and our inferiors to the end of time you will remain. But you are none the worse off for *that*.'[12] His audience, brave souls, dissolved in incredulous laughter.

Such academic prejudice manifested itself – especially at Oxbridge – in universities' refusal to judge men's and women's achievements on equal terms. At its most extreme this meant ignoring women completely, like the (probably terrified) professor mentioned at the beginning of the chapter who walked out on a lecture room of ladies. Different male lecturers had different strategies. The architect and artist John Ruskin mischievously doubted women, or 'bonnets', could cope with his classes:

I cannot let the bonnets in, on any conditions this term. The three public lectures will be chiefly on angles, degrees of colour-prisms (without any prunes) and other such things of no use to the female mind, and they would occupy the seats in mere disappointed puzzlement.[13]

C. S. Lewis grew ill-tempered and muttered petulantly when there were women present; J. R. R. Tolkien was quiet and subdued in the lecture room, his Anglo-Saxon sounding faintly threatening, like 'gentle swearing'. One tutor at Somerville College serially proposed to all his female students except one (who was mortified); another, supposed to be teaching six women maths, was slapdash and lazy. He gave them dispiritingly difficult problems to solve, without the background knowledge to tackle them; he never gave them individual attention; and if he had corrected a mistake on one girl's paper, would never correct the same on another's. They were left, bewildered and panicky, to compare notes, which took time, and none had the confidence or expertise to understand why she had gone wrong. His written comments were entirely indecipherable. His poor students, not surprisingly, were 'in a terrible commotion about their prospects'.[14] All they learned from this tutor was to hate maths.

Inevitably, discrimination posed practical problems. Durham University was desperately short of ladies' cloakrooms, forcing women students to arrange depots of chamber pots in strategic locations around the chilly city. Even though the huge and overwhelmingly splendid Royal Holloway College for women offered science degrees, they had neglected to build any laboratories; until the 1920s, women studying science at Oxford were bundled into a basement of Balliol College to do their practicals, with noxious results. Rachel Footman was a chemistry student in 1923–6:

Balliol . . . was rather dangerous as we studied poison gases there under Professor Thompson and we only had tiny windows below pavement level. I remember one day being seized round my middle by the Professor himself who threw my head and shoulders out of this tiny window – apparently I was making C.O. [carbon monoxide] and my gas cylinder was very inadequately sealed. He said 'another moment of that my girl and you would be dead.'[15]

Arts students at Oxford, in the early days, met for lectures in a poky little room above a baker's shop, with yeasty aromas filtering through the dust. At least they had no need of chaperones there.

Even though several of the civic universities were founded for men and women on an equal footing (except for the latter being initially barred from courses such as medicine, theology, or law), their male undergraduates seem to have been among the most chauvinistic in the country. At Birmingham, someone facetiously suggested opening a faculty of Feminology, so that students could have a crack at learning the arcane customs and thought-processes of the genus *Bluestocking*, also known as 'modern girl'. Another wag composed a 'Song for Maidens' (1915):

Napoleon knew a thing or two, said he, 'Les femmes tricottent,'
Which by interpretation is 'Let women till their plot.'
But they hold meetings nowadays and talk an awful lot,
And while they blag with politics the race just goes to pot . . .

When you disdain your strait domain, your scroll of life you blot.
If envy men you must, pray do – but emulation's rot.
We've seen your pictures, read your books, we COULD say
      quite a lot,
But chivalry forbids, – why, that's another thing you've not![16]

One might assume the author of the following little ditty to be some high Victorian misogynist, with Aristotelian sympathies:

> You modern girl, you chit of legs and wings,
> You walking palette of deceitful things,
> You mannequin who, with such subtle aid,
> Make every walk you take a dress parade.
> Prevaricator, holding flaming youth
> For all you say and do, a good excuse.
> Between a hat and shoes you fill the gap,
> They call you Miss, they're right in this:
> > > > Mishap.[17]

In fact, it appeared in the Birmingham University magazine, *The Mermaid*, of 1934.

At Cambridge there were riots in 1897 when the Senate addressed a vote on whether or not women students should be allowed official membership of the university, including the right to a degree. Oxford and Cambridge were by now the only universities in the country not to confer them. Tension was high on the morning of the ballot. Special London to Cambridge trains were laid on by the opposition, to encourage as many choleric graduates as possible to return and cast their votes. University Square filled with overexcited male undergraduates wielding screaming banners and placards – 'No Women', 'Down with Women'– and someone rigged up a caricature bluestocking, immodestly dressed in her underwear, on a bicycle suspended high above the crowds. According to Winifred Pattinson, up at Newnham at the time, things got very nasty very quickly. Effigies of Miss Clough and Miss Jex-Blake, the Girton secretary for the Committee for Nominal Degrees for Women, were set alight in the Square and burned, to whoops of atavistic glee from the men. Students at the two rowdiest colleges in

Cambridge, Caius and Jesus, were gated for threatening to fire-hose anyone voting for the women. Newnham girls were not allowed out of college after 11.00 a.m. Several escaped, however, and watched the proceedings unharmed, although oranges, lemons, eggs, bags of flour, and exploding fireworks were being pelted at anyone suspected of blue-stocking sympathies.

When the results were declared – 662 for allowing women 'in', 1713 against – all hell broke loose. To great cheering and jeering, the cycling mannequin was torn down by crowds of crazed undergraduates and marched to the locked gates of Newnham, where it was ripped to pieces and poked through the railings. They tried to plant their placards all over the college (when one student had the bright idea of propping one up in a tree, the loyal Newnham gardener's boy kicked away his ladder and left him stranded). More fireworks were lobbed at the girls' windows, with threats and obscenities, until at 10.00 p.m. men from Selwyn College lit a huge bonfire outside, subsided a little, sang 'God Save the Queen', and then went to bed. 'It was most kind of them,' noted Winifred, 'to provide us with so much amusement.'[18]

What would have happened had the women won? What appalled the Establishment, of course, was Girton's implicit demand for sexual equality. But it is worth remembering that Miss Clough at Newnham had never sought equality with the status quo. She wanted an improved system of university education everyone could share, according to individual strengths and ambitions. London and the civic universities concurred. The vast majority of women involved in developing higher education, staff and students alike, did not strive to be like men, nor even to be treated in the same way as men, except in terms of opportunity and just reward.

Some did not even want that. Kathleen Courtney at Lady

Margaret Hall in Oxford wrote to her mother on 23 May 1897 that she was glad Cambridge had just voted against giving women degrees, for if the motion had been passed, 'there would have been a renewal of the discussions here, and we are very well satisfied with our present position'.[19] Another LMH student, Eglantyne Jebb, agreed. She thought those clamouring for degrees were being hasty:

I cannot help thinking that the higher education of women is of too recent a growth, for us to be quite sure as yet what we do and what we don't want. If we bound ourselves down to it, it would probably prevent for ever the possible development of a separate and perhaps better system of our own. We are in such a hurry . . .[20]

The Establishment had an answer to that idea, too. 'If women require a university,' ran a newspaper article, 'by all means let them have it. Let one be founded at some suitable spot, say Land's End or the Scilly Isles, and let it turn out female Bachelors by the hundred. But on Oxford and Cambridge women have no just claim whatever.'[21]

The critics of unrestricted university access for women were relentless in pursuit of prohibition. Few girls, in the period before the Second World War, were able to study at university without their family's consent. So, as well as attacking on medical and academic fronts, the opposition attempted to claim the moral high ground by alarming undecided parents with threats of domestic catastrophe and social collapse. Their battle cries invoked duty, reputation, and obedience. If the medics and academics were right, they argued, and university really was a potentially ruinous environment for women, who in their right mind would send a daughter there? Think what might happen! At Oxford she might degenerate into that abhorrent 'type' so maliciously recalled by the author Christopher Hobhouse, who was there in the 1930s. His undergraduettes are sheep-witted creatures, content to flock to every lecture and scribble down every word, to read every book they are set, obey every rule, and dutifully to parrot every little gobbet of received wisdom they are fed. They have no sense of style, decking themselves in 'hairy woollens and shapeless tweeds'.

Instead of claret and port they drink cocoa and Kia-Ora [orange squash]. Instead of lordly breakfasts and lunches which a man can command in his own rooms, they are fed on warm cutlets and gravy off cold plates at a long table decked with daffodils.

In this setting the mind of the Oxford woman grows narrower day by day.[22]

Elsewhere the 'Oxford woman' was characterized in stinging little epigrams: on being told about someone's new boyfriend, the typical Somervillian would immediately ask, 'What does he read?'; the student from LMH, 'Who's his father?'; from St Hugh's, 'What's his sport?'; and from St Hilda's, 'Where is he?' In another version, LMH was supposed to be for ladies, St Hugh's for girls, St Hilda's for wenches, and Somerville for women. St Anne's did not feature, not being a cohesive college until the 1950s, and therefore deemed (in certain circles) unworthy of notice.

If your daughter went instead to a civic university, people might think her common. Rules there were more lax than at Oxbridge, but only because their students were snobbishly perceived to be somehow less valuable and weaker-willed. A large proportion of them, according to a 1909 report, belonged to a different class, and suffered from the 'marked contrast' between what was expected of them at university, and at home.[23]

Send her to Birmingham, where they taught technical subjects, and she would be corrupted in days:

> Miss Georgiana Washington's life went in whirls,
> She caught all the vices of 'Varsity girls,
> She smoked in capacity,
> Drank with audacity,
> Her one saving grace was her utter veracity.
>
> Georgiana's virtue scarce lasted a week,
> Since then horrid rumours have started to leak,
> Fate seemed to design her
> To find life diviner,
> When dancing with dentals or even a miner.[24]

At Manchester she would quickly curdle into a graceless 'new woman'. An article in the Owen's College magazine in 1895 describes this unlovely species: she smokes, rides a bicycle (while *not* wearing a skirt), demands a vote, a public voice, and total independence. She agitates for political recognition, and bruits her so-called learning like a hyaena. 'To be short . . . she is no longer content to exert the sweet influence of her sex, but stakes her hopes upon power. She is therefore odious.'[25]

At *any* university, she would be exposed to infectious social diseases, and put in mortal danger of contracting feminism, nymphomania, asceticism, atheism, or eternal spinsterhood. It was patently irresponsible, declared the critics, to condemn one's daughter to an expensive, unproductive interlude at university, which would probably rob her of charm and eligibility, and spoil her for family life.

To counter that negativity (somewhat feebly), articles

were published in the pictorial press suggesting the possibility of regarding scholarship as just one more asset in an accomplished young lady's repertoire. It need not compromise her essential womanliness. A Newnham student wrote an article to prove it:

Never have I heard it more consistently and reverently asserted that a woman's true sphere is the home. Most of the ladies [at Cambridge] rather pride themselves in their domestic accomplishments. Among my own contemporaries were some whose nimble fingers could wield the needle as well as the pen, and produce with equal ease a copy of Latin verses or a fashionable bonnet. Others could send up a dinner not to be despised by the most fastidious of College Fellows.[26]

Parents and students alike obviously required a measure of strong-mindedness – itself an unattractive quality – to brave certain quarters of public opinion. Perhaps the cleverest students were those who could disguise their intelligence and appear normal, like the Girtonian encountered at a dinner party in the 1880s: 'My dear, she was such a *nice* girl, with rosy cheeks and nice manners and nicely dressed and you wouldn't have thought she knew *anything*.'[27]

The steady increase of women undergraduates from the 1880s onwards proves that more and more parents, fortunately, were confident enough in their support of higher education, and sure enough of their girls' integrity, to withstand the gainsayers and satirists. They were at worst not particularly bothered, and at best honoured by the idea of an undergraduate daughter, even if her chosen course were non-vocational. What were the alternatives for an intelligent, unmarried young woman? Florence Nightingale and

Elizabeth Garrett Anderson warned of the corrosive effects
of sitting at home doing nothing. The *Girl's Own Paper* suggested some late nineteenth-century pastimes to fill what it
deliciously called that '*mauvais quart d'heure*' in a girl's life
between school and marriage (in an article 'by the author of
How to be Happy Though Married'). 'There is such a thing as
adult education,' asserts the writer, but it need not involve
university. '[W]e may learn from everybody and everything
until the day of our death, so that nothing is more ridiculous
than to speak of a girl's education being "finished" when she
leaves school.'[28]

She should try an essay club, a reading or study club, an
'Early Rising Society' (activities unspecified), a 'Question
Society', a lecture or discussion group. The poor are always
with us, so there is plenty of charity work to be done, and
'there is no household work such that a girl should deem it
beneath her position to know how to do' – if only to set the
servants a good example. If she keeps herself thus occupied,
'she will be able to wait in dignified tranquillity until the
right man comes to claim her'.[29] Oh, good.

Vocational courses became available at teacher-training colleges, schools of nursing, art colleges, or academies of music
during the second half of the nineteenth century. But only at
university could a girl really explore learning for its own sake,
or as one student put it, distinguish what she knew from what
she did not, 'which is the beginning of wisdom'. Sympathetic
parents recognized this. Even unsympathetic ones might be
persuaded, given a little diplomacy and determination on the
part of the ambitious schoolgirl. She had only to draw attention away from the negative arguments (which sound either
quaint or chillingly familiar to modern women students), and
concentrate instead on the many positives.

It was usually the father, if still alive, who made the final decision about whether or not his daughter went to university. If he had no particularly strong opinions on the matter, he might be swayed (as Constance Maynard's was) with skill, and made to think he was humouring a mildly wayward daughter. As we saw in Chapter 2, Constance was offered a pony in the 1870s to distract her from applying to Cambridge. Lucy Addey, sixty years later, was tempted with £1,000 by her father to give up the idea of Oxford.[30] Both girls preferred the adventure of university, showed their steadfastness by refusing to be bribed, and eventually made their bemused parents proud.

Hannah Cohen longed to go to university in the 1930s to escape the shadow cast by her sister's terminal illness at home in Sunderland. The possibility had never occurred to her Jewish parents (whose sons were sent for their higher education to the local Talmudical College). Hannah got a place at nearby Armstrong College in Newcastle, allied to Durham University, and persuaded her parents by promising to live at home and take extra classes in Hebrew. So she caught the train from Sunderland to Newcastle at 7.15 every morning; from Newcastle to Durham (a journey of about half an hour) for Hebrew later on, then back to Newcastle, dashing up the tower-block stairs to be in time for the last classes of the day. All this meant she did not get home to Sunderland until the dangerous hour of 11.15 p.m., and as the stress was beginning to give her nosebleeds, she was allowed to give up the Hebrew. Her parents chose not to attend her graduation ceremony in 1938, but that hardly worried Hannah. She loved every minute of a frenetic, fulfilling university life, and vowed to pass the opportunity on to her own children – as long as they stayed close to home, as she had.[31]

Essex girl Kathleen Lonsdale had nine elder brothers and sisters; her parents had separated while she was a child, and her mother (like Trixie Pearson's in Chapter 1), recognizing a spark, fought to keep Kathleen at school, even though her siblings all left at the age of twelve. When Kathleen was offered a place at University College, London, in 1922, it was acknowledged as Mrs Lonsdale's triumph as well as Kathleen's.[32] Daphne Harvey, who matriculated in 1937, relied on her father's support, in the teeth of active opposition from everyone else. 'My mother did not believe in education for girls . . . and I disliked living at home where, apart from my father, the family was anti-Bluestocking.'[33] When her contemporary Edith Wood won a place at Oxford, her father refused to pay, until her headmistress sent for him and gave him a brisk talking-to. He gave no trouble after that.[34]

To girls like Trixie Pearson, Hannah Cohen, Kathleen, and Daphne, university meant escape. Not all escapees found a better life, however. Doris Maddy's lonely path to university was strewn with obstacles. She had always (improbably, given her background) dreamed of going to Cambridge. Her single mother, by whom she was brought up, 'didn't agree' with school, let alone university, and refused to pay Doris's fees when she became a teenager. So Doris left home and became a pupil-teacher. With the support of her school she won a place at a teacher-training college, and then a teaching post in Grimsby, where she saved all her money while studying Greek for 'Little-Go' in the evenings. After two years, in 1919, she finally had enough money to afford the entrance examinations for Girton, which she stormed through, with the award of one of the highest open scholarships available.

She carried on working in the vacations as a supply teacher, or selling souvenir gift books of Grimsby to tourists (a meagre occupation): it was hard keeping her head above water financially, but her pride in fulfilling her ambition should have made the struggle worthwhile.

It did not. Doris had expected too much of Cambridge.

She perceived that to fit in you must either be a bright young thing or an earnest 'dowdy'. The former was out of the question: she was too exhausted, and hated the strenuous posing of those around her, refusing to 'dance at the crossroads under a full moon' with the others. She could not afford membership of any college or university societies: they all needed subscriptions. Nor could she afford an evening dress. Even the 'earnest set' demanded money: they went round relentlessly 'doing good' to those students they judged less fortunate than themselves. Once, they tried to recruit Doris for a college campaign 'to make Hermione happy'.

She was a fat, plain fresher, slow of speech with a complacent ox-like gaze. There was no pretence that any of us liked her. 'We're inventing little treats for her. She must feel she has friends.' Notes were passed under my door. 'We're giving a late feast for Hermione. Do come, and bring a banana.'

I did not go. Next morning I was told 'Hermione was such a stodge. But at least she must have enjoyed it. Do let's plan something more for her.'

I could not enjoy any of this. Soon, with more sorrow than anger, I was dropped by the whole group.[35]

Doris was too experienced, too different. So was an anonymous 'Miner's Daughter' who wrote a bitter little piece for the *Daily Herald* in 1935, complaining that her student career at St Hilda's College, which she must have fought to achieve, had ruined her prospects and happiness. It had seduced her with inappropriate ambitions; she mistook its intellectual glamour for real life; except to those who could afford to love learning for its own sake, it was no use. Worse than no use: 'Oxford, the city which destroys in order to construct . . . certainly destroyed most of me.'[36]

Those of us inspired by the first few generations of uni-versity-educated mothers or schoolmistresses must be grate-ful that there were not more people like Doris and the girl from the collieries, nor more who listened to the critics and doom-mongers; whose parents had neither the money, courage, nor imagination to support them; who were pre-pared to fill the *mauvais quart d'heure* – which sometimes lasted for ever – with the requisite round of dull duties. We had the benefit of precedent, but it takes true conviction to break the mould.

5. What to Do if You Catch Fire

There is a story that the only child of a particularly intellectual family not to get to university was apparently so mortified that she never managed to complete a sentence for the rest of her life.[1]

Before the Second World War, when admissions processes had not yet been formalized, parents were expected to play the decisive part in their children's further education. That, of course, was when eighteen-year-olds were still officially children. Christina Roaf was a student at Somerville during the 1930s. It was entirely her mother's idea that she should go to Oxford, and when the time came to choose a college, Mother smartly made appointments with the principals of Lady Margaret Hall and Somerville. LMH was impressive; it had tasteful modern pictures on its walls and an air of brisk efficiency, and Miss Grier, in charge, was polite and businesslike. Somerville, however, 'was another kettle of fish. Miss Darbishire had forgotten the appointment, her sitting room, full of books and papers, was austere, but when she did arrive she was very friendly, if rather vague.' The decision was easy: '"I think you will be happier at Somerville, darling," said my mother. So to Somerville I went.'[2]

Christina was indeed happy at Somerville, both as an undergraduate and a Fellow. Hers was the academic equivalent of an arranged marriage, and it worked very well. Her parents had a stake in the success of her university career; she

*A woodcut by a student at one of the women's colleges at
Oxford, illustrating their joint magazine,* Fritillary, *in 1924,
when academic dress was still something of a novelty.*

was absolved of the responsibility of making a life-changing
choice; the whole venture became a family affair.

Thanks in part to the close involvement of far-sighted
parents, and the proactive support of teachers, as the first
few decades in the history of university education for women
slipped by, the idea of sending a daughter to college gradually became less shocking. Other factors contributed to
progress, so that the image of a drab, maverick bluestocking
began to metamorphose into a far more luminous creature,
the 'undergraduette' who worked hard but also enjoyed herself. By the 1920s, an undergraduette was what more and
more girls aspired, and were likely, to be.

The cumulative effect of precedent was bound to play a
pragmatic part. Graduate mothers tended to produce undergraduate daughters. Learned aunts took clever nieces to
their proud bosoms, and thrilled them with iridescent tales
of college life. Sophisticated friends seduced impressionable

girls (like Katie Dixon in 1879) with the promise of arcane glamour:

While I was at the High School, I used to do my prep. upstairs in the old school room. One evening my mother brought in a visitor whom she had met abroad, and plumped her down at the table with me. That was Sarah Prideaux . . . Sarah you might say was all in with the new way of dressing. She wore a cotton gown with a blue design, clinging rather, but what took me by storm was that she had stockings to match, the same blue . . .[3]

Sarah was a Newnham girl; so, within a very short space of time, was Katie.

The increasing number and value of endowments to women's colleges, from the 1880s onwards, were vitally important in encouraging candidates to apply. More money for university and college bodies meant more places and better facilities, and the publicity generated by any ostentatious philanthropy to do with women was always useful. Although she is not connected to an English university, it is hard to resist introducing Mary Ann Baxter at this point. Miss Baxter was not famous, nor particularly political; she was simply a wealthy, curious, and far-sighted woman who realized what a difference it would make to her home town's prospects if its people had access to a university, women as well as men. Dundee College, which became the nucleus of a fine university, opened – thanks to her – in 1883.

Happy Miss Baxter was immortalized in verse by the peerless William McGonagall ('For the ladies of Dundee can now learn useful knowledge / At home in Dundee in their nice little College').[4] No one wrote odes to Anne Clough or Emily Davies, or even to romantic Oxbridge benefactresses like Margaret Beaufort or Devorguilla of Galloway.[5] But Mary

Baxter and her kind were local heroes: they brought university education, as McGonagall himself put it, 'to the ignorant masses', to women and working men, in other words.

Later, the period between the two world wars witnessed a growing number of scholarships offered to women by universities, schools, local authorities, the state, and a raft of charitable trusts and livery companies. Most of these were competitively awarded for academic achievement in public or entrance exams; others were available to anyone whose case was convincing enough. Adept, impoverished families became skilful at unearthing links to long-gone cordwainers or goldsmiths, so they could approach the appropriate guild for a grant. It was worth doing your homework before you applied. A pupil from the Mary Datchelor School (London) in the 1930s was sent to the Drapers' Company by her headmistress. Her mother went with her, and the pair took pains to look 'sort of clean, poor and well darned'. The chairman of the company interviewed them, and asked why the girl was aiming for Girton, which had offered her a £50 scholarship, rather than Westfield College in London, which offered £80. 'So my mother put her foot in it, in a big way, because she said: "Oh well, of course Cambridge for maths is considered the best." We discovered afterwards that the chairman was a governor of Westfield – and I didn't get anything.'[6]

With judicious research, and a certain amount of charm, it was possible to build up a portfolio of awards from various sources until not only were university fees and accommodation covered, but there might be a modest profit left over. Awards like these widened social catchment, and for many girls meant the difference between going to university and not. External funding relieved the pressure of family sacrifice, with all its hardships and complex obligations; it brought emotional as well as physical independence, and encouraged self-esteem.

It is humbling to realize what 'sacrifice' involved, and how valuable university education was perceived to be, especially during the Great Depression of the 1930s, by parents anxious to equip their children for a better future. There are tantalizing glimpses of domestic lives turned upside down by the determination to educate a daughter. Widowed mothers sold up, left friends and family, and moved to strange university cities so their daughters could live at home while studying, and lodgers be taken in. Daughters were consigned to more prosperous relations (and perhaps rarely seen again) to give them a better chance. Heartbreaking choices were made between equally keen and clever sisters in a numerous family, when there was only enough money to subsidize one. Opportunities were rarely bought without personal, as well as financial, expense.

Sometimes daughters had to fight for support. Neither Louisa nor Bella Macdonald knew any women graduates, but both were desperate, in the teeth of family opposition, to get to university. Their father had died and brother William was the head of the family. William did not hold with educating women, and refused to provide financial help (including senior schooling), so the girls enrolled on correspondence courses with their hoarded pocket money, walked miles to public lectures, and eventually graduated (bringing shame on the family, according to William) from University College, London, in the 1880s. Louisa went on to be the first Principal of the women's college at Sydney University, and Bella became a doctor.[7]

Bessie Callender's story was singularly unpromising. Her mother died a fortnight after she was born, when her father was in his early twenties. She was sent to her grandparents (strict Scottish puritans), since her father was a farmer and had no time to care for her. Financial struggles soon resulted in Mr Callender having to sell the farm, so when Bessie was

told at school that she should try for a place at Girton, the
plan was immediately rejected. What about Oxford, then?
That was out of the question, too: the place was riddled
with Anglo-Catholics. But so passionate was Bessie to escape
that she was eventually allowed to sit the Cambridge exam
on the bleak understanding that even if she got a scholarship,
she could not afford to accept. She did get a scholarship, the
only one the college possessed at that time (1899), and was
forced to refuse it.[8] Fortunately, as we shall see, that was not
quite the end of her story.

The academic barriers so strenuously erected in the early years
to keep bluestockings well corralled began to founder once
women gained the confidence to demand a wider range of
degree courses. All medical schools were open to women by
1894, and (with very few exceptions, such as law or theology)
they could study what they liked from then onwards. It took
some lobbying to win degree status for practical subjects like
horticulture or 'home economy' (domestic science), but by
the 1930s women were emerging from university as virtually
anything from aviation engineers to professional academics.

    With higher achievement came higher expectation. For
girls apt to 'catch fire' intellectually (the chapter title comes
from an article in the *Girl's Own Paper*),[9] it became a duty, a
right, for the good of society, not to extinguish the spark, but
to fan the flames. Many of the first few cohorts of women
graduates became inspirational teachers, with the expertise
to coach promising pupils for entrance exams, and spot
'unsuspected brains in out-of-the-way places'.[10] The pioneer
bluestockings fought battles, proving points for 'the cause';
their successors were therefore comparatively free to concentrate on themselves, and on scholarship, undistracted.

    During the first two decades of the twentieth century, the

significance of going to university, usually leaving home to do so, changed subtly. Commentators were still keen to stress how much better value women graduates would be to their husbands and sons: that attitude did not disappear entirely until after the Second World War. Qualification was important – vocational and non-vocational – but so, paradoxically, was the idea of intellectual accomplishment as some sort of moral ornament. After 1918, however, women felt able to acknowledge the need to escape oppressive or unsympathetic families, to enjoy time to themselves, take charge of their own lives, be proactive. What is more, there began to emerge a heady sense of obligation on women to use their learning to change not only their lives, but the war-torn world. Virginia Woolf, speaking somewhat wryly to Newnham and Girton students in 1928, chided her audience for not taking advantage of growing opportunities in education and the workplace to make their mark on society:

Young women . . . You have never made a discovery of any sort of importance. You have never shaken an empire or led an army into battle. The plays of Shakespeare are not by you, and you have never introduced a barbarous race to the blessings of civilization. What is your excuse? It is all very well for you to say, pointing to the streets and squares and forests of the globe swarming with black and white and coffee-coloured inhabitants, all busily engaged in traffic and enterprise and love-making, we have had other work on our hands . . .[11]

Role models like Woolf (although she was not university-educated herself) were undeniably influential in advancing the progress of 'the undergraduette', but none worked as hard for the cause as dedicated, ambitious teachers. As we saw in the previous chapter, some schoolmistresses were quite irresistible, like Edith Wood's in London, sternly hauling Edith's reluctant father into her office and convincing him that, contrary to his own impression, he did want to pay for his daughter's place at college – and so he did.

Florence Rich's headmistress was determined her prize pupil should try for a university scholarship. Miserly Mr Rich refused to let her sit the exam, saying the journey and administration fees would be too expensive, and that even if Florence were successful, he was not prepared to waste the balance of funds required for life at college. Nothing daunted, the headmistress marched Florence off to Oxford, treated her to an opulent private suite at the Randolph Hotel and, when she duly won the scholarship, demanded of her truculent father that she be allowed to accept it. He capitulated.[12]

Some parents needed only gentle persuasion. There were ten sixth-formers at Kathleen Edwards' single-sex grammar school in 1934, most of whom were traditionally destined for teacher-training colleges. But her headmistress had other plans for Kathleen, and suggested the possibility of university to Mr and Mrs Edwards. 'Neither I nor my parents had considered this,' remembers Kathleen, 'but they liked the idea, and so did I, though I knew nothing about universities.'[13] Kathleen lived in Walsall, about ten miles from the University of Birmingham; if she lived at home and took the bus to the campus each day, the family could just about afford this unexpected venture. The local authority came up with a scholarship to fill the gap, and off went Kathleen. She flourished.

Another Kathleen, Kathleen Byass from Driffield in east Yorkshire, would never have got anywhere near university had it not been for vigilant teachers throughout her school career. She was a farmer's daughter, born in 1898, whose primary-school teacher insisted that instead of leaving with her friends at eleven she should be sent to the local grammar school; her headmaster at the grammar had taught previously at a school near Oxford, and recognizing Kathleen's potential, he suggested she try for Somerville. Kathleen had not heard of Somerville, and had no idea where Oxford was, having never been further away from home than a day trip up the road to York. After a bewildering interview she was invited to sit at High Table with Miss Penrose, the Principal, and was terror-stricken on being asked 'and what are your feelings, Miss Byass, on the Turks' reported treatment of Santa Sophia?'[14] Still, she got her university place. So did Mariana Beer from a small village in Cornwall, the first in her family (and the only one of eleven siblings) to go to university. As soon as she heard she had been accepted to read English at Bristol in 1921, her proud headmistress declared a half-day holiday for the whole school.[15]

When Margaret Atkinson was offered her place at university, she had to decline. It was during the Depression, and without subsidy there was no chance of her parents affording it. She stayed on an extra year at school to try again for a scholarship and, on failing a second time, was assured by her teacher that she should not worry: funding had been found for her after all, and she could go. It was only years afterwards that Margaret discovered the 'funding' had quietly been paid by the teacher herself.[16]

Ideally, the path to academia would be smoothed by teachers and family working together, but occasionally pupils were propelled along against their will. 'I didn't want to go to university,' remembers one disgruntled daughter from Liverpool. 'I couldn't be bothered, and I argued solidly with my father for a whole year . . . I told him it would be a waste of money.'[17] Father won – and it was. Another girl rebelled after her doting papa sent her a postcard, when she was tiny, of Girton College, on which he'd written 'This is where you will be some day.'[18] It was not a very convincing rebellion: she merely went to LMH (in 1912) instead. An academic who had recently relinquished a senior position at a women's college once told me that she bitterly resented being sent to university as a girl in the 1930s. It straitened her life, imposing expectations she was too submissive at the time — and later too inexperienced — to resist. From matriculation to retirement, she lacked the confidence to leave. She had never really wanted to go in the first place.

Miss Amy Buller was the Warden of University Hall (the women's hostel) at Liverpool during the 1930s. She maintained that there were only three types of parents: supportive ones, who allowed their daughters to make well-informed choices; domineering mothers who interfered; and fathers reliving their own ambitions through their daughters. The ones who had always coveted a university education themselves were the pushiest, like the man who sent his infant daughter the Girton postcard.

Stella Pigrome's father had always given the impression he was an Oxford graduate himself; in fact she later discovered he had only ever been on vacation courses, and his insistence on her going to university there in 1934 was a matter of vicarious fulfilment for him, as well as fond ambition for his daughter.[19]

The three Fredericks sisters, Grace, Julie, and Daphne, were the only children of a Baghdadian Jew living in Shanghai. As an intelligent and ambitious anglophile, he bitterly resented never having been offered a chance to go to university himself. So the three girls were sent to school far away in England, staying with friends or paid guardians, and in due course Grace went to Oxford in 1926, and Julie and Daphne to Cambridge soon afterwards. 'My father pretty well ruined himself sending us to university,' Grace realized. 'And do you know? I never thanked him.'[20]

Attending university was compulsory in some academic families. Not that this necessarily made preparations straightforward. When your grandfather, two uncles on your father's side, five on your mother's, two aunts, and a brother and sister had all been to Oxford (as in the case of one of my correspondents), the weight of expectation could be hard to bear. Especially if, like this particular young woman, you were not even sure you wanted to go to university at all.[21]

Dressmaking and cooking were her favourite subjects, with art and music, and when LMH turned her down in 1934, it was hardly a shock. The Society of Home Students refused her too. But the following year, Oxford University was told to build up the proportion of women to men students to an extravagant 1:6. It also formulated a new social sciences course. Trawling its list of recent rejects, the Society of Home Students noticed this young lady, and offered her a place. It would have taken considerable courage not to accept.

Within fifty years of Girton College opening at Hitchin in 1869 with five students, universities all over England were turning scores of perfectly well-qualified young women away, despite the increase in places available. And so alluring was the image of the undergraduette by now that plenty of unqualified young women were applying, too. The Vice-Chancellor of the University of Liverpool took an astonishingly personal interest in candidates for courses there; in 1918, a mother wrote to him to request advice on how her daughter should apply. After checking the girl's school record, he sent the following answer:

She is almost at the bottom of the form, and her work in every subject – including those that, as a rule, are taught well in the elementary

schools – is weak. I looked through the term's marks in each subject, and found that she did not reach 40% in any one of them.

It is clear, therefore, that there is not even the remotest possibility of her passing a qualifying examination this summer.

Have you thought of physical training as a possible career? I
believe that the qualifying conditions on the scholastic side are
less rigorous than in most other cases . . .[22]

For young ladies (like this one) patently unfit for academia,
there was always the university of life, a virtual establishment
celebrated in a long, oleaginous, and anonymous poem,
'Our B.A.', in 1893.[23] The gist of it is that the most radiant of
all girl-graduates must be she who passes the test of Christian piety. Academia's pinchbeck lustre is worth nothing
compared with the sterling qualities of humility, obedience,
patience, and forbearance learned in dutiful everyday life.
Those whose honours are conferred at the Pearly Gates are
more fortunate than any earthly high-achiever.

Meanwhile, for those with the brains and the backing to try
for the real thing, there was serious work to be done. The
orthodox route to university admission was via school. Teachers identified likely candidates, coached them carefully,
crammed them and drilled them if necessary, made inquiries
about scholarships and grants, and arranged the entrance exams
and interviews. Their support was invaluable – although not
always obvious to the candidates in question. Daphne Hanschell
was told nothing at all about university by the nuns at her convent until the morning of her entrance exams for Oxford in
1929, when she was given a poached egg for breakfast instead
of porridge, and cheerily told not to fret over what lay ahead:
'the Holy Ghost will fix it'.[24] And that's what happened.

Leeds and Sheffield universities had a reputation for industrial or commercial subjects. You got degrees 'in making jam,

at Liverpool and Birmingham'.[25] London and Manchester were good for the physical sciences and medicine. Those weak at maths tried for Oxford rather than Cambridge. Each applicant was advised to use any influence available from family or friends. Diana Murray blithely arrived at Sheffield in 1933 to read chemistry, physiology, and physics; not only was this her first visit to the university, but she had never had a physics or physiology lesson in her life. None of this mattered, since she was recommended to the university registrar by a friend of her father's, who happened to be Professor of Surgery at the university. Diana was welcomed in.[26]

Contacts were particularly useful if you were an overseas student, as in the case of Martha Kempner. She was born in Berlin, and went to school there until leaving 'because of Hitler' in 1938. Martha was obviously academic, and anxious to continue her education. Her father (still in Berlin) was acquainted with Oxford's Member of Parliament at the time, Sir Arthur Salter, who offered to write to the city's women's colleges on Martha's behalf and ask if they might consider her as a student. Three of them replied that they would welcome her application, but not until the following year. Grace Hadow, Principal of the Society of Home Students (later St Anne's), was about to reply in a similar vein when her secretary recognized Martha's name. The secretary's daughter had once spent time with the Kempners in Berlin as an au pair, and been very happy. So Miss Hadow changed her mind. She invited Martha to an interview, then organized for the girl to sit entrance papers in the room she was renting in London. Her puzzled landlady was persuaded to supervise the exam, the papers were posted back to the college, and Martha was immediately accepted.[27]

Entrance exams – even official ones – were often rather haphazard. During the 1880s, some of the London ones

were held at the Natural History Museum, where the candidates crouched at their desks like prey among the looming
dinosaurs. Katie Dixon remembered delicious peach tarts
being provided at half time in Birmingham in 1879, and
when her contemporary Mary Paley wept with horror at
the questions on conic sections in her Cambridge maths
paper, the invigilator – Miss Clough herself – was quick to
scuttle down the aisle and dab her cheeks.[28]

Bessie Callender, the farmer's daughter forced to forgo a
scholarship to Girton, refused to abandon the idea of university altogether, and eventually persuaded her father and
grandparents to let her try for the local one, at Durham.

In those days Durham held its open scholarship examinations in
October during the week before term, so you came up early, sat
for the exam., and if successful stayed on. In the autumn of 1899
therefore I arrived with almost all my worldly goods in a massive
brown trunk with a rounded top. I dared not unpack, for fear I
should not remain.[29]

Bessie was not expecting there to be many other students in
the hostel when she arrived for the exam: university education for women was still in its infancy, and at Durham had
only been on offer for the last four years. Perhaps there
would be forty or fifty girls, she imagined, and they would
live in a large dignified house somewhere in the city. In reality, Bessie was driven straight through Durham to the slums
of Claypath beyond, and deposited at a highly unprepossess-
ing house, which was 'pleasant enough' when you got inside,
but with room for only a handful of inmates.

The scholarship examination took most of the week, and on the
Friday night the results would be posted on Palace Green. On

Friday, trembling with excitement and anxiety, two of us crept up Queen Street. 'Yes,' said the 'Bulldog' [university official], 'the list is up.' And he took us along to a passage by the lecture rooms. Our hearts in our mouths, we read the list. Both our names were there; we tore back to the hostel, nearly getting run over in the Market Place, and unpacked.[30]

Perhaps it was a good thing, in Bessie Callender's case, that there was no time to ponder (or ask the family) whether or not to accept: if you passed at Durham, you were in, straight away. Elsewhere, playing one acceptance against another, or an offer of a place against the promise of a scholarship, could be tricky. Groups of Oxbridge women's colleges held their entrance exams at different times of the year. It was therefore possible to keep trying every few months in the hope that someone, somewhere, would finally accept you. Barbara Wright understood from her academic parents during the 1930s that not only was she expected to go to university, but she must win a scholarship, too. Time was no object. So she happily settled down to a round of regular entrance exams during the year or two after leaving school, getting accepted each time, but with no award, until Newnham finally came up with the goods.[31]

Before the Universities' Central Council on Admissions was developed in 1961, the number of universities to which you might apply was limited only by preference, the expense of entrance exams, and time. Some of them maintained waiting lists, so you might not know where you were going until the very day before term began. The uncertainty was hard to manage. Extracts from the crowded diary of Joan Morgan, living in Halifax during the edgy prelude to the Second World War, reveal how one ordinary adolescent girl coped with the pressure. Joan applied to King's College in

London, Leeds, Birmingham, Manchester, and Liverpool.

5 Jan. 1939. Went to King's for interview by man & woman for about 5 minutes, and then saw Warden of Hostel – very nice and friendly – gave me application form. Only there about 20 mins. altogether.

18 Jan. Got 1.19 train to Leeds . . . At University from 2.0 to 6.0. Quite interesting but feet ached . . .

27 Jan. M.J. and A. Hutchinson [school friends] have to go to Manchester for interview, but [I] haven't had letter. Shouldn't be bothered really if didn't go.

1 March. Waited for post in a.m. Not got in at King's or Manchester – on waiting list at Leeds & Birmingham. Not heard from Liverpool at all . . . Everyone else in. Went to tell [the Headmistress] and started crying – silly fool – also in cloakroom – in form room & Biology lab – M. Dawson did as well, though . . . Letter from Liverpool a.m. 'I regret to inform you . . .' Just feel as if I don't care now . . . hell.[32]

In fact, Joan had been offered a place at Liverpool: it was her grant application that was rejected. So her mother suggested writing to ask if she could still take up the place if the family paid for everything – which would involve considerable financial sacrifice. The answer was yes.

26 April. [Mother] says we may not go for holidays this year & I can't say a word because lack of £.s.d. [funds] is because of me. Oh, damnation . . .[33]

Joan's interview at King's sounds like a depressing sort of speed-dating exercise. Surely they might have managed more than five minutes, even if they were certain they did not want her? After all, the trip down from Halifax was time-consuming and expensive. Poor girl, to have been dismissed so carelessly.

Research suggests that pre-war interviewers were not the most socially adept people in the world. Nervous candidates sat in dreary studies for long minutes waiting to be asked something – anything – by a tutor so shy herself that she could hardly bring herself to speak. Such occasions were excruciatingly embarrassing. Daphne Hanschell remembered being deeply discomfited by one of her tutors at Somerville: she was a modern linguist who solemnly insisted on dressing in the style of a northern French matelot, in a blue blouse and a beret with a red pom-pom.[34] A female tutor elsewhere wore a cassock, and yet another was never seen in anything but shocking pink. The matelot had a pronounced squint, incidentally, which made it difficult to know whether she was looking at you or not. One university only passed candidates forward for interview (allegedly) if the admissions secretary liked their handwriting;[35] an interviewer elsewhere would not accept anyone who did not 'look clean'.[36]

If there were a prize for history's most bewildering admissions interview, it would have to go to Elizabeth Smedley of St Hilda's College, Oxford. She was bidden to the study of Miss Rooke in 1928, after applying to read English:

My interview with Miss Rooke was . . . agonising. She sat in a dim light, by the fireside, making the shadows of different animals appear on the wall by manipulation of her hands. I was full of carefully prepared brilliant thoughts on Shakespeare etc. and was utterly taken aback on being urged to try and make a rabbit or an elephant appear beside hers.[37]

Elizabeth was accepted – and must have wondered what on earth she had let herself in for.

6. Freshers

How I ache to get home! And how I ache to stay here![1]

Few young women began their university careers in quite as bemused a state as shadow-puppeteer Elizabeth Smedley. The majority of freshers, or first-year students, had a clear (though not necessarily accurate) idea of what academic life would be like, and their descriptions of it were coloured, gaudy or muted, by how far from the truth that idea turned out to be. They hurried home their first impressions in reams of news for parents and friends anxious to hear what was going on in this parallel, exclusive world.

It may not prove so easy to archive the emails and text messages dispatched by today's undergraduates, or to connect the attenuated and intangible threads of modern communication. But during the seventy-year span of this book, each student's weekly routine, unless she lived at home, inevitably included solid time put aside for letter-writing. Some documents were extravagantly florid, especially during the Edwardian period. On creamy notepaper complacently embossed with a college crest, adoring parents were addressed in a sophisticated hand as 'Lambkin-boo', 'Dearest Daddie-wee', 'My own darling sweetie lovie'. Others had a childlike simplicity about them – 'Dear Mamma and Dadda' – and were scrawled blottily on pages torn from lecture notebooks.

Gwendolen Freeman's letters home from Girton in the 1920s were in the latter category. She found them sixty years after they were written, bundled at the back of a forgotten drawer, and at first failed to recognize the 'thin Woolworth's paper and round juvenile writing' as her own. Gwendolen was fascinated, on re-reading her letters, to realize how immature she was on leaving home at eighteen. Her mother had packed her off to college as though it were a particularly spartan boarding school, with industrial supplies of woolly knickers and thick-seamed bodices. But someone else had given her a powder compact: essential, apparently, as glamorous undergraduettes were obliged to powder their noses several times a day. She had no idea how to use it. She understood that now her school days were behind her, she was expected to wear her hair up, but it was slippery and disobedient, despite being stapled all over with hairpins. Glamorous undergraduette she was not, and it was worrying.

Infected by the boarding-school idea, Gwendolen, who had rarely been away from home before, began to panic. How would she cope living in such an alien community?

I imagined a women's college to have rows of suddy washbasins where we should wash in company, as in our school cloakroom. Perhaps the lavatories would be almost public. I was so worried about the hypothetical college lavatories . . . I was also certain that everybody at college would dislike me and that I should never find friends . . . I had always been a 'swot', and as potential university material, had always been a little apart. Now, I thought, that sense of being an outcast would return.[2]

Her fears were unfounded: she loved Girton from the very beginning. There were a few rather intimidating glamour-girls, but most of her peers were ordinary young women like her, a little afraid, but enthusiastic and not judgemental. Gwendolen settled in quickly.

It usually took freshers a little longer to get used to the newness of life at university, or – even more difficult to cope with – the familiarity. You could still spot slightly musty spinsters striding or mincing along cold linoleum corridors, just like teachers. Gloss-painted walls echoed the screeches and giggles of excitable girls doing their prep and having emotional crises. Community life continued to be governed uncompromisingly by rules, routine, and obligation. Students were even encouraged to join a local branch of the Girl Guides for healthy recreation, and to clamber into their knickers and gymslips for regular 'drill', which was supposed to tone the body alongside the intellect, and to divert energy away from those passionate 'special friendships' so characteristic of single-sex establishments. And there was so much work to be done. Where was the novelty, the exhilaration, in all this?

Disillusioned freshers failed to appreciate that universities were not there solely to provide them with novelty and exhilaration. They would find both for themselves in due course. Student opinion never counted for much before the 1960s, anyway. Parents were the important ones: if they were to continue supporting this enterprise, they needed reassurance that their daughters were safe at university, both morally and physically. Knowing the basic routines of college life to be much like those of school gave parents confidence in the system. Until the age of majority changed in 1970, anyone under the age of twenty-one was still legally a child, after all, and the university authorities had an obligation to act *in loco parentis*.

Social intercourse was considered the most perilous activity in which students were likely to engage while away from home. Therefore it was even more strictly controlled at university than at school. Calling cards punctuated companionship, even as late as the 1920s. They were presented to your college Principal before consulting her, and exchanged between students who planned a social engagement. In the union building in Liverpool, which accommodated meetings of various men's and (separate) women's societies, an elaborate ritual was practised between 1913 and 1925, revolving around the stout figures of Mr and Mrs White, employed by the university as male and female chaperones-in-chief. Again, it was heralded by the traffic of calling cards. Then, '[i]f men and women wanted to meet, Mrs White sent a message to Mr White (or vice versa), and the meeting took place on the strip of carpet that protected the polished floor between the doors from the two sides [of the union building: the men's and the women's], the said doors remaining open during the interview.'[3] No risk of any hanky-panky there.

Hanky-panky was a real concern, however. Innocence was the accepted prerequisite of purity, which is ironic given the necessary intellectual curiosity and independence common to so many bluestockings. Parents used to supervising their children's lives worried that their daughters had only to be presented with the vaguest of opportunities, to plunge inexorably into the depths of degradation. Liberal supporters of university education for women pointed out what a boon it was for them to be living away from home, from the demands and strictures of domestic life, and to have time and space to themselves. But student malcontents found any freedom they enjoyed at college so heavily circumscribed that they might as well have been in the tower with Princess Ida.

Practically, polite society's policy of not telling girls about anything to do with sex was cruel. It meant the 'curse' of menstruation came as an horrific shock, and while sanitary towels, or 'bunnies', were provided and disposed of at home or at school by your mother, matron, or a maid, at college girls suddenly had to manage their periods themselves. For those too embarrassed to go to the chemist for anything personal at all – even deodorant – the prospect was mortifying.

Any contact with boys was fraught with apprehension. One undergraduate, who 'had only just stopped having dinner in the nursery, rather than with her parents', was convinced she had fallen pregnant after her cousin kissed her goodnight one evening.[4] Few of her friends had the confidence to persuade her otherwise. Freshers at Durham were informed when they arrived that under no circumstances should they use each other's Christian names in public. Even in private it was only to be done following a 'proposal', when a senior student would formally ask for the privilege (and being 'propped' by someone one admired was hugely thrilling). In public it was considered reckless: a *man* might overhear (as distinct from a gentleman), and who knew to what dark uses he might put his precious knowledge?

Despite the moral safeguards in place, and physical ones like the broken glass garnishing the tops of women's college walls like aspic, if parents still fretted about their daughters' vulnerability during their first few weeks at university, they were welcome, within reason, to come and visit. Mothers travelling alone lodged with the Principal or Warden. But they only stayed long enough to see their daughters comfortably settled in. There was work to be done, after all.

Comfort was a relative term, depending on where you were. Students could take a maid from home to help them settle in to their Oxbridge college, and were allowed to keep horses or pets (usually dogs, but occasionally the odd goldfinch or rodent of some sort). They were able to write in advance and ask their Principal the colour of the wallpaper in their allotted room, so that matching accessories such as cushions and lampshades could be chosen before they arrived.

Rooms in the hostel for King's College, London, were lavishly and precisely furnished in the early 1920s with the following: 1 couch-bed and bedding, 3 blankets, 2 green rugs, 1 oblong table, 1 chest, 1 mirror, 1 green wardrobe curtain, 2 green window curtains, 1 basket chair, 2 wooden chairs, 1 basket, 1 bookcase, 1 cream net blind, and 1 blue-and-white bedspread.[5] By contrast, when girls arrived at Durham in the 1930s, they were advised to bring all their tea things with them (china and cutlery), two pairs of sheets, pillowcases, table napkins, a napkin ring (not silver), face and bath towels, an eiderdown, rug, and easy chair.[6] They were liable to share a bedroom. They slept on settees which turned into beds at night, with 'a well-used 2" flock mattress over chicken-wire', dingy with coal dust, and they used one of only two bathrooms available in college. The bathroom floors were of bare concrete with duckboard mats, and they were *so* cold.[7]

Gwendolen Freeman was grateful to find her rooms at Girton rather better than she had expected. They were on the ground floor, distinguished by a stern, blank-eyed bust of Gladstone stationed outside the door. Gwendolen felt she owed a great deal to Gladstone. Girton's corridors were so long, so numerous and uniform, that she relied on the sight of him, standing sentry, to guide her home.

In her first letter home, she proudly drew a plan of her rooms (most students at Girton, as at Royal Holloway, had two). Her study was plain, carpeted in blue, with 'pale nondescript walls' and its own little fireplace. The bedroom was more cheery, with flowery wallpaper, a red mat and eiderdown, a large Victorian washstand complete with its old-fashioned equipment, and a curtained-off area for hanging up Gwendolen's (two) dresses, and stashing the woolly underwear. The windows, strangely, had no curtains; only bars on the outside to prevent the recurrence of an incident involving a 'tramp' who, according to Gwendolen the ingénue, 'once tried to get in thinking it was the work-house'.[8]

Gwendolen's first job, the evening she arrived, was to unpack and personalize her suite. Up went the picture-wire and watercolours she had brought from home; she scattered her favourite cushions, arranged the dressing-table set her mother had presented her with, and ceremonially placed a sturdy new mantelpiece clock above her fireplace. That clock, she noted as it belted out the hour, 'was going to be very useful to both me and neighbouring students'.[9]

In Manchester's Ashburne Hall, you were allowed a chair each which, in the early days, you were advised to carry about with you wherever you went and were likely to want

An imposing corner of Royal Holloway College in about 1886.

to sit down. A girl in one of the hostels run by the Society of Home Students at Oxford brought her own chair: it came from her Uncle Jim's cabin on HMS *King George V*, and was, like him, a venerable relic of the Battle of Jutland.[10] University Hall in Liverpool was humbly furnished with a hotch-potch of donations by local well-wishers. In the 1908–9 session alone, it was given some china for the dining room, various magazines, fruit trees for planting, some concert tickets, cushions, a croquet set, garden seeds, a sewing machine, a mowing machine, novels for the library, and some curtain material – all received with delight.[11]

Royal Holloway College in Surrey reclined complacently at the opposite end of the spectrum. Founded in 1883 by a local businessman, in memory of his wife, it carried a £200,000 endowment – equivalent in today's money to about £9.5 million – and accommodated 250 young women in wings of magnificent bedrooms with separate studies. Its opulence persisted well into the 1930s, when Audrey Orr remembers dressing for dinner each evening and gathering at the chime of the dinner gong (sounded by Pine, the butler) to process through the library and museum into Hall, each student with another – or a member of the tutorial staff – on her arm.[12]

Freda Taylor had the unusual experience of witnessing her university, Hull, coming into being:

[I]n 1926 I saw the first pile driven into the marshy ground bordering Cottingham Road. On October 11, 1928 I was one of the twenty or so first students waiting for admission on the steps of one of the two unfinished red brick buildings then standing on the same site. There were . . . eight women at Thwaite Hall (four of them called Kathleen . . .) under the watchful eye of a female Cerberus, Miss Murray . . . We were to discover there were almost as many staff as students.[13]

Settling in here, with the first ever cohort, was easy. The
students set their own precedents. Conforming to the customs and strictures of long-established and insular institutions elsewhere could be extremely difficult, especially if,
like Beryl Harding, you felt you did not fit. Her family,
described as 'lower middle class' and mostly 'clerks and bank
officials', had no interest in academia, nor any knowledge of
what life as a student was like. Beryl arrived at Oxford in
1929, propelled there by forceful schoolteachers, without
confidence, money, or much hope of happiness.

She disliked the culture of discipline at college intensely.
She felt the maids (appropriately known as scouts) were
encouraged to spy on students and inform on misbehaviour.

The rules laid down that a student, meeting a young man, had to
have an approved companion. The Principal had to give her permission and kept a book outside her door for these requests to be
entered. We filled one in, now and then, 'to keep her happy,' as
we said. Otherwise the rules were ignored. I still think an institution whose rules are held in contempt, is not a healthy one.[14]

Beryl's most sickening memory of college discipline involved
a friend, Elizabeth, who had been brought up with the four
boys of a neighbouring family. Elizabeth had known these lads
all her life: they were as close as brothers. One of them, John,
was studying theology at Keble College. When his mother
visited Oxford one weekend, Elizabeth – eager to show her
gratitude and affection – asked her Principal for permission to
invite John and his mother to tea in her college room. The
mother was welcome, allowed the Principal, but definitely not
John. Men were safe enough in company, Elizabeth was told,
but John 'might find his way back again later'.[15]

★

Navigating the choppy waters of college regulation was a perilous business for freshers. Who could anticipate, for example, some of the abstruse house rules at Royal Holloway, issued during the early decades of the twentieth century? No hair to be thrown out of windows; permission to be sought for biking on Sundays; chapel doors to be shut on the fourth strike of the bell, and all students not inside by then to be punished; smoking only allowed in the afternoons in the remotest part of the grounds, and only after 4.00 p.m. in public corridors; no tennis on Sundays; stockings to be worn at all times and in all weather, even on the river; tennis shorts (in the late 1930s) to be no shorter than one inch off the ground when kneeling, and cut in pleats to hang like a skirt; and so on. Transgression, at some point, was almost inevitable, and became a matter of honour to a feisty few.

The system still in use today (in an expanded form) of college 'godparents' was designed to support bewildered students. New girls were allotted individual seniors to look after them for the first few days, and give them guidance. Occasionally this worked well, but too often hapless ingénues were abandoned after a single meeting, or even a hastily scribbled note ('Dear Alison, I hope you are not too frightened . . .').[16]

Nothing mitigated the strangeness or intimidating nature of one's fellow freshers, who tended to be categorized into types. An undergraduate at Somerville in 1935 decided they were all either As (with more sex appeal than she), Bs (a fair fight), or Cs (the rest):

Group A girls had a comely and bespoke look. They tended to wear suede waistcoats and gold earclips pointing upwards like ivy leaves. Their conversation was of champagne breakfasts and how ideas were more rewarding than people.[17]

★

At Durham, and elsewhere, there were popularly only two categories: 'the studious sister or the dashing damsel';[18] in other words, clever girls who patently worked too hard to get their beauty sleep, and 'fast' ones who were stupid. You called girls you liked 'chaps', and those you didn't, 'females'.

Meeting chaps and females en masse was even more terrifying than one by one, and mealtimes were particularly alarming. Vera Brittain's first dinner at Somerville was almost unbearable. Everyone (but she) seemed to be screeching instead of talking, and the noise shrilled around the lofty hall like a siren. Everyone (but she) looked dowdy, dressed in joyless, long-sleeved frocks. The food was dull, the crockery depressing, and the thought of this night after night was unendurable.

Actually, the immature Vera was not intimidated by her peers – they disgusted her:

It required all my ambition, and all my touching belief that I was a natural democrat filled with an overwhelming love of humanity, to persuade me that I had never really felt the snobbish revulsion against rough-and-readiness which my specialised upbringing had made inevitable.[19]

She was lonely, feeling physically detached and socially isolated. There were plenty of girls who perceived university to be dangerously elitist, educating them – as one put it – 'out of [their] real class in society', before spitting them out as misfits and strangers. Others, like Vera, considered themselves too self-contained, too sophisticated (in the purest sense of the word), to relax. Shyness works both ways.

Traditionally, of course, everyone you encounter on your first day at university seems much more brainy, worldly-wise, and self-assured than you. Sometimes they really are: several students remember Gertrude Bell, at Lady Margaret Hall, as the most brilliant woman of her generation. She went on to excel as a traveller, writer, and diplomat; at Oxford she was remarkable as a vibrantly beautiful and intelligent student who achieved a first in modern history after only two years' study, at the age of barely twenty. Apparently she had corrected one of her own examiners during finals, but with such grace and self-assurance that nobody minded.

It is also a truism that once you have recovered your confidence, you recognize that here is an exhilarating opportunity to make friends unencumbered by the preferences of your family or the confines of your school. To some this was disconcerting: 'I find it bewildering deciding if I like people by myself. I have been used to them labelled.'[20] Others found it faintly distasteful, like Vera Brittain. She had chosen Oxford in 1914 because there, she hoped she might 'begin to live and to find at least one human creature among my own sex whose spirit can have intercourse with mine'. There was no such creature in her cohort. In the preternaturally academic atmosphere at college, she considered herself unique, 'one of the "lions" – perhaps the "lion" of my year'. She realized such intellectual superiority was likely to seclude her from her peers, but that was not important. 'I might be hated by all my year at the end of a term,' she admitted, 'but I do not think I shall be, as people here are not jealous & resentful as they are at school.'[21] That last comment was somewhat naive.

Unlike Vera, most girls relaxed into the novelty of directing their own relationships, and remember endless evenings fuelled by cocoa, cakes, and helpless giggles in the company of girls from all over the world. Academic work was a duty; being silly in company with other silly people was an unalloyed delight.

Mary Applebey went to St Anne's in the days when it was

the Society of Home Students, just before the Second World War. She was billeted in a hostel with eleven other girls, all of whom became part of the fabric of her future. She lived with one of them for fifty years. The survivors still keep in touch, and their children, and children's children, treat each other as family. Yet this was a completely random group of people. Mary herself had an academic upbringing: her mother had been at Somerville, and married her chemistry tutor. Of the others, a few were from clergy families; one was a rich builder's daughter from Birmingham; one was an overseas student from Hong Kong; one a bright, rebellious girl from Wales; another followed a family tradition into Oxford. Two took pass (two-year) degrees, the rest took honours.[22] They explored Oxford together, comrades in academia, and their shared experience proved stronger than their disparate histories.

These bluestockings may (to a diminishing extent) have belonged to an academic elite, but socially, culturally, religiously, politically, sexually, even physically, university was open to all comers, provided they behaved themselves and pretended to be tolerably normal. An unsophisticated girl from suburbia or the provinces – like Gwendolen Freeman – was unlikely to have encountered before the lesbians or communists or atheists she would come across at college, and certainly not in an atmosphere of respect and high expectation. She could never have imagined making close friends with people of a different class, religion, or race.

As for meeting men: an undergraduate in the 1930s maintained that it was still perfectly possible in that late era to go through your university career without conversing with someone of the opposite sex. It would take some doing, though, and for those brave enough to take it, advice was available on how to cope with male attention:

Don't run away. This rouses the spirit of the chase. Don't faint. This rouses the protective impulse. Look him slowly up and down, smiling cynically. This will make him think he's improperly dressed . . . However, if you feel you would like to talk: talk about yourself . . . If he tries to talk, don't listen. Or change the subject. Either way you'll stop him; he'll give up . . .

If all else fails . . . follow the advice of all the sex appeal and beauty experts – and all the advertisements. This won't leave you any time for meeting men.[23]

Not much of this was relevant to freshers anyway: most of them had neither the opportunity nor confidence to discover sex (if they ever discovered it) until their first year was behind them.

Even though rules and restrictions held women undergraduates in such a tight embrace, students were still paradoxically encouraged to use initiative on occasion, which could be daunting. Being uprooted from the strict routine of family or school life was disorientating. Daphne Hanschell had loved her convent during the 1920s. Bells rang to tell you when to do things, you clanked softly with enamel badges declaring your duties or your place in the school hierarchy, and friends were neatly divided into those on your side, those not. She remembers longing to ask her fellow freshers at university to be on her side on her first day. She was so lonely. Her tutor had told her to go to a lecture, but Daphne dared not ask for directions to the hall, and so missed it. She was supposed to do an essay based on books in the library, but no one explained how to locate them among the miles and miles of shelving, and she gave up.[24] Vera Brittain once said that being a fresher felt like being in quarantine; to Daphne, and shy girls like her, it was more like solitary confinement.

Communication should have been better. Very few institutions took the time – right up until 1939 – to produce the sort of vade mecum its female students needed. They were endlessly being forbidden things, but nobody explained where to go, how the system worked, whom to ask for help. One bluestocking remembers waking at 4.00 a.m. each morning of her first fortnight and being physically sick with loneliness and apprehension. Another nearly died, she says, of homesickness, and sat for hours at a time in her room anxiously wondering what she should be doing. And despite what Vera Brittain said about the lack of jealousy and resentment, insecure freshers were quite capable of sniffing out victims in their midst, like Margery Morton at St Hilda's.[25]

Margery was older than her peers, coming to university in 1914 following three years at the Royal College of Music as a harp scholar, and a year's cramming at Oxford High School. She was ostracized as a sneak because she already knew the college bursar. She could not reciprocate tea parties because she had so little money and disliked the ubiquitous cigarettes (banning others from smoking in her bedroom). She declined to join Sunday bike rides, because she was church-bred and considered them frivolous. And she weighed twelve stone. 'I found a shop which sold damaged chocolate – floor sweepings – very cheaply, and made good use of it.' Her addiction to sugar was considered pathetic and disloyal, in an era of rationing and national sacrifice. Poor girl.

A little advice on budgeting would have been useful. Few students, before leaving home for university, had occasion to manage their own finances, apart from small amounts of pocket money spent or saved. Now they were suddenly responsible for all the sundries of life, and cutting their coats, as the saying goes, according to their cloth. Even though main meals, accommodation, and tuition fees were covered by parents, and supplemented by scholarships and grants, there were still plenty of expenses left. Fragrant cakes in greaseproof paper were regularly sent in parcels from home, and occasionally new or mended clothes and books, and most students sent home their dirty washing, since the postal service was so swift and cheap. Local laundries proved unreliable and unfeasibly expensive.

When Kathleen Courtney went to college in 1897, she carefully itemized her monthly payments for her father's approval. They totalled £1 11s 6d (about £100 at today's rate), and included 7s for laundry (the costliest single item), 2s for the church collection plate, 2s 6d for stamps, 5s for gloves, 5s for books, 7s 6d for entertainment and club subscriptions, and 2s 6d for miscellaneous bits and bobs. She also paid £2 per term to hire a bicycle.[26] Forty years later, Joan Morgan went to Liverpool to read zoology. Her accounts were rather more varied, including 'tweezers for eyebrows and dissections', a powder puff, chocolates, nail varnish, toffee, powdered shampoo, and acid drops.[27]

No matter how lavish their budgets, few women had any funds left at the end of term. Their first vacation was a welcome chance to replenish the coffers. Before the First World War, young women were not encouraged to withdraw money from a bank account without a responsible male in attendance (although post-office accounts were common), and students were constantly writing home requesting a pound note or two to be sent in the post.

The fresher's first homecoming after being away for a term could be awkward. Family dynamics had altered, and expectations changed. There might be jealousy and resentment from siblings forced to make sacrifices, or suspicion from parents unsure what their daughters had become. But

usually everyone was eager to hear all about the adventure of
university life, while being reassured that their pet bluestocking still loved home best of all. The trouble was, many
did not. They preferred their student lives. With more time,
as their courses progressed, families adjusted, but some
remained fractured beyond repair. Rosemary Vickers had
never been particularly happy at home.[28] Her parents rowed;
she considered her father to be deeply unhappy, and her
mother a manipulative hypochondriac. As an only child,
Rosemary felt trapped. She had hoped that by going to university (in 1935) she would not only refresh her own life, but
give her parents a chance to come to terms with one another
in her absence.

Her first term was the happiest period of her life. She
made friends, who invited her to their houses in the holidays, and for the first time ever she felt warmly loved. It was
only when she returned home at Christmas that she realized
'the utter impossibility of these new friendships with my
particular background'. How could she bring people home
to these dreary, parochial people, still blindly bickering all
the time? And if she was unable to reciprocate her friends'
invitations, she obviously could not accept them either.
They would lose interest in her and think her rude. 'Life is
poisoned at the very root,' she wrote miserably in her diary.
'I'm being educated out of my real class in society and made
unnaturally critical of my own parents.'

It took Rosemary a long time to reconcile her two different worlds.

7. Women's Sphere

You know, Eileen, in spite of going to Manchester,
you're really quite normal.[1]

Perhaps the most obvious sign of continuity between their old and new lives for every undergraduette – unless they lived at home – was the ringing of bells. At each college or hall of residence, bells measured out the routine with reassuring authority. At Langwith Hall, Manchester, they rang nine times daily during the 1930s: for waking at 7.15 a.m., prayers at 8.00, breakfast ten minutes later, the first lunch sitting at 1.00 p.m., the second at 1.45, tea at 4.00, dinner at 7.30, prayers at 8.10, and a 'morality bell' at lights-out. At Leeds there was also a dressing gong before dinner, and bulbs were twinkled on and off a few times at 10.30 p.m. to prepare for 'quiet time' at 11.00. Any noise after that meant trouble. Senior students were recruited to police the corridors, and report misdemeanours to the authorities. It was an invidious job no one enjoyed.

Domestic orderliness was encouraged not only to ensure the smooth running of a college community, but to lend an air of familiarity to a strange environment. There was a certain cosiness about everyone eating together three times a day, praying together in the chapel, helping each other with dressing, shopping, hair-washing, mending. Coping with the mundane helped settle this rarefied, academic life into a homely context. Be it Durham or Exeter, 1880 or 1930, a

*A rather grumpy monitor summons her fellow
students out of bed at Manchester University in 1905.*

woman student's timetable remained remarkably uniform.
On weekdays it would be much as those Manchester bells
dictated, with chapel and then work in the morning, exercise and/or more work in the afternoon, meetings of various sorts in the early evenings, and private study after cocoa
at 9.00 p.m. (or a cocoa party, of course). There was more
socializing and less work on Saturdays; long walks or cycle
rides and two bouts of chapel instead of one on Sundays.

Conformity was everything. It was achieved (when achieved
at all) through a firm mixture of expectation and regulation.
Apart from the usual laws about curfews and the making and

receiving of visits, litanies of house rules circumscribed students' behaviour around the country. In Durham, for example, no 'Dove', or woman student, was allowed to take her elevenses in a café; at Royal Holloway College the borrowing of teaspoons from the kitchen was forbidden; at Manchester you were not allowed to do the washing-up in the bath; and no Girtonian was permitted eggs in her bedroom. Liverpool insisted hats and jackets be worn at lectures, while Somerville expected you to keep them on at tea. Nottingham was a little more pragmatic: 'Endeavour to behave in the common rooms as you would in your home. Don't wear "here-I-come" apparel. Don't do a day's work on Monday and then spend the rest of the week admiring it.'² Stick to the rules, was the universal message, and you will avoid making a fool of yourself and your university.

There were always going to be rebels and mavericks, especially in academic institutions peopled by thinking women. If the college authorities could not quell them with activity, disapproval, or threats, they were expelled. But the majority of bluestockings accepted this mildly conventual existence with good grace. A measure of physical restriction was a small price to pay for intellectual freedom. Sensible students worked with what they were given. Using imposed structure as an outline, they coloured the picture with originality and flair.

Katie Dixon, at Newnham in the late 1870s, welcomed the college routine. Every morning, after breakfast, she would go to the sunny library and start work (but never before nine o'clock: a point of honour). If she felt stiff or bilious sitting down for too long, she would wander down to the lecture rooms to stand and read at the lectern – providing, of course, it was not in use. After lunch she played tennis or, in summer, went boating – all 'white flannels and pink parasols'. Back to

Newnham for tea; then evensong at King's at half-past five, dinner, and perhaps a little more work.

I remember many a winter evening with a roaring little fire, (that divine cakey coal, you could heave up with the poker) lying in one straight line in my wicker chair, lamp . . . behind me, a vast lexicon lying on my middle, and a play of Aeschylus or what not in my hands. The silence, the being alone, and knowing everyone else was at it in the same way seemed to give one a great push on.[3]

It sounds wonderfully relaxed. Sometimes it is easy to forget that cynicism has not always been in fashion: an indiscriminate sense of wellbeing washes over so many memories of college life. A student in the 1920s confessed to feeling almost stupidly content, the whole time: 'I was very happy indeed at Girton, and so were most of us, but on looking back I do not quite know why. It seems to me now that we were not very enterprising and that life was not really so interesting as it might have been.'[4]

Being there was enterprising enough. As for interest: there was plenty on offer in academic challenge, sports, social activities, relationships, and all the triumphs and disasters of a young university career. This chapter, however, is not about adventure, but shared experience: the mechanics of a bluestocking's world.

If the bell did not wake you in the mornings, the maid would. Most domestic staff are mentioned only in passing in chronicles of university life. They were not supposed to do any personal service for students; they merely cleaned rooms, and provided coal and jugs of hot water. But it was not unusual for maids to run their allotted 'young ladies' a bath in the mornings, or bring them the odd glass of milk or cup of cocoa. In return, favourites were invited to tea, or asked to dances organized by student associations. Maids' children were sent presents at Christmas, and collections were taken for anyone known to be in distress. At the residential University Hall in Liverpool there was a popular character called Mary, who 'had a sailor brother and a parrot to whom she was not at all severe';[5] another Liverpudlian, Margaret the parlourmaid, had literary aspirations. She used to borrow books from the library and, on opening a student's bedroom curtains one foggy morning, famously commented that the weather appeared 'very detrimental to vehicular traffic'.[6]

In any establishment, the cook was a figure of great significance. Certain colleges built up a reputation (then as now) for irresistible menus. St Hilda's in Oxford was one of them, particularly during the 1930s. After years of school fish-pie and cabbage, the students there were thrilled to find fresh asparagus on the menu, and trifle studded with crystallized violets. At St Hugh's, a typical autumn day's meals were detailed by Ina Brooksbank in a letter home in 1917. Oxford water was 'not fit to drink unless boiled', she warned, but considering this was wartime, the food was remarkably good. For breakfast there was porridge and boiled ham; sometimes sausage too, or fish-cakes, scrambled eggs on toast, fried eggs or fish; on Sundays, kidneys 'with lovely thick gravy'. Bread, toast, butter, jam, and marmalade were always on offer. Lunches included a slice of joint or pie, fish, hash, or occasionally liver. 'Seconds' followed, of sago, rice or maize pudding, jam suet or pastry, or stewed fruit, and a cup of tea. More tea at four o'clock, with a slice of bread and margarine. Dinner was a three-course meal of 'soups of various kinds from white to black'; a choice of two main dishes – perhaps stuffed tomatoes or fishcakes, vegetable hash, curried rice, or pork and beans, with two vegetables and pota-toes; a dessert of fruit tart, pineapple slices, banana trifle, or fresh apples and pears. Later on, in students' rooms, there would be the inevitable communal cocoa, with any cakes or biscuits to be found.

Bad manners spoil good food, as everyone brought up properly will know. And not everyone who was at university *was* brought up properly, according to an anonymous diarist at the University of London. Writing in 1899, she confessed herself appalled by the chaos after breakfast was announced: 'I felt almost embarrassed when I saw people finishing their toilette down the corridor, but neither they nor the student who went flapping down the corridor in sloppy bedroom slippers and a dressing gown seemed to think they were doing anything unusual.' At lunch, people strolled from table to table with plate in hand, 'searching for better puddings', and '[d]inner was a hideous meal, its only redeeming feature was its astonishing brevity! The conversation of the old students amazed me.'[7] So dining-hall etiquette was not all evening gowns and Latin graces. At Bedford College, lack of space meant some bluestockings were forced to eat standing up, balancing their plates on the mantelpiece, and everywhere the noise was overwhelming.

Attendance at dinner was one of the 'rules of residence' at university: like signing the morning register, sleeping in your own bed, and going to chapel. Only a few exemptions were allowed each term; miss any more, and you were liable for a fine, or suspension. So there was no escaping college food, good or bad. Nor could you avoid regular assemblages of the college population. You could, however, choose with whom (as long as she was female) you enjoyed toasted teacakes on a winter's afternoon, a picnic lunch by the river, or a treat at the end of a hard-working day, like this student during the 1930s:

One thing I remember with particular pleasure was when we finished [studying] . . . we used to go down to the Martyrs' Memorial to buy hot meat pies from a caravan there. It wasn't there during the day, just in the evening. Two or three of us would go together. It seemed quite an adventure in the dark, and we had to get back by 10.30.[8]

A descendant of that meat pie van exists in Oxford still.

A student at St Hilda's in the 1930s considered one of the great pleasures of university life to be the opportunity to drink coffee and smoke black cigarettes with 'odd fish'. By odd fish she did not necessarily mean eccentrics, but women who were different. Living in a crucible – which every resident student did to some extent – meant more than self-discovery: it meant reinvention. To many young women, especially those frustrated by the parochialism of family and school life, this was the strongest attraction of all. The trick was to avoid regression into domestic anonymity, or intellectual compromise, when the adventure was over. Sarah Beswick's father was a Derbyshire mill-worker. She was a provincial ingénue when she arrived at Manchester University in 1927 (encouraged not by her parents but by a determined English teacher). The very first meal she sat down to in the refectory opened her eyes. She was alone, until a black undergraduate asked if he could come and join her. She generously – or naively – invited him to sit down, and by the time she finished her meal 'was completely surrounded by a sea of black faces'. According to her daughter, 'despite having previously never seen a black face in her Derbyshire life', Sarah welcomed the company.[9] It was a critical point in her life. University turned villagers into citizens of the world, passivity into proactivity, and predictable little girls into strong, surprising women.

Maybe that is what parents were really afraid of. Leaving home has always been a strange journey. The trouble is that women, before the liberating effects of the Second World War, were apt to be marooned on an unfamiliar shore afterwards. Society was not yet ready for female graduates, unless they taught, went into social or clerical work, or married and ignored their degrees altogether. Like pioneer homesteaders in far-flung corners of empire, these early bluestockings husbanded the fruits of their labours for the benefit of future generations. They endowed their daughters and grand-daughters with what they had been denied themselves: an expectation of educational achievement and confidence of success.

Odd fish had their attractions, but nothing meant so much to these university pioneers, nor lasted so long, as friendship. A few episodes of bitchiness emerge in diaries and letters: inevitable, some would say, in any female community. A young lady called Maud gleefully broke the news of her engagement in 1897, and although no doubt roundly congratulated to her face, was derided in private. 'I must say one would never have expected it of her, of all people; she is such a lump.'[10] There was trouble at a drama club when too many prima donnas turned up to rehearsals: 'About 12.30 I was informed by Miss Burstall that there would be no theatricals as Miss Armistead refused to act with Miss Easterfield who could not be made to look like Galatea.'[11] More trouble at the Debating Society when the earnest (po-faced?) secretary resigned, prophesying doom due to the unpalatable facts that the habits of the committee members were unbusinesslike, many of the professors disapproved of their 'doings', and they bickered too much.[12] An American at Somerville in the 1880s grew exasperated with her sister students: they were too giggly, obviously suppressed, lacked 'gush' (a commodity she perceived to be desirable), and considered calling each other donkeys to be the apogee of wit. 'You can't imagine how jolly it seemed to get out of Somerville cloisters for a whole evening and away from all "women's sphere of action".'[13]

These irritations aside, it is obvious that an esprit de corps pervaded college life. University was appreciated to be a communal experience, as well as a period of personal development, and the majority enjoyed it as such. When Beryl Worthing visited Belgium in the course of her studies at Queen Mary College, she was introduced to the Dowager Queen Elisabeth. Next day, Her Highness sent a lady-in-waiting to invite Beryl to tea at the palace. Beryl was astonished when both women confessed to feeling envious of the English girl, and her freedom to work as she wished. The queen would have loved to pursue a career as a concert violinist, and her attendant always wanted to be a professional artist. 'But our destinies did not allow.'[14]

A student at Reading just before the First World War loved the 'zest and comradeship' she found among the women there; at Leeds there were all sorts of rituals to make students feel they belonged:

One ceremony which seems to have long disappeared was the custom at the end of any social function for everyone present to climb on to the nearest chair or bench and yell as loudly as possible 'Kumati, Kumati, Kaora, Kaora, Hagi, Hagi, Hai!' – a Maori war-cry, I believe, adopted as a slogan by the Leeds students.[15]

Each cohort used its own slang, ebbing and flowing through written records across the country. Letters can be dated by the incidence of certain words. If a tiresome male undergraduate is described as a 'grim tick' instead of 'ripping', or 'topping', it's the early 1920s. 'Lekkers', 'brekkers', and (heaven help us) 'wagger-pagger baggers' belong to the previous decade.[16] 'Regimentals' are 1870s underclothes; 'trollies' are 1930s knickers; and you 'throw' a coffee, instead of drinking it, or 'fling' a library, instead of visiting it, in (precisely) 1923.

Groups of friends banded together to play practical jokes on one another (a sure sign of fellow-feeling). 'Some of us had this need to laugh and be very silly,' remembered an undergraduette in the 1920s. 'It was part of the emancipation from the responsibilities of being prefects at school and older daughters at home.'[17] Her speciality – not very original – was to go down the streets around college ringing people's doorbells, then run away.

Katie Dixon was less enthusiastic about japes. One of her friends was addicted to them, relentlessly filching things from Katie's room and hiding them, or tying her doorhandle to the banisters during the night. It was exhausting. Pranksters tended to acquire a reputation, if they went too far, of fecklessness. Once she was stereotyped, it was difficult for any student to emerge again as an individual, and stereotyping was rampant in college society. Between the wars, as well as the generic division (in all its variations) between dumb blonde in high heels and brainy brunette in glasses, every college had its distinct sets. The country set kept terriers, went riding before breakfast on their own horses, frequently got drunk, and had rowdy boyfriends. The religious set were apt to burst into your bedroom, fall to their knees, and pray for your conversion. This was 'embarrassing at best, and highly trying if one were busy'.[18] The sporting set honked at one another and forgot to close their knees when they sat down. Medics smelt faintly acidic and spoke of nothing but dissections and post-mortems. Aesthetes (and 'aesthete-spotting' was a recognized pastime in Oxford in the 1880s) wore weird clothes and looked impossibly aloof. They were also dangerously attractive, male and female, the mere sight of one liable to leave a girl 'smashed', or quite besotted. Gwendolen Freeman remembered a particularly charismatic one at Girton, who painted her walls brilliant orange, stained the floor dark brown, and filled her rooms with 'heaps of valuable things'.[19] She had been born in America, this paragon, and travelled widely; she was gorgeous. Miserable Doris (another Girtonian), on the other hand, used to sit all day by the fire, swathed in an unlovely dressing gown, and sniff noisily. She had never experienced an English winter before. Her hot-water bottle leaked. She hated the food. She hated Girton.

The impression left by their writing and reminiscences suggests that, despite a tendency to caricature, most blue-stockings not only tolerated one another, but delighted in the company of new-found friends. Domestic intimacies drew them together – such as sewing bees, when everyone would bring their mending to a common room and work on it to music; or hat-trimming and dress-refurbishment sessions, when ribbons, birds' wings, silken posies were chosen and attached to various garments. It was hard not to be friendly to someone you asked to fasten the blouse buttons down your back, or help you with your hairpins, because you had no maid, mother, or sister present, as you did at home.

Look at any group photograph of women university students, and although not one of them looks younger than about thirty, it will immediately be apparent that fashion played a significant part in their lives. It is as easy to date different cohorts by their dress as it is by their language. A Somervillian declared herself 'sick of big puffed sleeves and puckered waists' in the early 1880s — everyone was wearing them. In the 1890s, sleeves subsided a little, the plumpness migrating to high-necked bosoms. The fashion of the early 1900s was to wear 'brush braiding' around the hem of a skirt, to save the fabric from fraying; this (disquietingly) infuriated a male undergraduate at Leeds, who wrote a spiteful little poem about it in the university magazine:

> O England's sisters dear!
> O England's mothers and wives!
> It is not your dresses you're wearing out
> But human creatures' lives.
> Germ, germ, germ,
> Lurks in that murky dirt,
> You carry today with a double tread
> A sword as well as a skirt.[20]

It is safe to assume that here was not a supporter of higher education for women. Or of women at all.

Everyone looked very prim during the first decade of the 1900s, with collars and college ties, and hair balancing like a satin cushion on each head. The 1920s were loose and winsome, and the 1930s rather drab. Bluestockings tended to favour a uniform look, after the turn of the twentieth century, which involved dark skirts and plain tops, usually with a jacket. Coats, hats, and stockings were de rigueur, right up to 1939, and trousers only latterly encouraged on field trips or treks. The odd free spirit would buck the trend — as at St Hugh's in 1924, when a fresher appeared at dinner with her hair clipped on one side and curled on the other. She was dressed in a skirt so short and tight that the other girls gasped. The college Principal, Miss Gwyer, did not flinch; she merely turned to her companion at High Table and commented: 'If Miss [X] wishes to wear trousers, I do wish she would wear a pair: that one will soon split.'[21] A contemporary of Miss X's was expelled for dressing like a man; in that case wearing trousers was deemed to be assuming a disguise in order to *behave* like a man and visit men's colleges. Miss X was luckily considered eccentric rather than subversive, and allowed to stay.

A newspaper article in 1936 recommended essentials for a 'University trousseau', including 'an attractive tweed ensemble', a black or dark navy suit, a knitted outfit for college or lectures, chic trousers, blouses, belts, and bags; 'try to have a fur coat', it advised, a mac, a simple woollen dress, and 'one smart dance dress'.[22] This stylish little collection, it assured its readers, would see the undergraduette right through her university career. That was all very well for those with money: Bessie Callender of Durham could only afford a 'black artillery serge coat and skirt for 28 shillings at Debenham and Freebody's summer sale', with a white starched shirt.[23] The absolute minimum wardrobe was a dress to change into for dinner, accessories to titivate that same dress for dances, and a couple of outfits for daytime. Gwendolen Freeman remembered wearing the same dress for the whole of her first term, which lasted nine weeks.

A leitmotif throughout literature concerning women's domestic life at university is the 'combi'. Combis, or combinations – a garment incorporating a chemise and knickers – seem constantly to have been in a state of disrepair, being mended with white wool, patched with the relics of long-dead predecessors, sent home to Mother to be re-sewn or washed. No item of clothing is so often mentioned in letters and diaries, so troublesome, and so necessary. Freedom from combis, when it dawned, must have been a marvellous thing.

Academic dress was a contentious issue. At Oxford and

The first women graduates in England qualified at the University of London on 10 May 1882. Their achievement is celebrated in a graceful engraving from the Girl's Own Paper.

Cambridge, women were not full members of their university until they were awarded degrees in 1920 and 1948 respectively; therefore they were not entitled to wear the academic uniform of cap and gown customary elsewhere (not a mortar-board: that was reserved for the first-come, first-served of the intellectual elite). The prohibition had its positive points. No one could tell you belonged to a college, and therefore operated under disciplinary rules, if you were out and about at night in 'civvies'; nor could anyone distinguish between scholars (entitled to wear long gowns) and 'commoners' (condemned to a foolish-looking scrap of black with a flap at each shoulder). But no one could fail to acknowledge the lack of entitlement to academic dress, as to an official degree, to be humiliating as well as illogical. At London, women wore them right from the beginning. A contemporary magazine illustration, captioned 'A Scene at the University of London, May 10th, 1882', depicts the first 'Sweet Girl Graduates' in England. The accompanying article is fulsome in its praise not so much of the pioneers' scholarship, as their femininity. It imagines them as graceful acolytes at the altar of wisdom, bare-headed, wearing black silken robes, and carrying their caps like offerings in white-gloved hands. Their academic hoods are lined in jewel-like colours – dark ruby for the arts graduates and citrine for the scientists. Being womanly women (it is noted), they made the hoods themselves.[24]

At Manchester, too, bluestockings prided themselves on sewing their own dresses for Degree Day, even though their gowns were available for hire. Due to the volume of late Victorian and early Edwardian hair-dos, early undergraduates at Manchester (and everywhere except Oxbridge) found it difficult to find caps that fitted.[25] Choosing between vanity and compliance with the rules was a problem. Students were expected to wear their academic dress to lectures, chapel, dinner, in the library, on certain occasions in public, and for exams. It was even more important than the clothes beneath. When Ruth Wilson of Westfield College in London found herself running late for prayers after a hot bath one morning in about 1920, she decided to put on her gown 'over my knicks', and rush down to chapel. The hot bath and a lack of breakfast conspired against her: she fainted, and all was horribly revealed.[26] Incidentally, if the fire in your bedroom refused to blaze, you had only to hold your impenetrable gown spread out in front of it, and the flames would draw beautifully. Caps made excellent kettle-holders.

On the eve of the first degree ceremony for women in Oxford, the academic authorities held a mannequin parade to decide what headgear best suited female undergraduates. The soft black cap they chose — a sort of square beret — was considered a 'judicious compromise between Portia and Nerissa'. It had dignity, and perpetuated the distinction between male and female. Even then, in 1920, allowing women to graduate from Oxford was deplored by commentators as a radical and dangerous enterprise. Especially Cambridge commentators: a document circulating in the Senate there described Oxford's move chillingly as 'a dark and difficult adventure, the outcome of which no man can foresee'.[27] There was to be no female graduate of Cambridge, remember, for another twenty-eight years.

This obstinate tardiness on the part of the Oxbridge University Congregations was more demoralizing to tutors than to students. Not being officially integrated into the university precluded academic staff at women's colleges from responsibility, rank, academic influence, and a sensible salary.[28] While working behind the scenes with discretion and a great deal of diplomacy to accomplish full university membership for their student communities (not completely achieved at Oxford until 1959), most tried not to be too angry in public. Women students were still 'on approval', it was feared; if they and their wardens appeared too strident in the fight for academic equality, or demanded too much, all might yet be lost. So they comforted themselves that what really mattered was their work, and its personal significance. 'It is not for success in the next examination that we are teaching,' claimed one careful headmistress, 'it is not even for success in their future career . . . we are looking to eternity for the judgement on our work.'[29]

None of this politicking affected the final examinations themselves. At Oxbridge, as everywhere else, your university career climaxed in 'finals'; there was no assessment programme, no modules: everything depended on a week or so of exams in the summer of your final term. Results were classified then, as they are now (although women's results were not always published alongside men's), and the pressure to succeed was hard to bear. Success, for the conscientious scholar, meant justification of all the expectations and sacrifices of the past. It was a matter of pride, even if she knew it might be irrelevant in terms of a future career. Some students pretended finals did not really count. Gemma Creighton, from an academically illustrious family, expected only a third-class result in hers: 'I shouldn't mind if only old friends . . . didn't seem to think it rather a scandal for any of us to sink to 3rds. And really it doesn't much matter, as whatever happens I've learnt a huge lot here, and have loved it, and mean to keep it and not let it become a past episode.'[30]

Frances Sheldon felt the same: 'I don't care tuppence whether I get an English certificate [the paltry female equivalent of a degree at Oxford] or any other; but I'll get all the knowledge I can, in just the line I want . . .'[31] Knowing you could have done better was the worst outcome: a student in the 1920s wrote that she regretted her lack of application all her life: 'I belonged to so many societies, did far too many things, played far too many games, so that

although I was expected to get a 2nd I got a 4th: I deserved
it, but have never got over it.'[32] Leeds University decided to
relieve the pressure by reassuring its undergraduates that
they were not there to get firsts, but to be educated. But
with so much at stake, panic was never far from the examination halls, and stalked querulous students greedily. 'I don't
know if I shall ever believe in emancipated women again,'
wrote one student in 1938. 'Out of 13 starters, 5 fell by the
wayside during our [finals].' One walked out of the exam,
went home, and slept for four days. The second had gastric
flu and could not physically stay the course; another collapsed with fatigue. 'Doris went gadding about with men
and began revising a bit too late – used to sit up all night
with caffeine etc.' and faded away. The fifth drop-out felt too
tired to walk to the examination hall, fainted during the
exam, and then went out on the river, where she was seen
with a man at 11.00 p.m.[33]

Well-regulated exams do not usually throw up surprises.
Given the right preparation – eight hours' revision a day for
at least the couple of terms leading up to finals – and a calm
disposition, all usually goes well. Taking short cuts is risky,
and rarely works. That is why tutors welcomed the success
of their female students with such delight. Every good result
was one more little vindication of the 'experiment' in wom-
en's higher education that had been running since 1869.
When one girl got a first in Classics at Somerville in 1935,
after a colourful undergraduate career, her tutor could hardly
contain herself:

Now that's the way I like things done. Miss a term with tonsillitis,
go to a few Royal balls, and occasionally to bed with a clergyman,
throw in an *embarras gastrique* on the eve of Schools – and after
that it really is worthwhile to say you got a 1st in Greats.

You're quite the most sporting horse I ever jockeyed – as far as I can see you did it all in the last lap – and I'm hugely delighted . . . My best jubilations.[34]

That is an extraordinary response. Reactions were usually more measured ('Dear Miss Worthington, I wish it had been a third instead of a fourth but still it has been well worth doing').[35] Elsie Phare's reward, after becoming the first woman to win a starred first in her English Tripos (Part I) and the Chancellor's Medal for English Verse, was to recite her poem in the Senate House. Being a woman, she was not, of course, allowed to wear a gown: this was Cambridge in the 1920s. The most brilliant English student of her generation, she was still treated like a fish out of water.

For those (unlike Elsie) allowed to graduate officially, Degree Day was an iconic occasion. Its formality presented problems to those with little experience. Sarah Beswick – the unsophisticated girl from Derbyshire who had settled in so well at Manchester – remembered hers clearly. She invited her mother, a close female friend, and Miss Axon, the teacher responsible for getting her to university in the first place. The outing had been carefully budgeted by her mother: Sarah's father was on short time (during the Depression), and money was tight. There was just enough for the tram fares, and a cup of tea after the ceremony at Houldsworth Hall. It was only when the party arrived at the Hall that they were told white gloves were essential – and Sarah possessed none. Someone dashed off to the nearest draper's shop and managed to buy a pair in time – but that meant no money left for tea. For one last time, Miss Axon came to the rescue and treated them all. The day was saved.[36]

At Birmingham, Degree Day was one big party. Here is the programme for July, 1926:

11–12	University Organ
12–1	Ceremony
1.15–2.15	Guild of Graduates' Luncheon
2	Outdoor play
2.15	Tennis tournament finals
3.30	Band (Regimental)
4	Tea. Motor cycle gymkhana
6.30	Reception of Flannel [informal] Dance
7	Dancing
11.45	Lights out[37]

And after that? What might a degree lead to next? For women prior to 1939 (especially on non-vocational courses), despite all the efforts of the pioneers, it was best to assume nothing. A student at the Society of Home Students put it well: 'Oxford was the end of my youth, not the beginning of my adult life.'[38]

8. Blessed Work

Don't write anything you can possibly keep in.[1]

The novelist Dorothy L. Sayers was at Oxford from 1912 to 1915. Contemporaries remembered her as an intellectually gifted young woman; somewhat eccentric, but definitely a serious thinker. The impression she liked to give was different. When asked to describe a working day at college, she came up with the following unlikely timetable: eat breakfast at 9.30 (thus neatly missing a nine o'clock lecture); mess about cleaning tennis shoes, catching up on gossip, and collecting post from 10.00 to 11.00; enjoy a leisurely coffee with friends until 12.00; 'cut' a lecture in favour of composing a sonnet; have lunch at 1.15 and then go punting; tackle tea at 4.00; go canoeing and eat a picnic dinner on the river at 6.30, then attend a Bach Choir rehearsal; have more coffee and cakes in a friend's room at 9.30; finally, retire to bed at midnight, unless anyone should happen to fancy a chat. 'From time to time,' she observed, 'some unfortunate who had "got an Essay" – an affliction always referred to as though it were a kind of recurrent distemper – was forced to go into retirement to write the thing.'[2] But Dorothy herself – blithe spirit – claimed immunity.

It might be an attractive scenario, some sort of nostalgic remnant of *la belle époque*, but this cannot really be how Dorothy and her high-achieving friends whiled away their days at university. Always, chuntering along in the background, squatting immovable beside you, or soaring over everything, was work. Work, after all, was the undergraduate's raison d'être, the commodity parents paid for, the excuse for opting out, for a while, from real life. It *is* true that reminiscences of student life before the Second World War tend not to dwell on academic routine. Nevertheless, that routine, with the response it generated, underpins the history of the bluestocking.

A student's relationship with her work proved an emotional, private thing. She was judged both within and beyond the university by how successful that relationship was, and how intense; she judged herself by how fulfilled it made her feel. The stakes were high. Whether through cause or effect, those who failed academically in the early days of further education for women rarely found peace of mind in other areas of their university careers, and the pressure of keeping up with work, or even holding back, produced a significant rate of attrition (see Chapter 10). There is a sense in their documents that intellectual effort was the only currency many women students felt they possessed; squander that, or be caught short, and the shame would be overwhelming.

It was in everyone's interests, therefore, to make sure each bluestocking maximized her talent. A solid structure helped. There was an intractable rhythm to the days, weeks, and terms of the academic year, marked by lectures, tutorials or 'coachings' (at some universities), classes, and exams. No matter what subject they were reading, students could choose any course of lectures they fancied at Oxford or Cambridge, guided by tutors and their own inclination. Elsewhere lectures were prescribed. A typical weekly timetable might be five lectures, as many classes (group teaching sessions), and perhaps one or two tutorials, when students learned singly or in pairs. A minimum of six hours' academic work a day was encouraged, with Sundays off for church, exercise, and letter writing. Factor in travelling time to lectures (especially from home, out-of-town colleges, or halls of residence), waiting for chaperones, the hour or two's recommended leisure time, practicals for scientists or practice sessions for musicians, and the days were soon filled.

With such a hectic schedule, minor disasters were inevitable. Work always came first for the conscientious scholar, but sometimes at a cost. Molly McNeill's Irish temper was roused by one of her lecturers at university during the First World War who habitually droned on too long, making Molly late for lunch. When she eventually arrived breathless in the dining hall, there was 'practically nothing left': a poor return for her diligence.

I got some sort of carrots and onions and meat mixed in watery gravey [sic], and managed after much searching to secure the scrapings of a potatoe [sic] dish which amounted to a helping about the size of an egg. There was absolutely no brussel sprouts left at all. When it came to pudding there was some scraps of tart which I avoided and took some fig pudding. What was in it I don't know, but it sounded and felt like emery or fine sand. I was frightfully angry because really when you come in after sitting freezing in a cold lecture room you do expect something warming.[3]

Exams were held at strategic points during the course, arcanely known as 'inters', 'prelims', 'Little-Go', 'mods', 'responsions', 'collections', and so on. Some were more significant than others; most were frighteningly formal, and required the wearing of 'subfusc' or academic dress. More than one girl wore fake glasses to help her feel suitably studious, or simply went into denial. Maude Royden, a student during the 1890s, was in the latter category, never seriously believing her exams would materialize: 'I always thought I should die, or the sky would fall, or the process of manufacturing paper and pens fall into disuse, or something of the sort.'[4]

Freshers at Girton were informed soon after their arrival that if they failed to secure a first or second class in their first-year Tripos, they would be out. Elsewhere it was possible to re-sit elements of exams, as long as you had the time and money. Candidates for pass degrees took shorter, less demanding courses than those reading for honours. It was not necessarily intellectual ability that made the distinction between the two: many young women could not afford three years at university, so opted for one or two, and a pass. But no one could avoid finals, which leered over the last summer term, beckoning with an ink-stained finger. I still dream about mine, thirty years on.

Intelligent young women who chose to go to university, rather than those forced there, generally coped well with the work, finding their own level, settling down, and getting on with it. People like Dorothy L. Sayers – possessed of a brilliant mind – achieved the highest possible results without appearing to try at all. Disguised harmlessly in mannered college photographs as vivacious beauties, dumpy maiden aunts, or schoolgirls wearing gymslips and complicated woollies, such scholars were quickly labelled geniuses, and somehow untouchable. The girl-wonder Gertrude Bell, Agnata Ramsay (who got the only Class I, Division I result in Classics at Cambridge in 1887), Philippa Fawcett (placed above the senior wrangler, or top undergraduate performer at Cambridge, in maths in 1890), Marie Stopes (the first woman Doctor of Science in England)[5] – these were lofty role models, beyond the reach of normal intellects.

Girls who had grown up on the fringes of academia had a

natural advantage when it came to understanding the university routine. Mary Plant's father was a senior lecturer in chemistry at Oxford. She used to play in the laboratories as a child in the 1920s and '30s, growing copper-sulphate crystals, prowling among Florey's mysterious penicillin cultures, rolling wondrous balls of mercury around in the palm of her hand. When her father's former student Dorothy Hodgkin interviewed her for a place at Somerville, the great scientist's opening words were 'I last saw you in the bath.'[6]

Ordinary mortals tried to do what was required in the way of work as best they could – with the help, if necessary, of constant cigarettes, sugar lumps, swigs of Sanatogen (a tonic wine), and wet towels for the fevered forehead.

Success was sweet, as this Cambridge bluestocking found in the 1870s:

Work doesn't seem work, but rather some delightful form of amusement. I can't tell you how happy I am this term. All my imaginings of what it was going to be like to have nothing but mathematics to work at were small compared with the real thing. I do a little other work besides – my half-hour of Odyssey after dinner; and every day except Thursdays and Sundays I work at my embroidery for the two hours immediately after lunch.[7]

'Studying is really the nicest kind of work one can do,' declared Jane Worthington in the 1890s; 'the only difficulty is it may become a little too absorbing.'[8] Her contemporary Lettice Ilbert worked hard simply because she found it made her 'unreasonably happy',[9] a sentiment Eglantyne Jebb agreed with rapturously. One of Miss Jebb's letters, dated 1896, almost burns the fingers: 'But my work, oh Dorothy, my work, my work, my work! Dear work, blessed work, my heart and soul go into my work.'[10]

Emma Pollard of Somerville went to two universities at once. Oxford still declined to award women degrees when she matriculated there, so she enrolled at University College, London, too, nipping down to London periodically to fill any gaps in the Oxford syllabus. She sat two lots of final exams, and passed both. Another student, profoundly deaf, qualified in medicine at Leeds in the early 1920s to the delight of her peers. Blind students, the terminally ill, orphaned, or even widowed young women were not only accepted on to courses (if they passed the entrance qualifications), but much admired; sadly the shy, ugly, or over-earnest ones, like Mabel Fuller in Rosamond Lehmann's novel *Dusty Answer* (1927), were generally not. Nor were those who conspicuously struggled academically, or refused to seize the opportunities university offered them. The former group usually left, with relief or in shame; the latter stayed, and were simply unhappy. 'If I wanted to marry an explorer,' complained one of them, 'or bring up twenty sons, or head the suffragettes, or take up lion taming, I would feel it worth while being so bored here.'[11] The implication is, poor girl, that she anticipates life after college will be just as dull. A university education, for her, will lead to nothing. On the principle that you don't miss what you've never had, she thus avoids enjoying herself at all.

It was not always easy to concentrate on work, however passionate you might feel about it. Practical problems offered unexpected challenges. St Hilda's College library in Oxford was in the basement of a building next to the river, and Joan Hunt, working there one summer evening in about 1930, remembers it being inundated by hundreds of tiny frogs leaping wetly round her ankles. Irene Rowell's digs in the 1920s were fine until the show started at the cinema next door. Then all hope of work was lost, as waves of frenetic music from the piano accompanying the silent movie surged and eddied around the room for hours. Unimaginative tutors set class essays based on a text of which there was only one copy in the library, so all the students ended up having to take turns with it, a couple of hours apiece, day and night. You might easily be distracted at a lecture by the endless clacking of chaperones' knitting needles, by the sniggering of male students waving a pickled penis around in the biology labs (that happened at Durham in the early 1900s)[12] or covertly tipping back your chair with their feet till you fell, legs asprawl, to the ground.

Over-enthusiasm about work was rather bad form ('At Oxford we do not hold with zeal,' warned a St Hilda's tutor in the 1920s). Cynthia Stenhouse discovered how risky it could be, one evening in the early 1930s. She had been working on some geological specimens in the Pitt Rivers Museum, and was so engrossed that she forgot the time. An employee was supposed to come round and check that there were no stragglers anywhere, just before the museum closed, but either he missed Cynthia, or she was too busy to notice him. By the time she had finished her work, the doors were locked and everyone else had gone. She tried telephoning for help, but all the phones were on internal lines. She thought about trying to escape, but the windows were too high. So arming herself with a serendipitous tin of biscuits, she settled down for the long night ahead, worried that college would contact her parents when she didn't turn up for dinner, and not at all sure how she would cope with the Pitt Rivers collection of shrunken heads and voodoo dolls once it got dark. Slowly, she began to panic.

Luckily, it wasn't long before the Bach Choir turned up for its rehearsal, held in the booming acoustics of the museum's Gothic hall, and Cynthia was set free. She was never tempted to work so late again.[13]

As well as being frightening on occasion, work could be

downright dangerous, especially for inexperienced scientists. Rachel Footman, conducting a chemical experiment in a laboratory in 1924, was almost killed:

[A]s the sulphate was dissolved in ether I had to evaporate the solution over a water bath. I was getting on quite well but rather slowly and I wanted to go to a special tennis practice with the men's University Team, so to hurry things up I lit the Bunsen burner under the water bath . . . Whoosh! . . . the whole apparatus went up in flames and me with it. I shall never forget the strange sensation of being entirely on fire, my hair, my overall, a ring of fire.

Rachel lost consciousness, and when she came round in hospital, confidently assumed she had died, 'seeing all white ceiling and walls and hearing hymns being sung'. In fact a church service was going on in the ward, and the nurses had arranged white screens around her for privacy. She was in agony, and suffered hideous burns to her face, but with care and time, the scars wore off.[14]

More mundane distractions involved difficult tutors. One 'used to put newspaper down to save his carpets and in the middle of talking about the woollen industry he'd suddenly leap across the room to shift the newspaper because the sun had moved'. Another would reach for the phone, in the middle of an essay reading, and order 'four plump herrings and 3 fishcakes' for tea.[15] There could be other interruptions too:

During one tutorial . . . our tutor, Mlle. Hugon, excused herself because she said she had to change her dress. She had a 'date' she said with an African tribal chief. [We] were surprised and not a little amused that she had changed into another dress identical to the one she always wore. Then she went out and, in stately fashion, rode off on her bicycle![16]

Not everyone knew *how* to work at university level. Telling a fresher in 1910 to conduct a physics demonstration, without explaining some fundamental basics, was unkind: 'Dolly had great difficulty . . . rushing around the lab apparently trying to move faster than gravity – and it nearly led to her giving up – but happily not quite.'[17] Daphne Hanschell, who went straight to Somerville in 1929 from a small convent school, recalls being utterly nonplussed when her tutor issued her with an essay title ('The Primitive Sense of Law'), expecting not to see Daphne again until it was written. What did it mean, and where should she start? Barbara Hutton felt similarly at sea ten years later: 'I found my academic life rather disappointing. Only after most of my time was up did I discover how to search for original historical material, and reading other people's views was frankly dull. I never dared say anything about this to my tutors, my fault not theirs.'[18] *Not* her fault, nor Dolly's or Daphne's: part of a university tutor's job is, and was then, to equip his or her students for original thought. Poor teaching was a significant factor for those bluestockings who found work difficult, frustrating, or boring.

Perhaps the tutors themselves lacked instruction. They tended to be selected for intellectual prowess rather than communication skills, and are frequently described as shy, aloof, distant, even cold. For much of the period before the Second World War they were required to be unmarried women, or childless widows; they were poorly paid; at Oxford and Cambridge they were not even official members of the university until the 1920s at the earliest. Many swapped straight from student to tutor (like superior sort of pupil-teachers) and so never left academia at all. From their mid-fifties onwards they were either encouraged or obliged to make way for their successors. Little wonder, then, that some, especially in the ancient universities, felt socially ill-equipped, academically sidelined, and trapped.

Their appearance could be disturbingly eccentric. Undergraduates report being confused by female teaching staff dressed precisely as men from the waist up (as was the fashion at the end of the nineteenth century), with short-cropped hair and a gruff voice to match. Some neglected their appearance altogether. The first Principal of St Hugh's, Miss Moberley, lacked 'any conception of either comfort or beauty. She was always dressed in a great many thick black clothes and always wore a black silk apron that seemed a vestigial appendage of episcopacy.'[19] Miss Rogers, of the same college, was terrifying, according to former students. She was thickset and looked strangely menacing in her soiled clothes, bulky woollen stockings, and heavy boots. She wore the same outfit every day. She was also considered rather mean. When she invited students to tea in the 1920s, she was notoriously stingy with the food. It thus became a tradition that if you were asked to Miss Rogers' rooms, you ate beforehand. 'She became wise to this, so when it was time to cut the cake, of which there was always one, she would say "I'm not going to cut the cake, as I suppose you had your tea before you came!"'[20]

One tutor conducted interviews with her students entirely in Latin. One murmured into the fireplace. One made and served tea, forgetting to include the tea leaves. One boiled marmalade on her fire during tutorials. One laughed uproariously at her students' (very solemn) essays; another remained silent for the whole session. One cheerily warned everyone that 'my mind is going, you know' before the tutorial began, while another took students on her lap, 'which, as I was rather tall, and she was rather bony, was embarrassing'.[21]

Others were exciting and affectionate, of course, and

remained loyal to their students all their lives. Certain names recur in reminiscences with great fondness, and it is clear that inspirational tutors changed lives. The colonial historian Margery Perham, 'reputed to have shot a lion and published a novel', was 'young, energetic, full of vitality and enthusiasm for emergent Africa, none of which qualities impaired her scholarly integrity'.[22] One of the most popular tutors was Miss Ady of St Hugh's in Oxford. She was even approachable enough for student Molly McNeill to risk inviting her to tea one autumn afternoon in 1916 – although not without considerable trepidation:

About 2.30 I started my preparations feeling all the time as if I'd never be ready. I got the fire lit first of all, then I changed my dress, I put on the red tartan and it looked lovely. I thought I should try to appear as decent as possible for Miss Ady. After that I started getting the food ready, buttered the scones and laid the table. Then I tidied up my room, put my suitcase under the bed, it usually stays out for convenience sake, dusted my chest of drawers and altogether got the room to look very nice. I was all ready, kettle boiling and everything, by about 25 minutes to 4, and Miss Ady arrived quite punctually at a quarter to. As soon as she came I infused the tea and in a few minutes we started. She thoroughly enjoyed her tea. She had one scone, one bit of seed cake, 2 penny cakes, and a piece of my birthday cake, which was excellent, and three cups of tea. It was most delightful to see that she appreciated it. Everything did look quite nice and appetising. We also got on magnificently in the way of conversation. I was rather dreading that . . . She really is a perfect angel, and the cleverness of her is wonderful.[23]

Molly was pleased as Punch the next day when her essay for Miss Ady was declared 'almost alright'.

Intense friendships between female students at university

were common, and we shall come across several instances, healthy and otherwise, later in this book. Similar friendships between those students and their tutors, male or female, were not encouraged. This did not stop young women 'falling in love' with soulful-looking lecturers like Mr Moulton at Cambridge, who taught maths during the early 1870s. Emily Gibson, one of the first Girtonians, remembered her friend Sarah and herself being thoroughly distracted by Mr Moulton's 'dangerous fascination'; she even goes so far as to attribute her early departure from Cambridge, in part, to him (although there is no suggestion anything actually 'happened').[24]

Nor did discouragement prevent certain senior staff taking advantage, cynically or not, of star-struck and often vulnerable undergraduettes. Women's diaries and reminiscences of the first seventy years of university education commonly talk of 'pashes', 'smashes', and crushes on male and female tutors, and several make coy mention of having married a member of the academic staff soon after leaving. I have never come across a first-hand account of the developing sexual relationship, while *in statu pupillari*, of an undergraduate and her tutor before 1939 – which should not imply it never happened; just that it was rarely articulated on paper. No one speaks about sexual harassment; perhaps it was unworthy of note in an era of chauvinism and cultivated naivety. Yet one women's college Principal, when students went to her with worries or problems, used to take them to her bed, for 'comfort'.[25] And it is difficult to believe that there was not considerable stirring in the fusty loins of old-school academics once 'the ladies' arrived in their lecture halls. As far as I know, and possibly thanks to those ubiquitous chaperones, they kept continent. After all, if Philip Larkin is to be believed, sexual intercourse only began in 1963. But the inevitable frisson between certain relatively impressionable girls and their senior (temporary) guardians, of either sex, must have added something to the university experience of both.[26]

Parents were certainly aware of the impact a traditionally virile college education might have on ingenuous daughters. Their concerns, and those of the academic authorities, meant that pioneer bluestockings were rarely taught biology, let alone medicine, and Classics courses strenuously avoided mentioning *Oedipus Rex*. English literature had its risky moments: a letter in the Liverpool University archives from a Reverend Procter, dated 1927, complains to the Vice-Chancellor (no less) that his daughter has been asked to study Byron's *Don Juan* for her English course. He strongly objects, and asks whether she will be disadvantaged in exams if she skips it. The Vice-Chancellor courteously replies that while we are right to take exception to the lifestyles of Byron and Shelley, we should not censor their work. University teachers must be allowed to do their jobs in preparing students as conscientiously as possible for their finals. Personally, however, the Vice-Chancellor assures the reverend gentleman that he has 'the greatest possible sympathy' with his conviction.

Like reading someone else's diary, there is an illicit pleasure in eavesdropping on academic reports. These were transcribed by hand in huge ledgers, until the fuzzy violet-ribboned typewriter took over, and one or two university archivists were reluctant to let me see theirs. But provided I maintained anonymity, and did not stray beyond 1939, I was usually allowed access.

They are fascinating: as eloquent about the sensibilities of teaching staff as they are about students. The Warden of Weetwood Hall, a women's residence at Leeds, could be scathing. She noticed a clear split in the 1935 cohort of leavers between those with little money, heavy family responsibilities, and an eagerness to take part in the cultural and corporate life of the university, and those spoilt by too much cash and with too little imagination. The former group she encouraged academically, with extra tutoring; the latter behaved with 'characteristic stupidity . . . [and] the tastes and sense of humour of the average preparatory school boy'. It is significant, she wrote, that 'they left nothing behind them, material or otherwise, except two tattered schoolbooks'. A couple of years later, she commented on six 'very able but psychologically peculiar' students, and bewailed the modern tendency for undergraduates to be entirely absorbed by their private lives, to the detriment of their work. 'Sheer mental laziness' should *never* be tolerated.[27]

The record books at King's College London read more like a series of school reports. All the right phrases are there: 'has ability but lacks application'; 'weak'; 'very much improved'; 'good but must not overwork'; 'should do well when she gets into the spirit of her work'; 'able, but the breadth of her interests may sometimes be incompatible with detailed work in all subjects'. Some comments invite questions. What are the stories behind these, for example? 'Maths . . . failure probably due to fact that her father was dying during the exam'; 'Work interrupted by home anxieties'; 'Work much interfered with'; 'Rather disturbed by examinations'; 'Failed all subjects'.[28]

At St Anne's, formerly the Society of Home Students, remarks entered neatly into the Terminal Report Book for 1898 are a little more detailed. One tutor habitually damns with faint praise: 'capable at times of work of good 2nd Class quality'; 'exceedingly clever, but immature in mind'; 'has worked steadily, but is much hampered by not knowing any grammar, French or English' (and those were the subjects she was reading for her degree). Elsewhere we are advised that certain bluestockings 'ought to have had a good deal more teaching' before they came up. One is 'a hard worker, [but has] not learnt how to work. Wastes time through failing to grasp the essential.' Again, is that her fault? Another 'lacks polish and she has a strong tendency to diffuseness', while her peer is 'rather puzzling. Has intelligence and a clear head but does not quite rise to her work.' Finally, there is an overseas student who has clearly overwhelmed her director of studies. She has 'abilities of a very high standard. Quite remarkable grasp of leading principles and even of niceties and subtleties which a foreigner could not be expected to attempt to understand.' Clever, female, *and* a foreigner? She was obviously something special.

Academic record books were not only a means of monitoring individuals' progress; they were also used by the college Principal to help pad out the awful end-of-term interview she was obliged to hold with each student. You would be summoned to her room, where (according to her degree of eccentricity, gracefulness, or irritation) she might perch awkwardly and purse-lipped on a stiff-backed chair, slump rather grumpily in a chintzy settee, or loll in gleaming satin on a chaise-longue, like Eleanor Sidgwick used to at Newnham in the 1890s, looking terrifyingly elegant and artistic. You would be asked how you thought your work was progressing, then probably be told, in paraphrase or directly from the tutors' reports, how very wrong you were. The book at St Hilda's, full of scrupulously balanced observations, was obviously designed to be read from word for word. Substituting 'you' for 'she' makes it eerily personal: 'You have not given me an impression of much power, but with more knowledge you ought to do very fairly'; 'Occasionally you do a bit of work which surprises me, and I think surprises you. You underrate yourself habitually'; 'You have a clear head and a vigorous style, but are rather afraid to let yourself "go"'; 'Your work is strangely unequal, being at times quite promising. But you are rather too diffident and seem oppressed with the difficulty of arranging your ideas.'[29]

The most trenchant of all reports appear in the Royal Holloway College students' record books for the period 1907–22. These were patently not for undergraduate consumption, and today might be actionable. In fact precious few remarks concern themselves with academic ability at all. They attempt instead to encapsulate personalities in single phrases. 'Abrupt manner. Noisy'; 'Loud voice. Efficient'; 'Rather breathless in manner'; 'Quite nice, rather casual'; 'Curious accent. High voice'; 'Forward'; 'Pretty manners'; 'Rather antagonistic and obstinate'; 'Peculiar'; 'Rather difficult. A lady. Weak ankles'; 'Excitable and unbalanced'; 'Nice-looking'; 'Tiring to listen to'; 'Rather a cushion in character'; 'Tight'.[30] Thus Royal Holloway unfortunately (and unfairly) emerges in the early twentieth century as a slightly worrying institution, peopled by young women with a bizarre assortment of character flaws.

This was by no means an uncommon perception of women's colleges. With an echo of the misogynistic days when women first invaded academia, once they started achieving in finals at the same level as men, there were plenty of snipers at their backs. 'Women!' urged an article in the Birmingham University magazine,

why try to be so learned? Because in gaining knowledge you lose all else, and become to all intents lifeless encyclopaedias. We have enough Professors to cram this little all into us. Do we want the gentler sex to join them? I appeal to students, and I hear their gentle voices crying 'No! No! No!'[31]

The author of a piece entitled 'The Intellectual Inferiority of Women', published in the *Durham University Journal*, concurred:

Woman acts within her natural rights when she demands the opportunity at least of increased scholastic freedom; the mistake she makes is in imagining – as so many seem to do – that she can surpass or even equal the intellectual achievements of man. All history, all experience, goes to prove how great is the delusion.[32]

Critics were silenced for a while by the First World War, when women students were welcomed everywhere. Lacking male undergraduates, universities needed the numbers, and the money they brought with them. But after 1918, and for the next year or two, there was a backlash. The academic establishment felt it owed soldier survivors an education, at the expense of the current cohort – infestation – of bluestockings. 'They were glad enough to have us when they had no one else,' noted a student tartly in 1919; now she and her peers were literally being denied entrance to lecture halls because there was no room for them. Sixteen thousand men were admitted to Oxford that year; the number of women was limited to well under 750.[33] This pattern was repeated, to a greater or lesser extent, around the country.

Sometimes opposition came from closer to home. One young woman called Jane overcame considerable difficulties to join a prestigious women's college in the 1930s. She was an outstanding student, and embarked on her course with great confidence. During her second year she married, and was told by her husband that this disqualified her from being a student (it didn't). She believed him, and left. Her hard-won place at university had meant so much to this young woman; she was devastated.[34]

Despite outbreaks of jealousy and ill-will, it remains obvious that most bluestockings' experiences of academia were positive, and that they met with more support than opposition once within the university precincts. They might be teased about their preternatural cleverness, but it was usually with more fondness than disdain. Jessie Emmerson, one of the first students to join St Hugh's in Oxford, summed up this affectionate attitude perfectly, in her reminiscences of university life in the 1880s. She read natural sciences, but being a woman, was not allowed to study biology. The knowledge she might have picked up about the human body and its various systems might well have corrupted her morals, as well as her mind. So she concentrated on physics and chemistry:

I was amused to find that my chaperon always deserted me at the door of the laboratory in which I was to work for the rest of the morning and – as it were – 'threw me to the lions'. As I was the first woman to work in the . . . laboratories I felt that the responsibility for the future admission of women rested on my shoulders. Everything was done by my lecturers to make things easy for me.

Because Jessie was small, and some of the lab apparatus roosted well above her head, her tutor provided her with a set of library steps 'so that I could get up and down with ease and dignity'. She went back to visit the labs after leaving university, and in that tutor's office found the steps with something chalked on them: 'Sacred to the memory of Miss Emmerson. Never to be used again.' That made her feel decidedly proud and happy.[35]

When Constance Maynard arrived at Girton in 1872, having whimsically chosen a degree course in preference to a new pony, her intention was to read 'Mental and Moral Sciences', or philosophy. The prospect was pleasant: she looked forward to communion with keen minds and ancient arguments; to wisdom and enlightenment. Not only would she discover long-sought answers at university, but frame more searching questions. This filled her with an almost religious fervour for scholarship. What Constance had not grasped before arriving at Cambridge was that just as engaging as the subject of one's studies, was studying itself. That moment of realization – an epiphany – came on a visit to a sympathetic tutor, who, with the aid of rather thrilling props, conjured up in Constance a quality of curiosity and awe that lasted a lifetime. They pored over a human skull together, wondering at its perfect design; he showed her 'a real cheek, ear, tongue and throat all together' dreadfully preserved in alcohol, and then soothed her with an entrancing experiment involving 'bubbles of gas (phosphoretted hydrogen, I believe) coming up through water and bursting into flame, leaving behind lovely even rings of white smoke, which whirled round at a great rate as they floated gently upwards and remained unbroken'.[36] Constance was enthralled.

Women, during the earliest decades of university education, were not usually encouraged to make discoveries. They were there to learn received wisdom, in a suitable manner, to an acceptable standard. When they left, it was to regurgitate their learning for the nourishment of their own, or other people's, children. Constance's intellectual curiosity, and the privileges she enjoyed from indulgent parents and progressive tutors, led her beyond mere expediency. She shared with later women students the sense that a university education was more than the sum of its parts. Gwendolen Freeman, at the same college fifty years later, had her own way of putting it. 'Looking back now over the plains of life,' she wrote some sixty years after leaving university, 'I see the three Cambridge years as a walled garden separated from the rest – a garden full of voices, freedom and some intimations of immortality.'[37]

Gwendolen's garden, like Princess Ida's, may well have been enclosed and isolated, but the scent of it lingered all her life.

9. Spear Fishing and Other Pursuits

Joan took an Egyptian fresher out in a punt. After a puzzled silence, the girl asked Joan what fish she was trying to spear with the pole.[1]

Maintaining a brisk momentum during leisure time was supposed to invigorate one's studies. Idleness bred slothfulness, which not only corrupted the body and soul, but threatened exam success. Hence there was never a lack of things to do for bluestockings off academic duty. Participation in sports, membership of various college-based clubs, and a healthy (if carefully monitored) social life were all encouraged by university authorities, as long as young ladies conformed chastely to the maxim – coined at Leeds in the 1930s – of 'gloves, hats, and no funny business'.

Sports might not include the singularly ungratifying exercise Joan's Egyptian friend thought she was witnessing, but there were plenty of others. Before the First World War, hockey, lacrosse, and netball were ubiquitous, but also available were water-polo, diving, cricket, rifle-shooting, and fencing. After the war there were opportunities for (among other things) motor-cycling, competitive rowing, and international athletics.[2]

A staple diet of meetings and societies was offered daily, seasoned with exotica like the Sharp Practice Club, the Associated Prigs, or the secretive LSDS (Leaving Sunday Dinner Society).[3] You could visit cafés, concerts, the local 'bughouse' or cinema, and the theatre, as long as you accepted the restrictions, which in 1920s Oxford meant matinées only (unless you were prepared to buy a chaperone's ticket as well as your own) and seats in the gallery rather than the more ostentatious stalls.

Dances were held in colleges and halls of residence, at first exclusively for women, then, as time went on, for men too. Private bedroom parties, hosted by students in their dressing gowns after dinner, were dedicated to cocoa, giggling, and setting the world to rights. Alcohol was rarely consumed, and few hoped to 'achieve' heterosexual intercourse (as one undergraduette rather grimly put it): 'hanky-panky' and 'sleeping around' betrayed bad taste, and damaged prospects.

One of the most socially energetic women's colleges was Westfield, in London. All its activities for 1894 were logged in *Hermes*, the college magazine. Some appear more attractive than others. They include a conference of the Women's Total Abstainers Union (South Hampstead Branch) in the Bijou Hall, covering the legislative and medical aspects of alcoholism; another on 'Sanitary Science' for women, all about domestic (rather than personal) hygiene; and a sensational talk by a Chinese pastor, Mr Yen, on 'Heathen Ladies' and how many pieces they are sliced into when they murder their husbands. From time to time there are debates, and occasional parties, like a grand St Patrick's Day do 'for all those who had any Irish blood in them'. Marmalade bees, or working parties, are organized in conjunction with college singing practices; there are frequent meetings of the 'Innocents' Debating Society', and photographers arrive each term to take jolly group pictures of the staff and students. In summer there is a garden party for some 500 guests, and an outing to Greenwich for the college servants, whose places are taken for the day by the most senior of Westfield's students. It is convenient, notes a junior member of college, to be able to consult the temporary housemaid, while she dusts your room, about the intricacies of Latin grammar.[4]

The Westfield Tennis Tournament did not involve any mixed doubles. Such matches were prohibited within women's colleges until shortly before the First World War. Instead, strong players had to choose weaker partners, ironically known as 'ladies'. As soon as mixed doubles were allowed, they quickly became popular – except at Leeds, where male undergraduates refused to play in case they were forced to become engaged to their partners afterwards.[5]

Tennis was a relatively simple game to organize; team sports, encouraged for the corporate loyalty and good sportsmanship they fostered, were frequently compromised by lack of numbers. Marjorie Collet-Brown was among the first cohort of eleven women at Imperial College in 1924 – 'enough for a hockey team', which they formed immediately; but a student at Durham in 1914 found netball exhausting, principally because there were only three a side. It was suggested as early as 1898 in Leeds that bluestockings there should form a football team. The ladies' department of the students' union greeted the idea with rapture. 'Just contemplate it, O my Sisters! Shall it be Rugby or Association? Will you "scrummage" or "dribble"?'[6] Nothing happened. Most universities could field a women's cricket team, however, and lacrosse was always popular.

At first, women's university sport was a matter of health: *mens sana in corpore sano*. Exercise, especially outdoors, was supposed to temper the fetid tendencies of academic life for ladies. Too much sedentary scholarship was dangerous. It slumped internal organs and sagged the spirits. Fresh air and vigorous movement (within limits) got the circulation going again and braced the brain. Cerebral work and physical play, when properly regulated, were perfect counterbalances. Progressive girls'

Pupils at Miss Buss's North London Collegiate School practise in the gymnasium in 1882, with unlikely poise and finesse.

schools, like Miss Buss's and Miss Beale's, boasted elaborate gyms, in which young ladies in weighty woollen gymslips swung solemnly from ropes and rungs, and outdoor 'drill' was a sacrosanct part of the day's routine.

Once a competitive edge was introduced, especially in team games, women's sport became less about serious duty and more about serious fun. Teams bought themselves smart blazers and college ties; they posed for endless photographs and trained for hours; every victory was celebrated, every defeat resented, and a new breed of college heroine was born.

The river featured heavily in the sporting life of London, Oxford, Cambridge, and Durham universities. Rowing was preferred to the ungainly art of punting, and safety was paramount. Kathleen Proud was a student at Royal Holloway during the First World War, and remembered strict college regulations:

A swimming test had to be passed, including life saving and three lengths of the bath in clothes. Each rowing party consisted of 5 people: a Beginner, a Moderate, two Efficients and a Captain. One had to pass a test to get from one stage to the next, and the Captains were tested by a few very superior Captains who became Judges.[7]

Usually, a doctor's certificate of good health was also required. Sadly, these rules were not enough to prevent occasional disaster. There was a near-tragedy in Durham one morning in March 1922 when the St Mary's College boat, *Iris*, was taken out by some inexperienced students. They started before breakfast, 'because it was a very broad boat for amateur women and likely to be jeered at by the men'. The river was choppy and confused, and despite the women's best efforts, *Iris* was swept over a weir and capsized. News reached college quickly, but imperfectly; the rumour was that all the rowers had been drowned. Happily, that was not so. Instead, the boat grounded on a shelf by a second weir, and its crew was dramatically rescued. To celebrate their deliverance from certain death, the Archdeacon of Durham (who had presented the college with *Iris* in the first place) arranged a thanksgiving evening, at which each of the survivors was presented with a silver St Cuthbert's Cross. One of the recipients remembered feeling rather embarrassed: the archdeacon's daughter was her tutor, 'who must privately have thought us perfect idiots to have gone boating in a strong wind, on a river already high'.[8]

The Cherwell, Isis, and Cam are customarily more languid than the Wear, and nothing much worse than seasickness while punting, or accidentally subsiding into the water, seems to have beset the boatwomen of Oxford and Cambridge. They were advised to clamp their skirts around their legs with elastic bands while rowing on movable seats, to preserve their modesty from passers-by on the bank, and – in time – to wear bloomers. Racing was forbidden on the river until the late 1920s, much to the chagrin of the Somerville Rowing Club, as expressed in the following song from 1922:

ON REFUSAL OF PERMISSION FOR BUMPING RACE WITH THE REASONS THEREOF
(Tune: 'O Foolish Fay', *Iolanthe*)

Your strange request
We must refuse
When you suggest
With rival crews
Here to contest
Your strength of thews.
To show your face
In feats of skill
In public place
Most surely will
Bring dire disgrace
On Somerville . . .

The brawny arm
Is merely plain;
And with alarm
We view the strain . . .
And beg that you
Will keep in view
The future generation.[9]

20. A third-year student performance of *The Princess* at Girton, 1891, based on Tennyson's poem about 'sweet girl graduates'.

21. A group of Girton Classicists in 1891 counter the traditional image of the dowdy bluestocking.

22. Vera Brittain of Somerville College, Oxford, 1914.

23. Open-air revision in June, 1919.

24. The first women entitled to wear academic dress at Oxford University, at their matriculation ceremony in 1921.

25. Sisters Grace, Julie and Daphne Fredericks, who all became students at Oxford or Cambridge in the late 1920s and visited each other by bicycle.

26. Students of Lady Margaret Hall, Oxford, prepare for punting, *c*.1890.

27. The Oxford University ladies' hockey team, *c*.1900.

28. St Hilda's Boat Club members under instruction in the 1920s.

29. Exeter University's tennis team, 1929.

30. The entire student and staff population of Leicester University on its opening in 1921. The ratio of men to women is 2 to 10.

31. A student chemist at Leeds University, 1908.

32. Physics research in a temporary laborator Queen Mary College, London, *c.*1930.

33. A practical lesson in anatomy. Human bodies under dissection, 1911.

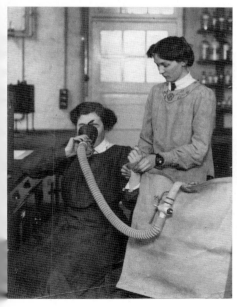

34. Medical students at Bedford College perilously demonstrate 'why weak hearts fail', *c.*1915.

35. A drawing class in the art studio, Bedford College, in the 1890s.

36. Trixie Pearson's Class of 1932, St Hilda's College, Oxford.

Individual pursuits suited certain characters better than team sports. Mountaineering was surprisingly popular. One student at Royal Holloway was skilled enough to be involved in the Ladies' Alpine Club in 1930. At Birmingham, ladies climbed closer to home. 'Joe's Folly', a tall brick edifice on the campus in Edgbaston (named for the university's leading light, Sir Joseph Chamberlain), proved irresistible. The daughter of students there in 1926 has photos 'of virtually every male member of my mother's "lot" and a surprising number of women too, hanging perilously from the fancy brickwork at the top of the tower. Absolutely forbidden by the authorities, of course, and with no safety measures what-soever!'[10] Royal Holloway and Girton colleges were both built with swimming pools, which sounds sophisticated, until we hear that the water in the latter place regularly grew 'green and soupy' before it was cleaned (although it did have a compensatory inflatable rubber horse).

For those who could not swim, and were neither com-petitive nor adventurous, there was always cycling. 'The most useful thing I learned at Oxford,' declared a satisfied student of St Hugh's, 'was to ride a bicycle in all circum-stances.' Colleges had bicycle clubs to encourage weekend expeditions. Some even provided the cycles, but funds did not allow more than one or two, which frustrated most of the members most of the time. Women thought nothing of pedalling long distances. The Fredericks sisters, Grace, Julie, and Daphne, were scattered between Oxford and Cam-bridge universities in the late 1920s; when Julie (Newnham) wanted to visit Grace (St Anne's), she simply climbed on her bike and rode across England.

Tricycles were recommended for beginners at the end of the nineteenth century, and there was naturally a dress code:

Wear as few petticoats as possible; dark woollen stockings in winter, and cotton in summer; shoes, never boots; and have your gown made neatly and plainly of C.T.C. [Cyclists' Touring Club] flannel (not the cloth, which is too thick and heavy for a lady's wear), without ends of loose drapery to catch in your machine . . .

If stays are worn at all, they should be short riding ones; but tight lacing and tricycle riding are deadly foes. Collars and cuffs are the neatest wear to those happy women to whom they are becoming. All flowers, bright ribbons, feathers, etc., are in the worst possible taste, and should be entirely avoided.[11]

If even cycling were beyond a student (perhaps she could not afford the equipment), the final resort was walking. College grounds might be extensive enough for reasonable exercise; Girton's took a good half-hour to stroll around, and eleven tedious circuits of the tennis court at Newnham equalled a mile. Sunday afternoon rambles to neighbouring village churches, or through the more picturesque quarters of the city, were routine. Gathering moss and fresh daffodils and kingcups to decorate your room, or sketching architectural curiosities, gave the walk a sense of purpose; at the end of it, there was usually a just reward in copious amounts of tea and cake.

Although sports clubs accounted for a good proportion of the Junior Common Room's activities (the JCR being the undergraduate body of a college or hall of residence), there were other things going on. The common room itself was the focal point of student relaxation, and was decorated with whatever resources were available. Each common room had comfy (if elderly) armchairs or settees, usually a donated piano, dubiously tuned, and in due course a gramophone with a small library of records. The minute books of JCR

committee meetings reveal what each establishment priori-
tized. At Manchester, Ashburne Hall's taste in pictures was
conservative: the students spent their £3 picture allowance
in 1902 on reproductions of Constable's *The Hay-wain*,
Millais' *The Gleaners*, and Watts' *Love Triumphant*. They cancelled their subscription to the *Daily Telegraph* that year
because no one ever read it, but the satirical magazine *Punch*
was so popular that back numbers were auctioned at the end
of each month. By 1938, two copies of the socialist *Daily
Worker* were provided; there was a cigarette machine (smoking had been allowed since 1919), and a Horlicks dispenser
in the basement. Still no alcohol, however.[12]

Leeds women's JCR was truly progressive. It acquired a
telephone and a Nestlé's chocolate machine in the mid-
1920s, and by 1930 a communal camp bed 'for use of any
student requiring to lie down', complete with hot-water
bottle and blanket. It set aside a 'small garret' for the private
relaxation of members who were nuns, and included – for
some reason – the *Indian State Railway Magazine* among an
eclectic array of periodicals.[13]

Debating societies were ubiquitous. In enlightened universities, male and female undergraduates met together, and
provocative motions stimulated some lively evenings' entertainment. 'This House believes that it is better to remain
single', for example, or 'Accomplished women give more
pleasure to others than strong-minded ones', or 'Pedestrians
should carry rear lights'. A proposal 'that the Parliamentary
Franchise should be extended to Women' was moved at
Manchester in 1898. One speaker pointed out that women
were patently unfitted for political life, and only the 'lowest
classes' would vote once the novelty had worn off. The
motion was defeated.[14] Eight years later, in Birmingham, the
subject came up again. Now the opposing argument was

that 'the excitement of voting would be detrimental to women's health'; this was parried by the ladies' Warden, Margery Fry (later Principal of Somerville), who 'failed to see why the [electoral] line should be drawn at "women, paupers, and lunatics"'. She thought her sex might just be capable 'of taking a walk to the polling booth' and surviving. This time the motion was carried – but only with the female president's casting vote.[15]

Not all debates were as sparky as Manchester's and Birmingham's. At University College, London, they had become so tedious by 1928 that guidelines were published in an effort to pep them up. Speakers were encouraged to make notes and strike points off their own list as they were made by others; to improve vocabulary and forgo slang; to avoid starting each sentence with 'I think'; and to 'take care of vowel sounds'.

Drama clubs flourished everywhere. Regulations against women wearing trousers meant an early preponderance of Greek plays, where male characters fortunately wore togas, and were efficiently differentiated from women by the attachment of impressive but anachronistic waxed moustaches. Freshers were expected to perform plays and charades to the whole college, and the 'going-down' play, usually some sort of mildly satirical revue staged by finalists, was an occasion not to be missed. Women were not encouraged, and at Oxford not allowed, to perform on the same stage as men until the 1920s, but this does not appear to have dulled the dramatic appetite. How much their performances would appeal to modern audiences is unclear. An evening of ladies' intercollegiate charades at Oxford in the 1920s sounds less than enthralling. Each of the college teams was supplied with one syllable of a charade. The word they had to guess was 'radiography'. Somerville did a piece from a medieval problem play with a princess, knights, and dragons; St Hilda's did a prehistoric trial scene; St Hugh's set the action in a French customs office; and Lady Margaret Hall did an extract from a play called *The Boys of St Winifred's*. 'There was only one Home Student there, so she did a sketch about hop-pickers, and the committee did the whole word.' I wonder how many guessed the answer – or cared.

In addition to all the college activities, each university faculty tended to run its own society. Modern languages clubs involved conversation and literary discussion; English scholars arranged reading weeks in the country; politics and philosophy students elected pretend parliaments and passed mock laws; geographers indulged in informal weekend field trips. These subject-related activities had mixed membership soon after women students arrived. Joining them presented welcome opportunities to meet students of the opposite sex on neutral, relatively non-judgemental territory. Subscriptions were expensive, but with careful economy most students could afford one or two. Biologist Marjorie Collet-Brown had nothing left over once she had paid her subs, so when an expedition to Mount Snowdon was proposed, she defied the order to purchase proper climbing breeches by sewing her own from an old pair of black velvet curtains. They were much admired.

Those who arrived at university with musical skill were soon swept up by choirs and ensembles of variable expertise. In Oxford the premier choral society was the Bach Choir. Angst-ridden weekly rehearsals (at the Pitt Rivers Museum, as we saw in the previous chapter) led to triumphant termly concerts. Dorothy L. Sayers and Vera Brittain were both Bach Choristers, and were captivated by its charismatic director, Sir Hugh Allen – especially Dorothy who, according to Vera, constantly gazed at him 'as though she were in

church worshipping her only God'. For those with more
modest musical ambitions, every college and hall of residence
boasted a repertoire of college songs, which students were
expected to learn and perform with gusto. When finals results
proved unexpectedly impressive, to celebrate a sporting triumph, or on a host of lesser occasions, new words to old
tunes were proudly belted out, and every so often volumes
appeared, printed or handwritten, like jolly college hymnals.
There was always an official anthem, rather pompous and
probably in Latin; supplementary songs were composed as
different cohorts of bluestockings came and went, either
witty or intense. I have come across a 'Bicycle Secretary's
Song', a 'Fire-Engine Song', songs to celebrate working hard
or being lazy. Most common are the songs that urge women
to scale the academic heights, thus joining or displacing those
men already there. Girton has the best, written in 1887. Its
chorus gets straight to the point:

> Come grant me the B., come grant me the A.;
> Come make me your equal without more delay;
> Then let each learned maid who loved Pindar or pi,
> Let her hasten to Girton that standeth on high.[16]

Women's suffrage societies featured prominently in university life before 1918. From fighting for academic equality
it was only a short step to agitating for political enfranchise-
ment. Membership was divided between suffra*gists*, who
promoted votes for women and tried to win support through
debate and ideological persuasion, and suffra*gettes*, attacking
the political status quo through physical protest and vio-
lence. Bluestocking suffragists affiliated themselves to
national societies, held meetings, wrote letters, sewed banners, and joined marches; the militant suffragettes courted

publicity by shocking the public into taking notice. Both these sisterhoods attracted ridicule, within their universities as well as in the world outside, and from women as well as men. The brilliant scholar Gertrude Bell, for instance, was Honorary Secretary of the British Women's Anti-Suffrage League, believing the majority of women too dangerously naive to be allowed a political voice. There seemed to be confusion about the cause and effect of supporting 'the vote': did those harridans who demanded it do so because they were ugly, or was it *being* a suffragette that turned them sour? A student writing in Leeds University magazine in 1907 claimed to know the answer:

> There was a girl in the days that were earlier,
> Not very handsome, and so became surlier;
> Ne'er had a lover, ne'er went to a tryst,
> Thus she became the first suffragist . . .[17]

Margaret Ker, a student at Liverpool, was a passionate suffragette. She set fire to a letterbox near James Street Station in 1912, using phosphorus which did little damage to the mail, but badly burned her hand. Margaret was arrested, charged with arson, and sentenced to three months' imprisonment in Walton Gaol. One would have expected the university authorities to be appalled by her behaviour, and glad to be rid of her. A dossier of correspondence in the university archive suggests otherwise. The Vice-Chancellor, Sir Alfred Dale, was undeniably shocked, and felt the university could not avoid suspending Margaret; after she had served her sentence, however, he wanted her back. He wrote to her mother (herself a militant suffragette): 'I cannot tell you what pain the whole affair has given me; for the fact that your girl is willing to suffer does not reconcile me to her suffering.' If

Margaret's education were sacrificed to 'the Cause', he continued, he would find it hard to forgive. In an appeal to the
Chairman of the Prison Commission at the Home Office, he
pleaded Margaret's case, and to be allowed to visit her. She
was only a girl of nineteen, he wrote, and easily led. If he, as
Vice-Chancellor, were allowed to talk to her, he could perhaps persuade her to put this peccadillo behind her, and
return to serious study and right-minded politics. Otherwise, he worried, 'enthusiasm without judgement, and conviction without knowledge, may carry her far into folly'. To
Margaret herself he sent words of comfort, assuring her she
was in his thoughts – 'indeed, on my heart'.[18]

Was Dale being overbearingly patronizing? Or did he,
like Gertrude Bell, recognize that what women needed in
order to achieve the vote and use it wisely was education?
Margaret Ker did go back to Liverpool, and graduated suc-
cessfully two years later.

Nineteen-eighteen was a momentous year for several reasons. Girton remembers it as the date the gentlemen arrived:
when the first dance to which Girtonians could invite male
partners was held. A few 'advanced' girls, in honour of the
occasion, ventured so far as to apply a little make-up. That
same year, permission to smoke in their own rooms was
granted to lady students: these were heady times.

At Girton and elsewhere, there was a strict code of etiquette involved in mixed parties. A male undergraduate
describes the drill in 1923:

One arrived at 7 (thereby having to do without dinner in one's
own College . . .). The Principal sat on the dais throughout and
each female undergraduate was expected to bring her partner up
to be introduced to the Principal at some stage in the evening.

Sitting out between dances was in the Hall or passages, <u>not</u> in undergraduates' rooms. At 10.55 an electric bell rang menacingly and after the next dance the Principal rose and said meaningfully 'Good night, gentlemen'. One's partner was allowed to accompany one to the front door, but not beyond.[19]

It was all very formal, even in the late 1930s. The ladies wore ball-gowns and the gentlemen, evening dress. Prospective partners' names were neatly entered on to wipe-clean dance cards, and there was, of course, no alcohol. If any bluestocking's room should be needed for sitting-out purposes, the bed was first removed, as a prophylactic.

Despite these restraints, dances were keenly anticipated by the students as highlights of university life. Whole afternoons would be sacrificed to clearing out dining halls and common rooms, pooling people's armchairs and arranging them downstairs; cushions were scattered on the stairs to provide extra 'sitting-out' berths, and festive coloured paper fixed to the light shades. Students donated their vases for fresh flowers, and 'as for our lovely selves', remembered Jessie Greaves of St Hilda's, 'of course, we looked charming'.[20]

Private dances for college or hall residents might be held as often as once a week (with dancing club meetings in between); open ones were generally termly. Inevitably, plenty of university romances grew from those termly balls. Despite the advantageous proportion of men to women at most universities (Leicester being a notable exception), it was never easy for a female undergraduate to meet and get to know a male undergraduate, so strictly sequestered were the women, and so lacking in experience. Their tutors, certainly in the early days, were single women themselves, and some colleges cultivated a conventual air that did nothing to boost social confidence. A student at Oxford in the 1890s found the atmosphere in college intensely oppressive. When she was invited to accompany a married lady friend to a musical 'At Home' one afternoon in another (men's) college, her Principal forbade her to go. Men's colleges were out of bounds unless you were escorted by an official chaperone, or your own parents. 'It is a bore. Don't you know the feeling when one wants to have a talk to a <u>man</u> and not everlastingly women – well, I have hardly spoken to a man this term, or been out socially at all.'[21]

This young woman was too early for mixed dances. The lack of men in the university lives of the first bluestockings did not, of course, preclude romance. But there was something delicious about meeting a very clever man, dancing with him, and falling in love. Winifred Carter was asked to a May Ball in Cambridge in the mid-1920s by someone she had only just met. He asked her to marry him that very night. She was somewhat surprised, but said yes, whereupon he imaginatively suggested she take off her dress, so that it shouldn't get too creased when he gave her a celebratory embrace. She refused: 'because of the narrow shoulder straps I had sewn my undies into my dress and if I had taken it off I would have been left in a very brief pair of briefs. So I didn't.'[22]

It is not just a matter of coyness or reserve: there really does appear to be very little sexual activity reported between male and female students at universities in England before the Second World War. Occasionally someone will mention hearing of an abortion, or even a baby being born to undergraduates; certain loose characters will be discussed at cocoa parties, and the odd renegade will be sent down, or expelled, from college for having stayed out all night (while her male partner will only be cautioned or fined):

[There's] a girl up here who shall be nameless but who was 'only a virgin for a fortnight'. She was indiscreet enough to tell someone. But this someone had indulged in these kind of adventures herself, and under the stimulus of 3 pints of beer, revealed everything! . . . I feel awfully shocked, but I suppose there must be some such people in every university. What idiots they must be.[23]

Men were undoubtedly useful, but not necessarily for sex. One student shrewdly remarked that the way she and her female contemporaries exploited their male undergraduate friends differed very little from prostitution, 'except that we give less than the people who walk the streets'.[24]

The lack of reliable contraception – and information – together with uncompromising expectations of unimpeachable morality from home, society, and the college authorities, meant that sex was very much a minority exercise for bluestockings, and rarely casual. One of them, for example, prosaically mentions her very first 'osculation' in her diary; it's the day she and her young man become engaged. Another wonders just where you need to be kissed to get pregnant. These women were institutionally naive.

Perhaps the romantic stakes were higher in the days when the brush of a hand betrayed a smitten heart, or a lingering look meant true love. Sometimes a bluestocking would be distracted for days by a man who asked to borrow a pencil in the library, or who sat beside her at a concert and smiled. The novelist Barbara Pym seems to have spent most of her university career in the 1930s in a febrile state of unrequited love, and several of my correspondents speak of their work being ruined by an emotional preoccupation with men, or one man in particular. The chasm between life at a girls' school, and at a mixed university (single-sex accommodation notwithstanding), could be fearsome, and hard to bridge.

Elisabeth Bishop of St Hilda's was so frustrated by un-
responsive men that she almost gave up on them altogether.
They were not worth the trouble. She spent the whole of
one Saturday in May 1938 getting ready for the college
dance, only to find her partner could hardly arrange one
foot in front of the other. He marched her stolidly up and
down the dance floor all evening, alternately treading on her
frock and kicking her. With a ghastly grin stretched across
her face, she kept assuring him she was enjoying herself terribly. In reality, she felt furious, and disillusioned.[25]

Weekly dances within college were frequently themed.
Fancy-dress parties elicited some bemusing outfits, as on this
occasion in 1888: 'Miss Saunders looked awfully handsome
as Coriolanus . . . Miss Tabor was a capital Heathen Chinee,
Miss Perkins a brown-paper parcel, and Miss Purdie a cocoa-
party.'[26] A book-themed party at Girton in the 1920s required
each person to come with an illustrated clue to her identity.
One sardonic character came carrying a self-portrait: she
was *Life's Handicap. Hard Times* was a girl with a notice about
the college coal allowance pinned to her breast. Someone
had pictures of a Roman soldier, Mussolini, and Stanley
Baldwin: *Hymns Ancient and Modern*; while 'Doris came
with a hopelessly muddled thing, a Russian spiritualist drawing or something like that, for *You Never Can Tell*.'[27]

Cocoa parties themselves, held in students' rooms after
work was finished for the evening, were a social institution.
The kitchens supplied milk, and guests brought contributions
of cake and biscuits sent from home; everyone got into their
dressing gowns (except for Trixie Pearson, of course, who
wore her black satin one-piece, as we saw in Chapter 1) and,
in the time-honoured tradition of undergraduates, talked 'till
the wee small hours'. Variations on the universal theme
included sardine parties at Liverpool, with coffee boiled in a

frying pan, and 'hate' parties at St Hilda's, where rebellious young ladies first placed a loud gramophone on the floor of someone's room, then crouched next to it under their eider-downs, and screamed until their throats burned.

Any outings to out-of-college parties, or to the theatre or concerts, required written permission, and a promise to be in by the stated curfew time. Transgression meant at least a heavy fine, and possibly suspension. There were ways round the rules. One hall of residence had a secret system involving apples. Before a group of friends went out, one of them would make sure the dining-room window was left ajar, and a row of apples – as many as there were girls in the party – placed inno-cently on the window sill. As each member of the group came home after hours, she would climb in at the window and take an apple. When the last person returned, she col-lected the remaining apple and shut the window behind her. It was a risky strategy, since it bypassed the 'signing-out' book altogether, and the penalty for being seen out of college with-out signing was severe. Being seen having neither signed, got permission, nor come home on time, meant catastrophe.

Another college had a system whereby friends would sign each other back in by proxy, and then the late-comers would climb over a discreetly located wall with the help (for a con-sideration) of 'a lady of the night' whose beat was in the street outside. Students in the hall of residence at Liverpool were more pragmatic: they were fortunate enough to have a somnolent porter. They arrived home at the last minute, woke him up to sign them in, and then simply waited till he had gone back to sleep before creeping out again, at liberty.

In some senses, female undergraduates enjoyed more free-dom than their male counterparts. Not being allowed to take degrees meant not having to wear academic gowns when out and about, so young ladies could walk around

Oxford and Cambridge in the evenings (before 1920 and 1948 respectively) unchallenged by proctors and 'bulldogs', the university police. Not being a full member of the university also meant avoiding the rules affecting students' ownership of cars. If an undergraduette was lucky enough to afford one, she was allowed to drive it from her first year, as long as it sported the regulatory green light; men had to wait until they were twenty-two, or graduates.

In fact life could be full of unexpected joys for the willing and enthusiastic bluestocking, no matter where she was at university, or when. Leta Jones, a student at Liverpool in the early 1930s, remembers the delicious occasional extravagance of a poached egg and cheese at Lime Street Station, tuppence-worth of chips from a shop near her hostel, or – an extra-special treat – some 'flamboyant ice cream' from Coopers, helped down by a penny bread-roll.[28] Sarah Mason mentions the excitement of a visit to Girton, around 1880, of four Frenchmen with two dancing bears; another Cambridge girl used to love to watch her dons skating soberly up and down the Cam during icy winters.

Sleeping outside in the summer was a frequent adventure:

It was great fun . . . stealing out [to the quad] in the dark with an armful of bedclothes and a mattress, and seeing other sleeping forms strewn about on the grass and stones. Miss Robinson and Miss Lord (our blind student and her companion) were having people to coffee, and it was jolly listening half-asleep to their talk and staring up at the stars which looked such funny twinkling dots in the sky . . . There was hardly any wind, just a breath of it cold against one's face, and the bedclothes were deliciously thick and warm. Waking up in the morning was rather fun too, with the air grey and raw, and the sun trying to warm it. I woke K . . . she was fast asleep with dewdrops shining in her hair.[29]

The great thing, almost everyone agreed, was not to frit-
ter away your time at university doing ordinary things. This
was an extraordinary place, full of extraordinary people: 'No
one wastes a moment — I don't mean that they work all day
— but they *live* . . .'[30]

10. Shadows

The change from schoolgirl to university woman is a very marked one,
and for many people it is too abrupt.[1]

It is clear that most alumnae remember their college careers
with fondness, but not all of them. Almost apologetically,
some will admit to having been miserable at university. For
them it proved a profitless exercise at best, and at worst a
period of deep unhappiness.

Personality played its part. Several women were crippled
by shyness. Without the confidence to socialize, they felt
isolated and out of place. Others were too cynical, too quick
to find fault with themselves and the system. The short but
vertiginous path from school to university was strewn with
critical decisions. No wonder some people got the balance
wrong: too much work, too little; too many friends, too
few. Brooding on mistakes, especially in the internalized
atmosphere of a women's college or hall of residence, could
be dangerous.

Elisabeth Bishop was a rather melodramatic student at St
Hilda's in the 1930s. During her first term, she wrote ecstat-
ically in her diary that now was the happiest she had ever,
ever been. But a series of complicated relationships (with
women as well as men), family problems, and pressure of
work soon combined to send her to the 'edge of an abyss'.
'Obviously fate does not intend me for happiness,' she
grieved. 'No home – no friends – and I could wager my

bottom dollar – no lover – no husband – no children.' She could not sleep: her compound discontent convinced her that life was 'poisoned at the very root'. Whenever she achieved a minor triumph – a good essay, a spontaneous smile from someone, a moment of self-belief – she could not help looking beyond it to the misery 'all banking up ready to descend on me . . . Is it worthwhile going on?'[2]

Bravely, Elisabeth persevered, but the university drop-out rate was significant, especially during the late nineteenth and early twentieth centuries. Most early leavers could only vaguely analyse what had gone wrong, pleading that university life 'didn't agree' with them, that they found their peers 'dreadfully depressing', or that work simply 'spoiled the head' and turned them hysterical. Others suffered secretly, unwilling to admit failure. Their college records too often close with a bleak verdict: *committed suicide*.

A designated 'moral tutor' was supposed to offer comfort and constructive advice to those distressed in any way. Miss Wordsworth of Lady Margaret Hall memorably recommended in 1892 'something meaty beside your bed' – cold stock soup or a beef sandwich – to combat those sleepless hours spent worrying.[3] It was difficult for undergraduates to confide in the academic staff. Only a tiny proportion of tutors were parents themselves, and to their students they could seem aloof and impenetrably cerebral.

If a troubled girl should manage to unburden herself to someone in authority, who would comfort her comforter? On 10 October 1910, Elsie Bowerman contacted home from college to postpone a visit from her mother. One of her tutors had been found dead in her bed that morning. 'It may be heart-failure,' wrote Elsie, 'but they fear it is due to drugs. (Don't say anything about it to people outside.)'[4]

Staff and student suicides, and details of those who left

before they should, were naturally never publicized. Accusations of hysteria and moral flimsiness had been levelled at bluestockings from the beginning. There was no point fuelling the fire. Internal records were kept, however, to explain or extenuate disaster: 'She has a difficult temper, poor thing'; 'She is hysterical, not very clever, and one of her brothers is mortally ill'; 'Hopelessly bad sight and tendency to melancholia'; 'Miss Harrison has been ill and now her brain seems really to refuse to do anything'; 'Miss Muller has been told by her doctor, that it is absolutely necessary, she should not work next term'; 'This student's sister died suddenly aged 20. The student has not intermitted her work or indulged herself and is <u>angry</u>'; 'Leave of absence granted on account of ill health, sleeplessness, and an affected heart.' There is as much about their health as their academic progress on some students' end of term reports; what anyone did to make things better, other than send for a doctor, prescribe rest (or exercise), or send them home, is unclear.

Often, students preferred not to confess to feeling ill. The rules stated that if they were too poorly to get up to breakfast in the morning and sign the register, the maid or a friend told the bursar, and the bursar called the doctor. But doctors were expensive, and unless it was an emergency, such as a new case of flu, mumps, chickenpox, or smallpox during one of the epidemics that visited halls and colleges fairly regularly, it was wiser to keep quiet. The most frequent indisposition was 'the curse', but few appear to have been seriously handicapped by their period (despite what those medical Jeremiahs had prophesied – see Chapter 4); even fewer wrote about it. Occasionally someone discussed a friend's suffering – 'Letty Chitty has been in bed today, and I went over and read to her out of *Kim* for a bit. Apparently she gets very knocked up every month'[5] – but I have yet to come across a pre-1939 student referring to her own menstrual cycle with anything but the most fleeting exasperation.[6]

Disease, when it was present, tended to spread rapidly in close college communities. Whenever outbreaks developed, as notoriously with influenza in 1917, quarantine conditions were immediately imposed, sending students into a kind of germ-ridden purdah. The oppressiveness and sense of apprehension engendered by this were almost as bad as the physical illness. Eye problems were common, attributed to long hours' study in poor light, and cases of neuralgia, typhoid, pneumonia, bovine tuberculosis, jaundice, even 'sleepy sickness', or encephalitis lethargica, all crop up in reminiscences. Katie Dixon of Newnham came down with jaundice during her first term, and because her family, according to Katie, was annoyingly 'homeopathic', she was condemned to an exclusive diet of the best natural remedy in the business: celery. 'Celery, celery at every meal. I remember I was so famished I sneaked down at night to the housekeeper's room . . . and asked for a basin of bread and milk. With that I survived.'[7]

A student at the University of London during the early 1920s succumbed to encephalitis during her third year, and her obvious decline deeply affected her peers. They remembered her struggling to keep awake during work, collapsing at lectures, begging that no one should tell her tutors she was ill. Finally she was admitted to a neurological ward before returning to college for one last attempt at continuing her Classics course. She was not strong enough to cope; her mother arrived to take her home and, a short time later, she died.[8]

This was rather dramatic; generally, students' letters home were punctuated by nothing more alarming than nose-bleeds, trapped wind ('grunting away with flatulence all day'), constipation ('I have taken quantities of the cascara pills, with very little result as yet'), headaches ('frightful . . . after the College Dinner . . . wines, claret and champagne'), and generally 'feeling seedy' due to insomnia or – as one girl put it – 'down-in-the-dumpness'.

Poor health or death in the family beckoned students home as insistently as their own illnesses. It was as though daughters were only seconded to university, remotely 'on call' to return and cope with family crises when required. From the 1860s to the 1930s, there was a constant (though diminishing) rate of attrition as girls disappeared to do their domestic duty. When fathers died, they were summoned to go out to work. When mothers died they were needed to keep house. When sisters or brothers died, they comforted the parents. Having left university prematurely, they rarely returned.

Changes in financial circumstances also eliminated students; having a bluestocking in the family was too often considered an unnecessary luxury. Whenever economies were called for, through family illness, redundancy, incapacity, or business failure, a daughter's further education was an obvious target. Not all mothers were as far-sighted as Trixie Pearson's. As we saw in Chapter 1, she fought to keep her daughter at Oxford, though her family was well-nigh penniless, for the long-term benefit of a graduate salary.

Religion and politics cast shadows over university careers that extend to this day. One of my correspondents spoke with heartbreaking immediacy of being forced to leave college seventy years ago by her Jewish father, on her conversion to Christianity. She asked not to be named: the loss of her father's love, and of her university career, is too painful, still, to expose. Another, a German national, was deported at the outbreak of the Second World War. She could not bring herself to tell me how she felt, only that 'very sad and difficult years followed'.[9]

College authorities – or individual tutors – did what they could to help. The much-vaunted 'family atmosphere' of women's university residences came into its own on these occasions. Parents were summoned for interviews, to try to dissuade them from reclaiming their daughters, and students were offered loans and bursaries to tide them over financial storms. Rachel Footman had experience of this, when her father killed himself during her first term, in 1923:

I still feel cold all over when I think about it . . . It was the most crushing blow. He rang me up on Friday and said could he come up to Oxford the next day to see me. I said gaily 'Oh, no, not tomorrow, that is the college dance. Come later, Daddy.' I feel I can never forgive myself because he shot himself on Monday morning – was he coming to say Good-bye? Or could I have persuaded him not to do it? I shall never know.[10]

Rachel's father left no money to support his family, and it seemed certain she would have to leave. But her college came up with a scholarship, allowing her to continue her university career with the equivalent of about £15 a week for expenses. It was hard, but Rachel managed. Helpfully, there was never any question that she should leave on domestic grounds.

At Manchester, students themselves donated money to cover the fees of one of their number, and if an undergraduette had trouble paying bills, there was no shame in her doing odd jobs for others, to earn a little money. Favourites were hair-washing, stocking-darning, and errand-running. People appreciated the privilege of being at university, and were glad to help one another if they could. Wasting the opportunity, so hard won, was shameful. It meant letting down all those who had supported you in the past – especially proud parents.

A second chance occasionally offered itself to 'drop-outs': they returned to university as mature students and tried to take up the threads of academic life where they had left off. Reprises like this tended not to happen in cases of expulsion, or 'sending down'. Being sent down was the ultimate penalty, the ultimate shame. Once a university had issued a 'request to withdraw', because your residence was 'no longer desirable', you were cast out of Eden (the apple half eaten) and forgotten. Failure to pass exams was a neat, objective means of exit; altogether messier was dismissal due to assumed breaches of discipline or morality.

The Victorian press may have rattled on about bluestockings, labelling them fierce, desiccated harridans, or silly long-lashed lovelies; to the academic establishment at the time, the corporate body of female university students was imagined rather differently, as a spreading, flaccid figure in need of structure and support. The minute regulations to which that establishment subjected her were designed to act like stays. They laced her tight, kept her standing straight, and prevented unsightly slippages. Uncompromising discipline was generally accepted by the students themselves (with individual exceptions) until the First World War. Thereafter, intelligent and increasingly independent young women began to question such stricture, to break the rules, and agitate for freedom.

In a petition to the university establishment in 1924, 'the chief defects of the present regulations' were listed by Oxford's women students. The authorities demeaningly treated responsible young women like impressionable schoolgirls; they adhered to the outdated morality of the 1870s 'when several of the Principals of the women's colleges were of the age of their present students'; there were too many spurious restrictions; the current atmosphere of oppression created a culture of defiance and contempt, and encouraged an unhealthy, furtive attitude to sex and relationships; finally, this disciplinarian regime was condemning the university's young women to all the evils of co-education, and none of its advantages.[11]

In the early days, a zero-tolerance policy was rigorously maintained towards anything that could conceivably be construed as lax behaviour. At Durham, it was noted in 1908 that

a Senior Woman had been sent down for speaking to her brother on Palace Green, another student had been gated for the rest of term because she rang the doorbell just after, and not before, the last stroke of six had sounded from the Cathedral clock, despite the pleading of one of the clergy, with whose family she had been taking tea, that the drawing-room clock was slow.[12]

Scandal ripped through a university science department in 1895 when a reeling professor reported he had just 'heard a young man and a young woman engaged in conversation in a room darkened for the purpose of studying optics'.[13] Manchester students appear to have been particularly spirited: in 1910, two young ladies were excluded for having occupied with two gentlemen undergraduates a room in the students' union 'not used by the Music Society during a Social'; when asked to leave they refused, and stayed there 'with the light out for a considerable time', behaving in a blatantly 'unseemly manner'. A few years later, another Mancunian girl was expelled for unspecified 'misbehaviour' in a charabanc on the way home from a sports match against Liverpool university.[14] Incidentally, the punishment meted out to the males involved in these outrages was almost without exception more lenient than that inflicted on the females. Boys will be boys.

A draconian approach is hardly surprising, given the anxiety of those responsible for establishing university education for women about how their protégées would behave, perform, and be accepted. What is shocking is that undergraduettes were still being treated like recalcitrant children into the 1920s and 1930s. The Shawcross Affair at St Hilda's in 1935 is a case in point.

There had been a slightly shaky relationship between St Hilda's students and their superiors for a while. A bust of Miss Beale, the college's esteemed foundress, used to preside over the dining room; at the beginning of the 1920s, some skittish students decided it was too ugly to be borne, and commissioned boys from Magdalen College School, across the road, to sneak in and abduct it. The joke backfired when no one noticed it was gone, so the boys brought Miss Beale back. The morning after she was reinstated, the students discovered someone else had given her a gaudy overhaul in red, white, and blue paint. Miss Beale was immediately ordered to be scrubbed clean. Soon afterwards, as the final act of an anonymous and sinister comedy, the bust was smuggled down to the River Cherwell, poked beneath the surface with hockey sticks, and drowned.

Such mutinous behaviour boded ill, and for the next few years various japes, such as booby-trapping dons' doors, or hiding people's gowns before chapel, erupted and subsided like dramatic preludes to Dorothy L. Sayers' *Gaudy Night*. The apotheosis of this grumbling rebellion was the Shawcross Affair. One evening in May 1935, the Principal of St Hilda's was (according to which report you read) locked either in her room, out of her room, or in the lavatory.

Furious at the indignity, she demanded to know who was responsible. She also cancelled the May Dance, to which the whole college had been looking forward all year. When an article about the episode appeared with suspicious promptitude in *Isis*, the university student magazine, the Principal was even more incensed. She blamed the editor, a sophisticated St Hilda's student called Edith Shawcross, for the leak. Miss Shawcross, along with her friend Lady Katherine Cairns, offered to take the blame for both the prank and the leak (without acknowledging responsibility) so that the dance could go ahead. Both were asked to leave the college. But then one of the national newspapers got hold of the story – 'Earl's Daughter Sent Down' – and within a day or two St Hilda's, its choleric staff, and glamorous, naughty students were being talked about not only in British papers, but in America, India, Australia: all over the world.[15] The dance, by the way, remained cancelled.

Despite the general heavy-handedness, the spirits of most English undergraduettes remained robust. There were still plenty of 'noises off' behind the scenes. In different locations around the country, girls screamed down college staircases on tea trays, slept illicitly on the roof, consumed secret bottles of sherry, or canoed down streams in the dark. Life as a bluestocking was rarely bland.

All reminiscences of living in a women's college or hall of residence, whatever the date, are punctuated by minor mishaps and inconveniences. Snow blew down the chimney and settled on the bedroom floor; dyspeptic plumbing kept you awake all night; fires smoked, coating the walls with a bloom of soot and calling forth chilblains and cold sores. Sometimes burglars or unspecified 'madmen' broke in, or exciting accidents occurred. Sarah Mason and some Girton

friends were nearly killed in 1880 when their carriage drove
on to the kerb in Cambridge, the horse keeled over, and the
girls were pitched into the path of oncoming traffic. Women
fell off their bicycles with tedious regularity, and sustained
impressive injuries from hockey sticks or skate blades: such
little disasters are remembered fondly.

Food generally looms large in letters and diaries. Although
they were rarely too awful (in peacetime, anyway), it has
always been fashionable to complain about college meals. In
the face of such harsh criticism, those who planned and
cooked students' fare must have despaired. A 'Bursar's Song'
from the Somerville archives suggests it is not the quality of
the food that spoils its enjoyment, but the illogical conviction on everyone's part that somebody else's college cuisine
must be so much tastier:

> I've tried and I've tried but you're not satisfied,
> I can't sympathise with your attitude.
> You disdain kedgeree, you want cake for your tea,
> You want grapefruit for breakfast each morning.
> Caviare for your hall, but it won't do at all,
> For the whole kitchen staff would give warning.
> I don't like to boast but there's plenty of toast
> And it's only your greed that reduces it.
> In my College the food is remarkably good,
> And 'tis envy alone that traduces it.[16]

The worst food, and most difficult conditions, were experienced during the First World War. None but the most
selfish complained, when they realized what their male contemporaries had to deal with on the front lines. But however
stoical you were, there was no denying the food really could
be dreadful – and less and less plentiful as the war dragged

on. Unfeasibly yellow bread and margarine were increasingly substituted for 'real' food, and a single sardine each was welcomed as enthusiastically as a banquet. Qualified people to cook meals were in short supply, as more women disappeared into munitions factories. 'I once found the cook's blouse button in my rice pudding,' lamented a wartime student, 'and then the safety pin that had replaced it.'[17] Another described how

It became so difficult that wages had to be increased to get enough staff to keep things running. When food became very scarce, and very horrid, the students' ration books would be used to make things more pleasant for the kitchen staff. We were very near a starvation diet. There seemed to be an abundance of artichokes [and rabbit, carrots, and macaroni] which I detest, and I also have memories of very hard pink pears, stewed for hours but still hard as pebbles.[18]

Fuel was scarce during the war; a good idea was to pool resources (two lumps of coal each per day), work together with friends by a single fire, and in winter, to wear your coat and fingerless gloves indoors. When academic work was done, there were always socks to be knitted for the soldiers and plenty of other war work. Lists on JCR notice-boards across the country asked for volunteers for the university Ambulance Corps, Nursing Corps, canteens, hospital laundries, digging land, breeding rabbits, wheeling wounded soldiers around the streets, reading to them, and – in the vacations – flax-pulling in the fields.

While most women students were pleased to stay at university and do their bit, some found the enormity of the war too much to bear – especially students in the ivory towers of Oxford and Cambridge. They could not justify 'standing and waiting' in academia, so far removed, or aloof, from the action. Vera Brittain remembered arriving for the summer term of her first year – in 1915 – the day after Rupert Brooke was killed. Her college at Oxford had been commandeered as a military hospital, and the students evacuated to another college; the city was empty of undergraduates, full instead of cadets and wounded soldiers, and news was filtering through of the second battle of Ypres. Vera's brother and lover were both away fighting. Her university career, in these circumstances, seemed obscenely irrelevant, and she left.[19]

Those who stayed knew they were 'living in a changing world', according to a Cambridge student in 1917: 'The youngest-looking of the Newnham students reading my subject was a war widow.'[20] She and her friends bitterly resented paying for the mistakes of the previous generation, and vowed to do all they could, as educated and enlightened citizens, to make things better for the next.

This meant practically as well as ideologically. Everywhere there was an annual 'rag week', a festival of fund-raising when 'gown' donned bizarre costumes and performed various stunts for the amusement of 'town', and collected money. Women's colleges also offered opportunities for voluntary charity work during term and in the vacations. This might be fairly small-scale, such as inviting children from the slums to tea in the dining hall, or going carol singing; it might also involve serious commitment of time and energy. Inner-city 'women's settlements' were sponsored by individual colleges, or national, university-based associations, to which students were seconded to work (on social welfare projects) in the holidays.[21] During the Spanish Civil War, and the lead-up to the Second World War, undergraduates aided refugee camps around the country, and raised money to support Jewish students and their families. There is evidence throughout academia of a muscular social conscience among women, and the will to act on it. They acknowledged the flipside of privilege to be responsibility.

One of the keenest delights of university life for the blue-stocking was friendship. After a degree (or its equivalent), friends were the most precious legacy of this heady period in her life. Friends formed her college 'family', and her happiness depended on how satisfyingly relationships developed. As Elisabeth Bishop discovered – she who found herself 'on the edge of an abyss' at St Hilda's – 'mucking up' socially could be profoundly upsetting. Those who had been to boarding school, had large families or a wide social circle at home, coped better with the vagaries of popularity and commitment than loners. There was no advice available on how to cope when things went wrong. In an atmosphere lacking the fresh air of self-reliance, close friendships, or 'pashes', could soon curdle and turn sour.

Popular nineteenth-century literature throbs with examples of loyal, loving girls who demonstrate their sentimental affection for one another by stroking, kissing, and embracing. They might be even more intimate, without losing their innocent charm. When two boarding-school mistresses were charged with 'improper and criminal conduct' in 1819, for climbing in with their pupils at night, lying on top of them and 'shaking the bed', they were acquitted because the judge blithely declared that 'according to the known habits of women in this country, there is no indecency in one woman going to bed with another.'[22] Constance Maynard was actually advised by the college doctor in 1883 to bring one of her students at Westfield to bed with her, to calm the girl's nerves:

[Maynard] then had to lie down with her on the bed, which gave the girl the opportunity to grasp her tightly and to declare that they were now married. In 'solemn tones' she insisted 'we are two no longer. I am part of you and you are part of me . . .' The next day the girl was quickly taken away and returned to her family for care.[23]

The emotional stakes were high, for those who were not equipped to make a distinction between 'healthy' (that is, platonic) friendship, and a homoerotic 'pash'.

Constance is an interesting example. She was always a highly religious woman, very loving too, and she considered it her duty to act on that love for the mutual spiritual development of herself and her closest companions. In the cultural (and linguistic) idiom of the day, she expressed her love for special colleagues and students in terms of a wife's for her husband, often giving them male nicknames. She writes about the end of an affair with a tutor at Westfield most movingly:

['Ralph'] was not very well, and I went up to see that she was rightly attended to. As I left she said with gentle hesitation 'You never bite my fingers now, as you used to do.' 'Oh no, never,' I replied lightly. 'And you never snarl and growl like a jaguar when you can't express yourself. I never heard anyone growl as well as you.' 'No,' I said, 'it's useless. I've been cured of that.' The sweet low voice went on, 'And you never rock me in your arms and call me your baby.' 'No,' I said in the same even tone, 'I've been cured of that, too.' 'Oh!' she said, with quite a new meaning, 'oh, I see.' Here was a spot too painful to be touched, and I said 'Goodbye, dear,' and left the room. I will not go into the desolation I felt when alone again. I was like a pot-bound root all curled in upon itself, like an iron-bound bud that has lost its spring, and now no rain and no sunshine can open it.[24]

Was this a lesbian relationship, or just intimacy of the sort women like Constance were brought up to admire? Here was the dilemma of those trying to regulate bluestockings' sexual behaviour. Colleges and halls were full of animated, like-minded young women, hemmed in with one another and sharing the same new experiences and sense of self-discovery. 'Pashes' were bound to develop. A student at Oxford in the 1880s learned that 'sentimental devotion' was all too apt to degenerate into emotional obsession: every girl about to go to university should guard against worshipping another, she warned, or becoming an object of worship herself. There was too much 'loss of dignity and self-respect' involved.[25]

Parents, and those at university *in loco parentis*, were unwilling to spell out to their charges (if indeed they recognized it themselves) the moral danger of such intensity, in case they corrupted them. It is as though young women — even the intelligent, independent thinkers who got themselves to university — had only to be aware of perceived immorality to commit it themselves. Sexual gratification should not even cross their minds, subconsciously or otherwise, before marriage (and maybe not even then). But what would happen, wondered those responsible for the moral and academic welfare of women students, if they let such 'pashes' be? Might that prove injurious? Perhaps women needed a physical sexual outlet, as well as men? Marie Stopes, herself an undergraduate at University College, London, before lecturing at Manchester University, believed they did. But 'unsuitable friendships' were not the answer. 'Solitary self-abuse' was preferable to mutual masturbation, she advised, which was 'very apt to lead to grosser and more abominable vices . . . against which a warning is not superfluous in these days when a cult is being made of homosexual practices'.[26]

The 'cult' she refers to was really a heightened awareness,

fed by a growing number of high-profile authors. A few examples might include the psychologist Havelock Ellis, whose *Sexual Inversion* – including references to lesbianism – was published in 1897; the popular novelist Clemence Dane (Winifred Ashton), who published the novel *Regiment of Women* in 1917 about a cruel lesbian schoolteacher; and, of course, D. H. Lawrence (*The Rainbow*, 1915). All of these have women physically and emotionally engaged in same-sex relationships. God forbid such Sapphic monsters should stalk the hallowed corridors of academia . . .

The following extracts, even though they might read like sensational fiction, are taken from the school and university diaries of a maths student at Royal Holloway College.

19th June 1906. Baby came and sat on my knee . . . but I will draw a veil over the rest of the evening . . .

23rd June 1906. We tried to find a secluded spot, so after a bit we got into a sort of wood and lay down under a huge tree, with my umbrella over us and, I am ashamed to say, flirted terribly . . .

20th February 1909. I met May who said all her family [group of friends] were going to Hockey Tea so I suggested we should have it together in her room. We were quite mad and the furniture kept giving awful cracks. Our snug tete-a-tete was suddenly rudely interrupted by an awful knock on the door and we heard Miss Thompson's voice in the passage. May gave a huge cackle of laughter and said 'Come in.' I, from May's account, went a vivid crimson and gabbled away as hard as I could to hide my confusion . . .

12th June 1909. [I] went up to May at about 11, just before, I think it was. We talked till about 12, and then proceeded to sleep but at first kept waking up, finally got off to sleep at about 2 or so. Awfully shocking behaviour.[27]

According to this diarist, girls often 'nighted it' with one another, and spent all day not working, but dreaming of what the dark would reveal. Tucking a friend into bed, or making sure she got up in time (or not) for breakfast, could be a lengthy process, and if it became obvious that love was unrequited – or, worse, unnoticed – the pain and frustration were hard to bear.

Sex loomed over friendships, according to Elisabeth Bishop, like 'a dark shadow'. For a long time, the only accepted way to dispel that shadow, for heterosexuals and lesbians alike, was to get married to a healthy young man as soon as possible. How a bluestocking, corralled in her college, was to meet and get to know such a man, and what she was to do with her useless degree once married, were questions society preferred to ignore.

11. Breeding White Elephants

The female undergraduate: Eve in the Home of Lost Causes.[1]

It may have been an odyssey, and the territory hostile, but led by some of history's most determined and diplomatic pioneers, the quest for women's higher education finally succeeded. Visionary retreats imagined like mirages by Mary Astell and Daniel Defoe resolved into adamant seats of learning. 'Bonnets' and 'pretty dominae' matured into rigorous scholars, and by 1939 every university in England (except one) awarded them qualifications on the same terms as men. 'There is a wonderful exhilaration about getting a degree,' wrote a female graduate of Manchester in 1926. 'It is something more than the degree itself. It feels like coming into an inheritance of tradition.'[2] Achieving a share in that tradition was a marvellous thing. But what did it mean? What was a university-educated woman for?

Teaching was the original raison d'être, and remained the most acceptable career for a female graduate until her real vocation expressed itself in marriage. At a time when choice was limited, teaching was a way of life thousands of strong, imaginative women relished, and at which they excelled. Thousands more were as miserable as their pupils.

The decision facing the majority of nineteenth-century bluestockings was not what they would be when they left university, but whether they would spend the period before marriage (which might never happen) teaching or at home. For those at the Leeds, Liverpool, and Manchester campuses of Victoria University, whose degree courses and further training were financed by King's scholarships from the Board of Education, there was no alternative. The conditions of those scholarships stipulated at least three years in the classroom. Even when I went to university at the end of the 1970s to read English, the widespread assumption was that afterwards I would teach. Teaching offered one of the few opportunities, I was told, for an arts graduate to use her 'book-learning' and earn a respectable wage. There is a remote possibility I might have been good at teaching, but I resented the fact that it was still the default career for every woman undergraduate (unless a medic or lawyer or similar): her apologia for indulging in a university education. This assumption had a dual effect. It put eligible students off a valuable and gratifying profession, and encouraged those who avoided it to clutch at any alternative, with sometimes feckless enthusiasm.

At least I could carry on working when I married: that was a luxury denied conventional students before 1939. Statistics suggest that had I been at university earlier still, marriage would probably have eluded me anyway. A survey of the 'after-careers' of Oxbridge alumnae published in 1895 reported that they were 'more likely to be a teacher than a wife'. Of the 720 students who attended Newnham College between 1871 and 1893, 16 died, 37 were foreigners who returned to their original countries, 155 married, and 374 (52 per cent) went into teaching. Of the rest, 230 were living at home (of whom 108 were married), five did medical work, two were missionaries, one was a market gardener, one a book-binder, and the remaining handful worked for charities or did secretarial work. Of the 335 who got degree certificates from Girton during the same period, 123 (37 per cent) taught, only 45 married, two were missionaries, six were employed by the government, four did medical work, and six were dead. The rest, presumably, did nothing.

Fewer Girton graduates married than Newnham ones (1:10 against 1:9); the subject least likely to produce a wife at both colleges was modern languages. The compiler of the report concluded that although its findings might be considered 'puerile and foolish', it did have its uses. The modern girl was free to decide for herself whether marriage should be considered 'an achievement or a come down, but mothers will be prudent if they realise that . . . marriage is [n]either desired [n]or attained by the majority of very highly educated women'.[3]

The implication was that anyone seriously ambitious to become a grandparent should not send their daughter to university. It is unclear where that leaves the mother who told her plain but earnestly intelligent girl that she was too ugly *not* to go to college, 'to increase [her] chance of a prize in the matrimonial lottery'.[4] If she did go, there was a vociferous argument that she should not be burdened further by a degree. That would surely threaten her tenuous femininity. Depend upon it, ladies, wrote a journalist in 1891, after the latest Cambridge revolt against admitting women to full membership of the university: no man in England wants a wife who would sooner concentrate on differential calculus than on him.[5]

The venerable philologist Walter William Skeat agreed:

If given the BA, they must next have the MA and that would carry with it voting and perhaps a place on the Electoral Roll . . . Even the BA would enable them to take 5 books out of the University Library . . . I am entirely opposed to the admission of women to 'privileges' of this character. And I honestly believe they are better off as they are.[6]

Dean Burgon of Chichester, whose sermon declaring women eternally inferior to men had caused such a stir in 1884, put it even more apocalyptically:

The admirable Ladies who preside over 'Lady Margaret' and 'Somerville' Halls, and the charming specimens of young womankind who have made those Halls their temporary home, – proved irresistible [to those Fellows who allowed them into Oxford]. The men succumbed. I remember once reading of something similar in an old Book. The Man was very sorry for it afterwards. So was the Woman.[7]

Back to square one.

Novelist Winifred Holtby remembered Burgon when she pictured the 'modern' undergraduette of the 1930s as 'Eve in the Home of Lost Causes': someone of whom so much was expected, and to whom so little was allowed.

Somerville College responded to critics like Skeat and Burgon by issuing what would now be called a mission statement, declaring its objective to be 'to afford young women, at a moderate expense, such facilities for their higher education as will enable them better to fulfil the duties of life, and, if need be, to earn an honourable and independent livelihood', preferably preparing or inspiring younger women to follow them to university.[8] Even in this fine and progressive declaration, duty comes first. It still did when I left the same college soon after its centenary year. My duty, I felt, was to teach; to use the education bestowed upon me in public service. I abdicated that duty, felt guilty, and so shared the unwelcome legacy of anyone who ever questioned the right of a woman to graduate from university.

It is ironic that, by the turn of the twentieth century, the forebodings of Henry Maudsley and his medical colleagues, that university education would render women sterile (see Chapter 4), had to some extent come true. Scholarship might not physiologically prevent conception, but it had an effect on the birth rate in other ways. Career women chose not to marry, apparently preferring independence to domesticity. Not that marriage and other careers were always mutually exclusive. During the First World War and occasionally thereafter, married women taught in schools and universities, and general practitioners who were wives and mothers were not unusual (although married female hospital doctors were).

Perhaps it depended on your husband. Fully dedicated tutors declared themselves married to scholarship, like Anna Paues of Newnham, who wore a wedding ring. It also depended on your employer's attitude. When Elsie Phare requested leave for 'a few days' from the English Department at Birmingham in the 1930s (in order to give birth), she was promptly denied it, on the irrefutable grounds that no *male* employee would ever ask for time off to have a baby . . .[9]

Gwyneth Bebb would appear to have got the balance right. She earned a first-class law degree at St Hugh's in 1911, and was a thorough pioneer. She campaigned for the admission of women to the legal profession, bringing a landmark case – *Bebb v. the Law Society* – to court in 1913. The case sought to define her as a 'person' within the meaning of the Solicitors Act 1843, so that she could be admitted to the preliminary examinations of the Law Society. Gwyneth lost, the court bewilderingly holding that women were not to be deemed 'persons' in this case, and therefore that they were disqualified from training to become solicitors. She appealed, but the decision was upheld. However, partly as a result of Gwyneth's case, the law was eventually changed. The Sex Disqualification Removal Act was passed in 1919 (which also

led to Oxford granting degrees to women); the day afterwards, Gwyneth was admitted to Lincoln's Inn to read for
the Bar. She was married by now, and gave birth to a daughter while studying at the Inns of Court; she then went on to
take a first-class degree in criminal law.

She sounds like the model of a successful working mother.
But even someone as feisty as Gwyneth could not renounce
the cruellest and most womanly of fates: in 1921 she died in
childbirth, aged only thirty-two.[10]

*How a fin-de-siècle cartoon imagines a Cambridge
alumna will conquer the old world, armed with a
degree, a pair of bloomers, and a golf club.*

For the entire period from 1869 to 1939, the question of whether a woman's degree was a social asset was argued, and remained unresolved. When Emily Davies founded Girton's mother-house in Hitchin, her aim was to offer students an intellectual refuge. Her college was an almost spiritual place of learning, removed from the distractions of mundane domesticity and meaningless accomplishment. 'The accepted idea was that we had come . . . because of our love of study and not in order to qualify for earning a living.'[11] Qualification was a distasteful concept for ladies – it smacked of commerce. No one in the early days of Girton or Newnham, Somerville or Lady Margaret Hall, imagined ladies would ever feel the sordid need to become professionals. Perhaps that is why Cambridge only offered its lady 'guests' a scrap of paper (rather grandly referred to as a certificate) recording their achievements in the Tripos, instead of ceremonially conferring the signed and sealed degree awarded to real undergraduates. When Oxford agreed to grant its female students degrees in 1920 (having not offered them *anything* before), the common rooms of Cambridge, yet again, went wild. 'We won't have women!' brayed the undergraduates – and nor did they, until 1948.

There is a distinction to be made here between ladies and women. In 1881, the constituent colleges of Victoria University declared that female students would be allowed to work for degrees on the same terms as men; henceforth they were no longer referred to as ladies, but women. London University welcomed ladies to lectures, but once they enrolled as undergraduates, they too metamorphosed into women. At Durham, incidentally, there were neither ladies nor women: only Doves, who inhabited their own little 'Dovecot' in 1901 (Abbey House on Palace Green) and fluttered about the city cooing prettily.

Females were further subdivided by the popular press into 'womanly' or 'true' women, and 'strong-minded' ones. The former, though perhaps spuriously over-qualified, were still reasonably attractive, and capable of benign moral influence within their families; the latter (cartoon bluestockings) were an embarrassment. As late as 1933, strong-minded female academics were described generically as 'enforced celibates, predestined spinsters. And women cunning enough to maintain complete secrecy in their sexual relations [that is, lesbians] . . . a prospect that fills a good many people with horror.'[12] But such bombastic over-generalization meant far less in the 1930s than in the 1870s. The number of women students had grown prodigiously, yet English society had still managed, somehow, to resist being brought to its knees.[13] Perhaps bluestockings were not as corrosive as first thought.

This gradual acceptance of women graduates was not supported by any imaginative careers advice. London and the civic universities had better services than Oxbridge (which is not saying much), but nowhere did aspiration seem to play a part in planning a female student's future. True, the First World War allowed women into professions left short-staffed by fighting men. Alumnae records of this period in women's college archives specify a professor of West African languages, an inspector at the Ministry of Labour, a medical officer in the British Army, a Deputy Directress of Public Instruction, a house surgeon at Clapham Maternity Hospital, an anatomy demonstrator at a teaching hospital in London, and a physicist doing research work at Woolwich Arsenal.[14]

Precedent is useful, but there was no guarantee that any appointments or promotions made during the course of the war would last. Once it was over, there was an obligation to move aside and offer your nice, warm seat to its rightful tenant. If positions were scarce, married men stood at the head of the queue, with families to support. Single men came next, then single women, and, last of all, wives. They had no need to earn money of their own, nor (it was argued) any right.

An exception to this pattern was Edith Morley. In 1915, she produced an important book on prospects for women graduates in the workplace;[15] even though the seven professions she listed in it were predictable – teaching, medicine and dentistry, nursing, sanitary inspection and health visiting, the civil service, secretarial work, and acting – the levels she considered women capable of reaching within those professions were unprecedentedly high. Miss Morley knew her subject, being (in her own words) 'the first woman to obtain the title of professor at a British University' on her appointment to a chair in English at Reading in 1908. She was a trenchant champion of career women. Her professorial colleagues – all male, of course – found her terrifying:

She was likely to subject even the most casual of remarks about the weather to acid criticism. Her driving was memorable . . . and her driving was a direct expression of her character. She was provocative, disturbing, aggressive, intransigent; others kept their distance to avoid collision and damage.[16]

No doubt she found their cowardice gratifying.

After the passing of the Sex Disqualification Removal Act in 1919, hard on the heels of the Representation of the People Act, passed the previous year and giving women over thirty the vote, legal barriers to women's progress in the workplace grew more permeable. Virginia Woolf, in *A Room of One's Own* (1929), is keen to point this out to undergraduettes who blame their poor prospects on prejudice, rather than lack of initiative. She reminds them that the cultural climate in England has changed dramatically, not just in the legal and political sense, but educationally (thanks to university access for women) and therefore economically. It is time, she says, to go out into the world:

[You] will agree that the excuse of lack of opportunity, training, encouragement, leisure, and money no longer holds good . . .

Thus, with some time on your hands and with some book-learning in your brains – you have had enough of the other kind, and are sent to college partly, I suspect, to be uneducated – surely you should embark on another stage of your very long, very laborious and highly obscure career.[17]

An interesting concept: did university *un*educate women? Certainly. It was Miss Davies, in the earliest days of Girton's history, who said that the value of being at a women's college lay in relinquishing the so-called accomplishments of a traditional female education, and learning sturdier disciplines instead. And a 'highly obscure career'? Choose fiction, urges Woolf. Subsidize your writing how you will, but write. Write your way out of obscurity and into history.

Despite Woolf's esoteric agitating, teaching was still the most popular post-war career. Sixty-nine per cent of graduates from St Mary's College in Durham chose it during the 1920s,[18] and the availability of more university posts created a floating population of women academics who surfaced and dipped in the records of colleges around the country, following one another around in a sluggish whorl of promotion. But now, robustly supported by the British Federation of University Women (founded in 1910), and inspired by regular features in the *Journal of Careers*, unlikely ambitions did begin to appear feasible. An article in the *Incorporated*

Secretaries' Journal for 1927 encouraged women (like its author, who had a doctorate in economics) to aim high.[19] No longer, she argued, was femininity regarded in the world of commerce and industry as an incurable disease; there were few corners of that world forbidden to enterprising women these days.

The *Journal of Careers* ran a series of pieces on new opportunities for women graduates; the January–June volume for 1928 – the year of the Equal Franchise Act – suggests metallurgy, chartered accountancy, advertising, publishing, film-making, financial consultancy, politics, journalism, and – puzzlingly – large-scale rabbit farming. Fewer marriages (after the ravages of the war) meant more potential career women, and among all the teachers, and an increasing number of welfare and social workers listed in college registers for the 1920s and 1930s, are some unorthodox occupations. Not only were bluestockings breaching the mainstream professions by becoming barristers, veterinary surgeons, insurance executives, and personal private secretaries; they were emerging – all around the world – as mining engineers, museum directors, industrial chemists, broadcasters, translators in the Foreign Office, et cetera.

One Foreign Office translator demonstrates a remarkable life lived without fanfare: she was a farmer's daughter, born in 1905, who read modern languages at Durham, then worked with the League of Nations in Geneva before becoming a secretary at the International Labour Office, also in Geneva, from 1930 to 1936; from 1936 to 1939 she was appointed French translator and Literary Secretary to the Rt Hon. David Lloyd George MP, and when the war broke out she worked for the British and American governments as a translator (French, German, and Italian) in London, Paris, New York, Brussels, and Jamaica. Her name was Erica Lea.[20] I wish I could have met her. I also rather wish I had met a certain general's daughter who studied maths at Westfield College, went on to win the *Croix de Guerre* for war work in France, and then, according to a terse college record, enjoyed 'a rather unsatisfactory period in her career during which she was wanted by the police. By now [1936] she may have made good.'[21]

All these livelihoods were patently possible, but that did not mean that women graduating in the mid-1930s had any sense that society owed them a career. The Great Depression re-inforced the pecking order, prioritizing married men. An *Evening News* journalist reported in 1936 that universities were every year turning out young women who had taken degrees 'and mastered half the "ologies"', but only the lucky few were 'able to find openings suitable to their attainments'.[22]

Academia was breeding white elephants.

When Gwendolen Freeman tried for a job with a high-profile publishing house in 1929, hoping to become a journalist, she was warned by her interviewer that to have any hope of success, she must forget Cambridge altogether. 'Blue stockings,' he scoffed, 'are not wanted here.'[23] In 1937, Joan Lovegrove of St Hilda's found her prospective employers in the Diplomatic Service depressingly preferred 'County' to 'Brainy' girls. Barbara Fletcher, who read social studies during the 1930s, found her degree useful in securing an interview, but not necessarily a job. Women were sooner considered over-qualified than men, even though they had exactly the same academic background.

Teaching, meanwhile, remained reliable. Hannah Cohen of Durham remembered how ridiculously easy it was for her to find a post. She was sitting in the college union waiting for the results of her finals one Friday in 1938 when the porter called her to the telephone. The headmaster of a local high school was on the line: he was looking for a Spanish teacher and had already spoken to Hannah's tutor, who had recommended her. Would she like the job, starting next Monday?

Hannah replied that she must ask her parents, and was shocked (but not affronted) to hear that the headmaster had already done this, and that they had agreed. 'He finished the conversation by saying, "I will send the chauffeur to meet you to take you across the ferry to Tynemouth at 8.30 a.m. on Monday morning. Goodbye, Miss Cohen. I look forward to meeting you."'[24]

As the Second World War loomed ever closer, the undergraduette enjoyed a new-found gravitas. It was clear that highly educated, well-organized women were going to be vital on the home front and in the services (particularly in administration and intelligence). And, as one mother put it as she encouraged her daughter to try for Somerville, an invading enemy might rob you of many things, but never your education.[25] Thus, ironically, dawned the golden age of the bluestocking – a period of astonishing achievement, personal heroism, and – afterwards – infuriating public pigheadedness. Its story has yet to be told.

It should be no surprise that most of the individuals featured in this book went on to be teachers. But not all of them. To give a few examples: Constance Maynard of Girton became the first Mistress of Westfield College, after helping found St Leonard's School in St Andrews. She died in 1935, aged eighty-six. The story of Bessie Callender, a pioneer of St Mary's College, Durham, is rather sad. She also went into education, but ended her days in an old people's home nearly blind, deaf, and tortured by arthritis, trying, after a busy life, 'to bear the boredom of having nothing to do'.[26]

The melodramatic and heartsick Miss Bishop of St

Hilda's had an unsettled career. She failed to get into the civil service, and so became a teacher, but later left to work in market research. She ended up a property manager in London. The novels she wrote were unpublished, and despite her yearnings at college and afterwards, she never found her life's partner.

Rebel Sarah Mason of Girton did marry, but it was an unhappy liaison. When her husband committed suicide, she was left with four children and a small allowance. She could not afford to offer a university career to any of her daughters. Rachel Footman, who nearly blew herself up in the chemistry labs, also married. She achieved her first ever paid employment at the age of fifty, when (thanks to her degree) she was appointed headmistress of a substantial girls' school in Worthing. Cynthia Stenhouse, so enthusiastic about work that she managed to get herself locked in the Pitt Rivers Museum, enjoyed several careers. None of them would have been thinkable, she says, without a degree. First she was a doctor's secretary, then an editor's assistant, a school librarian and secretary, and finally – a teacher. She also married and had an admiring family.

Trixie Pearson continued to inspire. After leaving St Hilda's, she took a teaching diploma, and earned enough (as promised) to raise her loyal family out of poverty and restore its self-respect. She married just before the war, and moved to Edinburgh, where she continued to work, coaching potential university applicants in her spare time to stretch their wings, as she had done, and fly.

Gwendolen Freeman got her job with the man who disapproved of bluestockings, and became a successful journalist, novelist, and poet. The most touching passages in her memoir, *Alma Mater* (1990), are about leaving university and coming to realize (only possible at a distance) what it really

meant to her, and how it changed her life. Those are questions I asked alumnae myself, and their answers were similarly moving. A maths and physics graduate of Liverpool
described her university career as a beacon, which lit up her
life. To Irene Peacock it was 'a wonderful treat', and to Miss
Bott, an experience of incalculable significance:

I came from a suburban non-academic background, was lucky
enough to get to a very good school, and so to Oxford. Oxford
and Greats [Classics] changed and classified my mental attitude
basically for the rest of my life, and I look back on those four years
as a major turning-point and a source of pleasure and stability
ever since.[27]

Barbara Britton appreciated the fun. Her abiding memory
was of cycling past a group of soldiers at the beginning of
the Second World War when her skirt blew up to reveal her
knickers, and the men swooning to the ground and cheering. She considered university to be 'like a game, not serious'.[28] Ruth Ridehalgh read history from 1938 to 1941, but
never counted herself a true scholar. It did not matter:

I look back on my university career with more than fondness. I
was not highly academic and made no contribution to Oxford as
some women did. I started as a shy, naive Lancashire girl. Oxford
gave me a vision, opportunities, a life I had never dreamed of, and
my gratitude is enormous.[29]

That is something so many bluestockings share: recognition
of privilege, and a deep sense of thankfulness, not just for
academic qualifications, but for minds opened, friends made,
and memories shared.

★

This book should close as it began, with the story of an ordinary young woman whose university experiences reached beyond her own life. I had never heard of Edna Green before receiving a letter from her daughter during the course of my research, but soon came to realize I may have much, personally, for which to thank her. Edna was the first in her family to be educated at university; she went to the London School of Economics in 1928, where she read geography, and then to King's College to train as a teacher.

Edna could not afford to live in college: the Depression had hit her (numerous) family hard, and although her parents supported her academic ambition, they could not afford to pay accommodation fees. So Edna stayed at home in Ashford, Middlesex, and caught the train each day to central London. After taking her teaching diploma at King's, she was offered an interview at Sleaford High School in distant Lincolnshire. This posed two problems: how to get there, and what to wear. Her father somehow found the money to risk her fare and a new suit 'to create a favourable impression', and – luckily for them both – she got the job. She stayed in Sleaford for four years, before moving back to London shortly before the war.[30]

Just starting out on her secondary-school career at Sleaford High, when Edna taught there, was a pupil called Helen Morton. Following Edna, Helen was encouraged to try for the London School of Economics, and succeeded in getting a place. Helen, in turn, encouraged her own children – two daughters – to aim high.

Helen was my mother.

Something else in Edna's story struck me as beautifully appropriate. She was apparently a very keen sportswoman at LSE, a member of both the cricket and the hockey teams. Her daughters remember her fine woollen hockey stockings with great fondness: for many years they were hung at the end of the girls' beds on Christmas Eve. When they woke in the morning the stockings were magically full of surprises, brimming with promise.

Their colour, of course, was blue.

Notes

For full details of sources quoted, please see the Select Bibliography.

INTRODUCTION

1. Rule, extant until the 1920s, from a London University hall of residence.

2. Dyhouse, *Students*, 4. See also Boyd, *St Mary's College*, 4, and Bremner, *Education of Girls*, 7.

3. Samuel Heywood, quoted in Turner, *Equality for Some*, 46.

4. I have come across another meaning of 'Bluestocking' in the course of my research. It's a cocktail, invented by the Roberts family to celebrate their daughter gaining a place at university: one tablespoon of gin, one of blue curaçao, three of clear apple juice, and a fat blue cherry.

I. INGENIOUS AND LEARNED LADIES

1. Makin, *An Essay to Revive the Antient Education*, 3.

2. Beatrix Walsh, Reminiscences (1932–6), St Hilda's College Archives. I have inferred certain characteristics of Ruth Pearson's personality and past history from her affectionate daughter's papers and from her family. See bibliography (under 'Walsh') for further details.

3. Hester Thrale (1741–1821) – at this stage still a brewer's wife – was ambivalent about what she called 'the Blues', and joined those who ridiculed them when it suited her. Later, after her marriage to the Italian musician Gabriel Piozzi in

1784, she was happy to relax into London's intellectual life.

4. *Westminster Magazine*, July 1773 (copy not seen), quoted in Myers, *The Bluestocking Circle*, 271.

5. From 'The Letters of Mrs Elizabeth Montagu', a review attributed to Sir Walter Scott in the *Quarterly Review*, October 1813, 38.

6. Wollstonecraft, *Vindication*, 296. Wollstonecraft's argument in the *Vindication* expanded a theme first published in her essay *Thoughts on the Education of Daughters* (1787), in which she argued that organized learning for girls was the only way for them to achieve rationality and mental independence.

7. Wortley Montagu, *Works*, vol. 4, 185.

8. Walter Map, *The Letter of Valerius to Ruffinus* (*c.* 1180), ch. 9, quoted in Blamires, *Woman Defamed*, 105.

9. Simon D'Ewes, quoted in Teague, *Bathsua Makin*, 31.

10. Makin, op. cit., 3, 23.

11. Ibid., 22.

12. Woolley, *Gentlewoman's Companion*, 67.

13. 'Elegy', *Letters and Poems in Honour of . . . Margaret, Dutchess of Newcastle*, 166.

14. Astell, *Serious Proposal*, part 1, 10.

15. Defoe, *An Essay Upon Projects*, 113, 114.

16. Ibid., 114.

2. WORKING IN HOPE

1. Frances Buss, quoted in Kamm, *How Different from Us*, 104.

2. Lloyd, *Memoir*, 57.

3. *The Princess* was published in 1847. Tennyson was inspired by taking part in a Mechanics' Institute (later Birkbeck College) summer outing to Maidstone, where students enjoyed

a garden fête and debated the accessibility of education to working men. Lectures at the institute were open to women at the time, too. In the poem, Tennyson's heroine dreams of an isolated, inviolable college for ladies where bluestockings like her might be immersed in the pursuit of learning. The scheme turns out to be impractical, of course: the heroine marries a prince who has managed to break in, and the college is promptly disbanded and turned into a hospital – much more useful.

4. Firth, *Constance Louisa Maynard*, 102–3.

5. Nightingale, 'Cassandra', *Suggestions for Thought*, vol. 2, 402.

6. Firth, op. cit., 43.

7. See Turner, *Equality for Some*, 58.

8. Weeton, *Journal of a Governess*, 13–14, quoted in Turner, op. cit., 68.

9. Turner, op. cit., 68.

10. Firth, op. cit., 22.

11. Marshall, *What I Remember*, 6.

12. From Helena Wells, *Letters on Subjects of Importance to the Happiness of Young Females* (1799), quoted in Broughton and Symes (eds.), *The Governess*, 63.

13. Maurice, *Queen's College*, 1, 5.

14. Cobbe, *Female Education*, 4.

15. Charlotte Yonge to Emily Davies, 'Davies Family Chronicle' (1830–1921), 622 (GCPP Davies 1), Girton College Archives.

16. Sewell, *Principles of Education*, vol. II, 219–20.

17. Martin, *Queen Victoria*, 69–70.

18. *The English Woman's Journal* was launched, with Bodichon as its editor, in 1858. In 1864, it continued as the *Alexandra Magazine*.

19. The University Extension Movement was developed in

the late 1860s as a network matching willing lecturers from the few established universities at the time with Educational Associations around the country.

20. Firth, op. cit., 55.

21. Quoted in Bradbrook, *'That Infidel Place'*, 10–11.

22. Firth, op. cit., 105–6.

23. The college was not called Girton until 1872; it moved to Girton village a year later. For a full and entertaining history, see Bradbrook, op. cit.

3. INVADING ACADEMIA

1. From the trio 'Gently Gently', Act II of Gilbert and Sullivan's *Princess Ida*, first performed in London, January 1884.

2. Sir Basil Champneys (1842–1935) was a friend of the Sidgwicks; he also designed Somerville library, and buildings at Lady Margaret Hall and Bedford College.

3. Dilys Lloyd Davies MSS (1877–8), Newnham College Archives.

4. During the 1930s, when chaperones were dispensed with, it was still customary to state on social invitations to undergraduettes the comforting assurance that 'Ladies will be Present'. The implication was that they should chaperone each other.

5. See note 3.

6. Dorothea Beale envisaged St Hilda's originally as a teacher-training college solely for Cheltenham Ladies' College students. During the early 1890s, however, too few Cheltenham Ladies applied to keep it financially viable, so admission was opened to others.

7. Jessie Emmerson's reminiscences, published in the *St Hugh's College Chronicle* (1931), St Hugh's College Archives.

8. *Schools Inquiry Commission Report* of James Bryce, Com-

missioner for Lancashire (1867–8), quoted in McWilliams-Tullberg, *Women at Cambridge*, 25.

9. *Punch*, vol. 80 (1881), 130.

10. Dyhouse, *No Distinction of Sex?*, 7.

11. The constituent colleges in the Victoria University federation gained their own charters in time: Liverpool in 1903, Leeds in 1904, and Manchester in 1935. Sheffield broke away from London in 1905 and Bristol in 1909, but Exeter, Hull, Leicester, Nottingham, and Southampton did not award their own degrees until after the Second World War.

12. The Taunton Commission was originally intended to investigate the state of elementary education for boys in England; Misses Buss, Beale, and Davies lobbied for girls' schools to be included, and gave evidence to the commissioners. One of the commission's eventual requirements was the establishment of a girls' grammar school in every town in England with a population over 4,000 people.

13. Edith Cass MSS (1909), University of Leeds Archives.

14. *The Mermaid* (the university magazine), vol. 1 (1904–5), 135, University of Birmingham Library.

15. Emmerson, op. cit.

16. Bertha Johnson, quoted in Bailey (ed.), *Lady Margaret Hall*, 48.

17. *The Macleod Family Magazine*, vol. 1, no. 11 (November 1881), typescript copy (GCRF 4/1/24) in Girton College Archives.

18. Bessie Callender's reminiscences, quoted in Bird (ed.), *Doves and Dons* (unpaginated).

19. Tylecote, *Education of Women at Manchester University*, 32; Tout, *Ashburne Hall*, 3; University of Manchester's Department of Women Archives UA/4/23 (reminiscences).

20. Constance Watson MSS (1909), Somerville College Archives.

21. Students' Record Books (1897–1918), King's College London Archives.

22. Students' Record Book, St Mary's College Archives, Durham.

23. *The Gryphon* (university magazine), vol. IX (1905–6), 12, University of Leeds Library.

24. Audrey Brodhurst MSS (1931), Somerville College Archives.

25. J. M. Upcott's reminiscences from a questionnaire to 1907–10 alumnae, Somerville College Archives.

26. See note 24.

27. Rathbone, 'The Dales', 77.

28. Sarah Mason, Diaries (1878–82), private collection; extracts also held in Girton College Archives.

29. See note 1.

30. Alfred Lord Tennyson's description of women in *The Princess*, canto VI, lines 290–91.

31. 'M.P.S.', 'The Disadvantages of Higher Education', *Girl's Own Paper*, February 1882, 333.

4. MOST ABHORRED OF ALL TYPES

1. *Yggdrasil* (magazine of Ashburne Hall, Manchester University), Christmas term, 1902.

2. Annie Rogers, secretary to the governing body for the Society of Home Students (later St Anne's), and the first Classics tutor at St Hugh's. Annie was a brilliant academic: her father – a professor at Oxford – entered her for the Local examinations in 1873, using just her initials; when the results were issued, she was top of the list, and therefore offered scholarships at both Worcester College and Balliol. There was considerable embarrassment when her gender was revealed.

3. 'A Woman's Reply', *Durham University Journal*, 10 June 1899.

4. Former Oxford High School pupil Margaret Fletcher puts it beautifully in her book, *O Call Back Yesterday* (1939): 'She must not trade with [her brains], but keep them in a napkin that she might one day hand them on unimpaired to a possible son.' Quoted in Avery, *The Best Type of Girl*, 55.

5. Maudsley, 'Sex in Mind and Education', 467, 472.

6. Quoted in Burstyn, *Victorian Education*, 94.

7. Turner, *Equality for Some*, 126.

8. Dr N. Allen, quoted in Maudsley, op. cit., 477.

9. Elizabeth Garrett Anderson, 'Sex in Mind and Education: A Reply'.

10. Ibid., 590.

11. 'The Intellectual Inferiority of Women', *Durham University Journal*, 13 May 1899.

12. Burgon, *To Educate Young Women*, 29.

13. Quoted in Mallet, *History of the University*, vol. 3, 447.

14. Frances Elizabeth Sheldon MSS (1880–83), Somerville College Archives.

15. Rachel Lily Footman, 'Memories of 1923–1926', private collection and Somerville College Archives.

16. *The Mermaid*, vol. 12 (1915–16), 132–3, University of Birmingham Library.

17. Ibid., vol. 5 (new series, 1934–5), 146.

18. Winifred Pattinson, letter dated 23 May 1897, Newnham College Archives.

19. Kathleen Courtney MSS (1897), Women's Library, London Metropolitan University.

20. Eglantyne Jebb MSS (1895–8), Lady Margaret Hall Archives.

21. Cutting, dated 5 March 1896, among a collection in the St Anne's College Archives.

22. Hobhouse, *Oxford*, 101–3.

23. *Report as to the Rules and Discipline in Force for the Women Students at the University of Oxford* (BURR 031/49; 1909), St Hilda's College Archives.

24. *The Mermaid*, vol. 2 (new series, 1931–2), University of Birmingham Library.

25. 'The New Woman', *Owen's College Union Magazine*, February 1895, 74–5.

26. *Girl's Own Paper*, September 1886, 770.

27. Maynard, *Between College Terms*, 189–90.

28. *Girl's Own Paper*, September 1886, 769–70.

29. Ibid., 770.

30. Author's collection (Addey).

31. Ibid. (Cohen).

32. Kathleen Lonsdale MSS (1914–22), University College London Archives.

33. Author's collection (Harvey).

34. Ibid. (Wood).

35. Doris Maddy is a pseudonym, as is Hermione.

36. *Daily Herald*, 21 June 1935.

5. WHAT TO DO IF YOU CATCH FIRE

1. A family anecdote related to me by Clare Passingham of Oxford.

2. Christina Roaf, 'Life Before Somerville', *Somerville College Report*, 2003–4, 88.

3. Rathbone, *'The Dales'*, 72.

4. Quoted in Shafe, *University Education in Dundee*, 15–16. William Topaz McGonagall (1825–1902), whose publisher advertised him as 'the greatest bad verse writer of his age . . . or of any age', was affectionately known as the 'Poet Laureate of the Silvery Tay'. His most famously awful poem is 'The

Tay Bridge Disaster', celebrating (if that's the right word) the tragedy in 1879 when a Scottish railway bridge collapsed, hurling train passengers into the river below. Seventy-five of them perished.

5. Lady Margaret Beaufort (1443–1509), mother of Henry VII, is honoured as the foundress of Christ's and St John's colleges in Cambridge, and Devorguilla (c. 1210–90) was the principal benefactress of her husband John de Balliol's foundation at Oxford.

6. Quoted by Pat Thane, 'Girton Graduates: Earning a Living 1920s–1980s', 350.

7. Conversations with the Macdonald family.

8. Bird (ed.), *Doves and Dons* (unpaginated), and St Mary's College Archives, Durham.

9. *Girl's Own Paper*, March 1886, 407.

10. A comment in *Yggdrasil*, Lent 1902.

11. Woolf, *A Room of One's Own*, 110–11. Woolf expanded her theme in *Three Guineas* (1938), an essay arguing for greater investment in women's education and employment in Britain.

12. Florence Rich, Reminiscences (1884), Somerville College Archives.

13. Author's collection (Edwards).

14. Kathleen Byass MSS (1917), Somerville College Archives.

15. Author's collection (Beer).

16. Ibid. (Atkinson). Margaret went to Manchester University.

17. Quoted in a University of Liverpool thesis by Lynn Patricia Edwards, *Women Students at the University of Liverpool: Their Academic Careers and Postgraduate Lives 1883–1937* (1999), 69.

18. F. M. Swann, 'Four-Score Years and More' (reminiscences), Lady Margaret Hall Archives.

19. Author's collection (Pigrome).

20. Ibid. (Fredericks). All three sisters (at the time of writing) are still alive, aged a hundred, ninety-eight, and 'the baby', ninety-six. My interviews with Grace and Julie were high points in the research for this book: it was a privilege to hear their history.

21. Author's collection (Fletcher).

22. Vice-Chancellor's Letter Book (S.2344, pp. 819–20, 29 April 1918), University of Liverpool Archives.

23. *Girl's Own Paper*, May 1893, 514.

24. Author's collection (Hanschell); see also Daphne Levens, 'Life Before Somerville', *Somerville College Report*, 2003–4, 75.

25. Epigram quoted in Rothblatt, *Tradition and Change*, 186.

26. Author's collection (Murray).

27. Ibid. (Kempner).

28. Marshall, *What I Remember*, 10.

29. Callender, *Education in the Melting Pot*, 12.

30. Ibid.

31. Author's collection (Dainton). Barbara Wright's mother, trained at the Royal College of Science in Dublin, was appointed the first married woman lecturer at the University of Liverpool. She was a physical geographer.

32. Ibid. (Morgan). Transcript of her mother's diaries generously supplied by Ceridwen Lloyd-Morgan.

33. Ibid.

34. See note 24.

35. *Yorkshire Ladies' Council on Education Reports, 1873–1920* (1874), University of Leeds Archives.

36. Author's collection (Emma Mason).

37. Elizabeth Gordon MSS (G 2; 1928–32), St Hilda's College Archives.

6. FRESHERS

1. Frances Sheldon MSS (29 January 1882), Somerville College Archives.

2. Freeman, *Alma Mater*, 2.

3. Eleanor Rideout, Reminiscences (1913–16) in *Sphinx*, vol. XLVI (June 1945), 12 (SPEC S/LF 372.5.S75), University of Liverpool Archives.

4. Elizabeth Gordon MSS (G 2; 1928–32), St Hilda's College Archives.

5. Hostel Expense Ledgers (1921), King's College London Archives.

6. St Mary's College Archives (Student Finance file, 1934), Durham.

7. Bird, *Doves and Dons* (unpaginated).

8. Freeman, op. cit., 8.

9. Ibid.

10. Author's collection (Stenhouse).

11. Reports of University Hall (1908–9) (SPRC LUP.903. UNI(PC)), University of Liverpool Archives.

12. Author's collection (Orr).

13. Lady Rolls MSS (1928–34), University of Hull Archives.

14. Author's collection (Harding).

15. Ibid.

16. Alison Graham-Campbell MSS (1929–32), Newnham College Archives.

17. Susan Hicklin MSS (1930s), Somerville College Archives.

18. *Durham University Journal*, vol. XI (18 May 1895), University of Durham Library.

19. Brittain, *Testament of Youth*, 76.

20. May Wallas MSS (27 October 1917), Newnham College Archives.

21. Brittain, *Chronicle of Youth*, 118.

22. Author's collection (Applebey).

23. *University College London Magazine*, vol. XVI (1938), 28–9, University College Library.

24. Author's collection (Levens).

25. St Hilda's College Archives; Margery Morton is a pseudonym.

26. Kathleen Courtney MSS (1897), Women's Library, London Metropolitan University.

27. Author's collection (Morgan).

28. Based on a diary in St Hilda's College Archives (PP3); Rosemary Vickers is a pseudonym.

7. WOMEN'S SPHERE

1. Eileen Hare, Reminiscences (1932–5), Ashburne Hall Archives, Manchester.

2. From the University of Nottingham *Annual Handbook* (1915), quoted in Wood, *A History of the University College Nottingham*, 163.

3. Rathbone, 'The Dales', 74–5.

4. Quoted in *The Girton Review*, May 1929 (GCCP 2/1), Girton College Archives.

5. *University Hall Fiftieth Anniversary* (1952), 47 (SPEC R/ LF379.5.U.T94), University of Liverpool Archives.

6. Ibid.

7. Anonymous, 'Memories' (1899), courtesy of Queen Mary, University of London Archives.

8. Author's collection (Stenhouse).

9. Ibid. (Beswick).

10. Kathleen Courtney MSS (1897), Women's Library, London Metropolitan University.

11. Sarah Mason, Diaries (1878–82), private collection; extracts in Girton College Archives.

12. Women's Debating Society Minutes (1879), University College London Archives.

13. Frances Elizabeth Sheldon MSS (1880–83), Somerville College Archives.

14. Author's collection (Worthing).

15. Goode MSS (1911–14), University of Leeds Archives.

16. One can probably guess that 'lekkers' are lectures and 'brekkers' is breakfast, but a 'wagger-pagger bagger'? A waste paper basket.

17. Petronella Snowball MSS (2002.0017; 1921–4), St Hilda's College Archives.

18. Rathbone, op. cit., 79.

19. Freeman, *Alma Mater*, 19.

20. *The Gryphon*, 1902–3, 53, University of Leeds Library.

21. Kathleen Hobbs, quoted in Griffin (ed.), *St Hugh's*, 107.

22. Article in *The Star*, undated cutting in a scrapbook, St Hilda's College Archives.

23. Quoted in Bird, *Doves and Dons* (unpaginated).

24. *Girl's Own Paper*, July 1882, 37.

25. *Iris* (university magazine), December 1887, University of Manchester Archives.

26. Author's collection (Wilson).

27. *The Times*, 7 December 1920.

28. For a revealing treatment of the subject of women academics in British universities, see Dyhouse, *No Distinction of Sex?*

29. From a speech by Miss Arnold, the Headmistress of Truro High School in the 1890s, quoted in Deneke, *Grace Hadow*, 17.

30. Gemma Creighton MSS (1910), Lady Margaret Hall Archives.

31. Frances Sheldon MSS (1880–83), Somerville College Archives.

32. Anonymous reminiscence (early 1920s), St Hugh's College Archives.

33. Elisabeth R. Bishop, Diaries (PP3; 1935–9), St Hilda's College Archives.

34. Mary Fisher MSS (1931–5), Somerville College Archives.

35. Jane Worthington MSS (1893), Somerville College Archives.

36. Author's collection (Beswick).

37. From a copy of the programme in the University of Birmingham Archives.

38. Author's collection (Britton).

8. BLESSED WORK

1. A tutor's advice on essay writing, from Sibyl Ruegg, 'Extracts from a Diary' (1911–12), Somerville College Archives.

2. Dorothy L. Sayers in an article, 'Women at Oxford', *Daily News*, 9 February 1927, quoted in Brabazon, *Dorothy L. Sayers*, 47.

3. Molly McNeill MSS (1916–17), St Hugh's College Archives.

4. Maude Royden (1896) in Marking (ed.), *Oxford Originals*, 14.

5. Gertrude Bell (1868–1926) went on to become a distinguished Arabist, diplomat, traveller, and writer. Agnata Ramsay (1867–1931) abandoned scholarship for marriage the year after her triumph in Classics. Philippa Fawcett (1868–1948) had an impeccable pedigree, being the daughter of the suffragette Millicent Fawcett and a Cambridge

professor, and the niece of Elizabeth Garrett Anderson. She went on to lecture in maths, and was eventually appointed principal assistant to London County Council's Director of Education. Marie Stopes (1880–1958), after her appointment as lecturer in paleobotany at Manchester, found fame – or notoriety – as the author of *Married Love* (1918).

6. Author's collection (Plant).

7. Hertha Marks writing from Cambridge to her sponsor Barbara Bodichon, in Sharp, *Hertha Ayrton*, 67.

8. Jane Worthington MSS (1893), Somerville College Archives.

9. Lettice Ilbert MSS (1894–7), Somerville College Archives.

10. Eglantyne Jebb MSS (1895–8), Lady Margaret Hall Archives.

11. Winifred Peck (1901) in Marking (ed.), op. cit., 23.

12. Author's collection (Gaskell).

13. Ibid. (Stenhouse).

14. Rachel Lily Footman, 'Memories of 1923–1926', private collection and Somerville College Archives.

15. Elisabeth R. Bishop, Diaries (PP3; 1935–9), St Hilda's College Archives.

16. Author's collection (Bray).

17. Ibid. (Morris).

18. Ibid. (Britton).

19. Evans, *Prelude and Fugue*, 69–70.

20. Griffin (ed.), *St Hugh's*, 69–70 (reminiscences of Dorothy Hammond, Ethel Wallace, Felicia Stallman, and Ina Brooksbank).

21. Florence Rich, Reminiscences (1884), Somerville College Archives.

22. Griffin (ed.), op cit., 94 (Renée Haynes).

23. Molly McNeill, op. cit.

24. Elizabeth Gibson, 'Reminiscences', *Girton Review*, May 1925, 2–11.

25. See Martha Vicinus's article 'One Life to Stand Beside Me', 616, wherein Vicinus names our friend Constance Maynard as the Principal (of Westfield College, London) who occasionally – and medicinally – sleeps with her students.

26. For an intriguing discussion of relationships in early women's colleges, see the note above.

27. Weetwood Hall Reports (1919–40), University of Leeds Archives.

28. Students' Record Books (1897–1903), King's College London Archives.

29. Taken from *Defining Gender, 1450–1910* (online publication – see Select Bibliography), sourced from St Hilda's College Archives (Student Record Books: BURR 022/1 (1898–1902) and BURR 022/2 (1902–10)).

30. Student Records (RHC/10/1; 1907–22), Royal Holloway College Archives.

31. *The Mermaid*, vol. 2 (1905–6), 115, University of Birmingham Library.

32. *Durham University Journal*, vol. XIII, no. 13 (13 May 1899), University of Durham Library.

33. Ina Brooksbank from St Hugh's notes the number of male students in a letter written at the beginning of Michaelmas Term, 1919 (St Hugh's College Archives).

34. Author's collection (name withheld).

35. *The Gryphon*, vol. XI (1907–8), 25, University of Leeds Library.

36. Firth, *Constance Louisa Maynard*, 116.

37. Freeman, *Alma Mater*, 102.

9. SPEAR FISHING AND OTHER PURSUITS

1. Joan Platt, Reminiscences (P 6; 1929–32), St Hilda's College Archives.

2. Kathleen Courtney remembers diving while at Lady Margaret Hall in the late 1890s (Courtney Reminiscences, Women's Library, London Metropolitan University); a motor-cycling demonstration was held at Girton in 1919 (Winifred Trenholme, Reminiscences, Girton College Archives).

3. Several colleges had a 'Sharp Practice' club, which held impromptu debates at which everyone, with no notice of the motion, had to speak for three minutes. The Associated Prigs were earnest Somervillians who discussed matters of mutual interest. The LSDS, run from Newnham, was set up by Alison Hingston (she of the extraordinary scrapbook – see Introduction). Every Sunday a small group of women met in a hired room in Cambridge to talk, eat a meal they took turns to cook, roll their own cigarettes, and occasionally sit up all night.

4. *Hermes*, July 1894, 20–23, Westfield College Archives.

5. *The Gryphon*, vol. XV (1911–12), 36, University of Leeds Library.

6. Ibid., vol. II (1898), 4.

7. Author's collection (Proud).

8. Marjorie Woodward, Reminiscences (1921–4), St Mary's College Archives, Durham, quoted in Boyd, *St Mary's College*, 177.

9. Quoted in Adams, *Somerville for Women*, 209–10.

10. Author's collection (Wilde).

11. Campbell Davidson, *Hints to Lady Travellers*, 38.

12. Minute Books for the Women's Union (1923, 1938), University of Manchester Archives.

13. Women's Representative Council Record Book (1930–39), University of Leeds Archives.

14. *Owen's College Union Magazine* (1898), 102.

15. *The Mermaid*, 3 (1906–7), 178, University of Birmingham Library.

16. 'The Lords of the Camus', composed by E. Wilson in 1887, 'College Songs' (GCRF 7/1/10), Girton College Archives.

17. *The Gryphon*, vol. X (1906–7), 64, University of Leeds Library.

18. Vice-Chancellor's Letter Book (S.2338, p. 684, 29 November 1912), University of Liverpool Archives; see also Marij van Helmond, *Votes for Women: The Events on Merseyside 1870–1928* (1992), University of Liverpool Archives.

19. Anonymous inter-war reminiscence (Acc 129; 1923), Brasenose College Archives.

20. Jessie Greaves, Reminiscences (1919), St Hilda's College Archives.

21. Private collection (Christine Burrows).

22. Winifred Evans, Reminiscences (GCRF 4/1/4; 1923–5), Girton College Archives.

23. Elisabeth R. Bishop, Diaries (PP3; 1936–8), St Hilda's College Archives.

24. Newman MSS (GCPP Newman; 1925), Girton College Archives.

25. Elisabeth Bishop, op. cit.

26. Mary Smith, Diary Extracts (1888–91), Newnham College Archives.

27. Freeman, *Alma Mater*, 35.

28. Leta Jones MSS (D.455/6/2, p. 5, 1929–33), courtesy of Leta Jones, University of Liverpool Archives.

29. Constance Savery MSS (1917–20), Somerville College Archives.

30. Anonymous, undated reminiscence (early 1920s), St Hilda's College Archives.

10. SHADOWS

1. Grace Hadow, Principal of the Society of Home Students, speaking to Oxford High School pupils in 1936, quoted in Deneke, *Grace Hadow*, 120.

2. Elisabeth R. Bishop, Diaries (PP3; 1936–8), St Hilda's College Archives.

3. Private Collection (Christine Burrows).

4. Bowerman Chibnall letters (1910–11), Women's Library, London Metropolitan University.

5. Mary Wallas letters (1915–20), Newnham College Archives.

6. I was surprised to find an advertisement in the *Girl's Own Paper* (dated as early as April 1902) for 'Hartmann's Hygienic Towelettes . . . Indispensable for Ladies Travelling and for Home Use'. They were available from chemists. Someone who could afford it might send her maid to purchase some; it's very difficult to imagine a student at that time marching in and buying her own. The normal equipment at the turn of the century would be a towel folded lengthwise, tied on with elaborate ribbons. A 'menstrual apron' was available from 1914: that was a pad attached to a belt with a rubber-coated flap hanging from the back of the waist. The Kotex Company offered ready-made pads, about 20 inches (50 cm) long and stuffed with wood pulp, in 1921. Tampons were not marketed until the early 1930s, and took a long time to become popular. See the website of the Museum of Menstruation (if you feel up to it), for further information.

7. Rathbone, *'The Dales'*, 74.

8. Author's collection (Wilson).

9. Ibid. (Haardt).

10. Rachel Lily Footman, 'Memories of 1923–1926', private collection and Somerville College Archives.

11. *Isis* (university magazine), 4 June 1924, 5.

12. Boyd, *St Mary's College*, 121.

13. Professor R. Case, *Against Oxford Degrees for Women* (*c.*1895), St Anne's College Archives.

14. Minute Books of the Women's Union (1910 and 1919), University of Manchester Archives.

15. St Hilda's College Archives hold scrapbooks of newspaper cuttings on the Shawcross Affair (reference: Shawcross 1).

16. From a Somerville College 'Going Down Play' (1933), quoted in Adams, *Somerville for Women*, 227–8.

17. Constance Savery MSS (1917–20), Somerville College Archives.

18. Author's collection (Proud).

19. Brittain, *Testament of Youth*, 145–6.

20. Anonymous, 'Impressions of Newnham' (1917), Newnham College Archives.

21. University settlements were based in large buildings in slum areas and designed to be a focus for voluntary social welfare work. Staff there offered advice and practical help, and ran clubs and societies. Most were founded between 1884 and 1897 in east or south London, but settlements were also established in Manchester (1895), Liverpool (1906), and Bristol (1911).

22. See Federman, *Surpassing the Love of Men*, 147.

23. Constance Louisa Maynard, unpublished autobiography (section 54, pp. 286–7), Westfield College Archives, quoted by Martha Vicinus in '"One Life to Stand Beside Me"', 616.

24. Ibid.

25. Faithfull, *In the House of My Pilgrimage*, 66.

26. Stopes, *Sex and the Young*, 44.

27. Winifred Mary Seville, Diaries (RHC/20/3; 1906–10), Royal Holloway College Archives; see also Megan Bosley, *Sexuality, Society and Style: An Analysis of the Diaries of Winifred Mary Seville* (MA thesis, Royal Holloway, 1997).

II. BREEDING WHITE ELEPHANTS

1. The caption for a photograph illustrating the article 'Should Women Go to Oxford?' by Winifred Holtby, published in the *News Chronicle*, 2 February 1934, 8.

2. Evelyn Rhoden, Diaries (1923/5), Ashburne Hall Archives.

3. Compiled by Alice Gordon in 'The After-Careers of University-Educated Women'.

4. Comment to author; see also Turner, *Equality for Some*, 208.

5. 'A Man', 'Thoughts on the Higher Education of Women', *Girl's Own Paper* (1891), quoted in Forrester, *Great-Grandma's Weekly*, 34.

6. Letter from Walter William Skeat to Henry Sidgwick (June 1887), Newnham College Archives.

7. Burgon, *To Educate Young Women*, 4.

8. Bremner, *Education of Girls*, 136.

9. Phare, 'From Devon to Cambridge, 1926', 149.

10. Author's collection (Bebb).

11. Griffin (ed.), *St Hugh's*, 115. This comment was made in the early 1930s: things had not changed much.

12. E. H. Neville, 'University of Reading', 8.

13. From scores of women in the 1880s, the numbers grew to 2,090 women at English universities in 1901 (15.1 per cent of the university population), of whom 535 were Oxbridge students (9.1 per cent). By 1938 there were 7,969 women (21.9 per cent), with 1,398 at Oxbridge (13 per cent). Source: Dyhouse, *Students*, 4.

14. Student Record Books and Registers, courtesy of Queen Mary, University of London Archives and St Mary's College Archives, Durham.

15. Morley, *Women Workers in Seven Professions*.

16. Holt, *University of Reading*, 88.

17. Woolf, *A Room of One's Own*, 111.

18. Boyd, *St Mary's College*, 196.

19. M. Miller, 'Women in the World of Commerce', *Incorporated Secretaries' Journal*, June 1927.

20. Student Record Book, St Mary's College Archives, Durham.

21. Register of Students, vol. 2, courtesy of Queen Mary, University of London Archives.

22. *Evening News*, 19 March 1936, quoted in Dyhouse, op. cit., 88.

23. Freeman, *Alma Mater*, 95.

24. Author's collection (Cohen).

25. Author's conversation with Rosalyn Page.

26. Bessie Callender MSS (1899–1901), St Mary's College Archives.

27. Reminiscences (1934), St Hugh's College Archives.

28. Author's collection (Britton).

29. Ibid. (Ridehalgh).

30. Ibid. (Willatts).

Select Bibliography

Adams, Pauline. *Somerville for Women: An Oxford College 1879–1993* (Oxford: Oxford University Press, 1996)

Anderson, Elizabeth Garrett. 'Sex in Mind and Education: A Reply', *Fortnightly Review*, vol. 15 (January–June 1874), 582–96.

Astell, Mary. *A Serious Proposal to the Ladies* (1694/7), ed. Patricia Springborg (London: Pickering and Chatto, 1997)

Avery, Gillian. *The Best Type of Girl: A History of Girls' Independent Schools* (London: André Deutsch, 1991)

Bailey, Gemma (ed.). *Lady Margaret Hall: A Short History* (Oxford: Oxford University Press, 1923)

Balsdon, D. *Oxford Life* (London: Eyre and Spottiswoode, 1957)

——*Oxford Now and Then* (London: Duckworth, 1970)

Bates, James, and Ibbetson, Carol. *The World of University College London Union* (London: UCL Union, 1994)

Beale, Dorothea. *Address to Parents* (London: G. Bell, 1888)

Bettenson, E. M. *The University of Newcastle-upon-Tyne: A Historical Introduction 1834–1971* (Newcastle: Newcastle University, 1971)

Bird, Marilyn (ed.). *Doves and Dons: A History of St Mary's College 1899–1920* (Durham: St Mary's College, 1982)

Blake, Catriona. *The Charge of the Parasols: Women's Entry to the Medical Profession* (London: Women's Press, 1990)

Blamires, Alcuin (ed.). *Woman Defamed and Woman Defended:*

An Anthology of Medieval Texts (Oxford: Oxford University Press, 1992)

Boyd, Elizabeth. *St Mary's College University of Durham 1899–1999: A Centenary Review* (Durham: St Mary's College, 1999)

Brabazon, James. *Dorothy L. Sayers: The Life of a Courageous Woman* (London: Gollancz, 1981)

Bradbrook, M. C. *'That Infidel Place': A Short History of Girton College 1869–1969* (Cambridge: Girton College, 1969)

Bremner, C. *Education of Girls and Women* (London: Swan Sonnenschein, 1897)

Brittain, Vera. *Chronicle of Youth: Vera Brittain's War Diary 1913–1917*, ed. Alan Bishop (London: Gollancz, 1981)

—— *Testament of Youth* (London: Gollancz, 1933)

—— *The Women at Oxford: A Fragment of History* (London: Harrap, 1960)

Broughton, Trevor, and Symes, Ruth (eds.). *The Governess: An Anthology* (Stroud: Sutton, 1997)

Burgon, Dean John. *To Educate Young Women like Young Men, and with Young Men, – a Thing Inexpedient and Immodest* (Oxford: Parker, 1884)

Burke, Barbara (Oona Ball). *Barbara Goes to Oxford* (London: Methuen, 1907)

Burns, C. Delisle. *A Short History of Birkbeck College* (London: University of London Press, 1924)

Burstall, F. W., and Burton, C. G. *Souvenir History of the Foundation and Development of the Mason Science College and of the University of Birmingham 1880–1930* (Birmingham: University of Birmingham Press, 1930)

Burstyn, Joan N. *Victorian Education and the Ideal of Womanhood* (London: Croom Helm, 1980)

Butcher, E. E. *Clifton Hill House [Bristol]: The First Phase 1909–1959* (no imprint, n.d.)

Callender, Bessie. *Education in the Melting Pot* (Norwich: Crowe, 1971)

Campbell Davidson, Lillias. *Hints to Lady Travellers at Home and Abroad* (London: Iliffe, 1889)

Chapman, Arthur. *The Story of a Modern University: A History of the University of Sheffield* (Sheffield: for the University of Sheffield by Oxford University Press, 1955)

Chorley, K. *Manchester Made Them* (London: Faber and Faber, 1950)

Clapp, B. W. *The University of Exeter: A History* (Exeter: University of Exeter Press, 1982)

Clarke, Edward H. *Sex in Education; or, A Fair Chance for Girls* (Boston: James Osgood, 1875)

Climenson, Emily J. *Elizabeth Montagu, the Queen of the Bluestockings* (London: John Murray, 1906)

Clough, Anne. *Ladies Wore Hats: A History of the University of Liverpool Women's Club* (Liverpool: Liverpool University Press, 2001)

Clough, Anne Jemima. *Women's Progress in Scholarship* (1890), reprinted in Spender, *The Education Papers*

Cobbe, Frances. *Female Education and how it would be affected by University Examinations* (London: Emily Faithfull, 1862)

Courtney, Janet E. *Recollected in Tranquillity* (London: Heinemann, 1926)

Davies, Emily. *The Higher Education of Women* (London: Strahan, 1878)

——*Women in the Universities of England and Scotland* (Cambridge: Macmillan and Bowes, 1896)

Defining Gender, 1450–1910: Five Centuries of Advice Literature for Men and Women (online publication), www.adammatthew-publications.co.uk/online/Defining-Gender

Defoe, Daniel. *An Essay Upon Projects* (1697), ed. Joyce

D. Kennedy, Michael Seidel and Maximillian E. Novak (New York: AMS Press, 1999)

Delamont, Sara. *The Nineteenth Century Woman* (London: Crom Helm, 1978)

Deneke, Helena. *Grace Hadow* (London: Oxford University Press, 1946)

Dyhouse, Carol. *Feminism and the Family in England 1880–1939* (Oxford: Blackwell, 1989)

——*Girls Growing Up in Late Victorian and Edwardian England* (London: Routledge and Kegan Paul, 1981)

——*No Distinction of Sex? Women in British Universities 1870–1939* (London: UCL Press, 1995)

——*Students: A Gendered History* (London: Routledge, 2006)

Edwardes, Mrs Anne. *A Girton Girl* (London: Bentley, 1885)

Evangelisti, Silvia. *Nuns: A History of Convent Life* (Oxford: Oxford University Press, 2007)

Evans, Joan. *Prelude and Fugue* (London: Museum Press, 1964)

Faithfull, Lilian M. *In the House of My Pilgrimage* (about the Cheltenham Ladies' College) (London: Chatto and Windus, 1924)

Federman, Lillian. *Surpassing the Love of Men: Romantic Frendship and Love Between Women from the Renaissance to the Present* (New York: Morrow, 1981)

Firth, C. B. *Constance Louisa Maynard, Mistress of Westfield College: A Family Portrait* (London: George Allen and Unwin, 1949)

Fitch, J. G. 'Women and the Universities', *Contemporary Review*, vol. 58 (1890), 240–55

Forrester, Wendy. *Great-Grandma's Weekly: A Celebration of the Girl's Own Paper 1880–1901* (Guildford: Lutterworth, 1980)

Freeman, Gwendolen. *Alma Mater: Memoirs of Girton College 1926–1929* (Cambridge: Girton College, 1990)

Gardner, Alice. *A Short History of Newnham College* (Cambridge: Bowes and Bowes, 1921)

Glenday, N., and Price, M. *Reluctant Revolutionaries: A Century of Headmistresses 1874–1974* (London: Pitman, 1974)

Goodbody, Margaret. *Five Daughters in Search of Learning: The Sturge Family 1820–1944* (about Bristol University) (Bristol: Goodbody, 1986)

Gordon, Alice M. 'The After-Careers of University-Educated Women', *Nineteenth Century*, vol. 37 (1895), 955–60

Griffin, Penny (ed.). *St Hugh's: One Hundred Years of Women's Education in Oxford* (London: Macmillan, 1986)

Griffiths, Sheila (ed.). *Yggdrasil: Anthology 1899–1909* (Manchester: Ashburne Hall, 1999)

Grimke, Sarah. *Letters on the Equality of the Sexes and Other Essays*, ed. Elizabeth Ann Bartlett (New Haven: Yale University Press, 1988)

Hale Bellot, H. *University College London, 1826–1926* (London: University of London Press, 1929)

Harrison, Jane Ellen. *Reminiscences of a Student's Life* (about Newnham College) (London: Hogarth Press, 1925)

Harte, Negley, and North, John. *The World of University College London* (London: UCL Press, 1991)

Hearnshaw, F. J. C. *Centenary History of King's College London, 1828–1928* (London: Harrap, 1929)

Hirsch, Pam. *Barbara Leigh Smith Bodichon 1827–1891: Feminist Artist and Rebel* (London: Chatto and Windus, 1998)

Hobhouse, Christopher. *Oxford*, 3rd edn (London: Batsford, 1945)

Holt, J. C. *The University of Reading: The First Fifty Years* (Reading: Reading University Press, 1977)

Holtby, Winifred. 'Should Women Go to Oxford?', *News Chronicle*, 2 February 1934

Hughes, Kathryn. *The Victorian Governess* (London: Hambledon, 2001)

Hunt, Felicity (ed.). *Lessons for Life: The Schooling of Girls and Women 1850–1950* (Oxford: Blackwell, 1987)

——and Barker, Carol. *Women at Cambridge: A Brief History* (Cambridge: Cambridge University Press, 1998)

Ives, Eric. *The First Civic University: Birmingham 1880–1980* (Birmingham: University of Birmingham Press, 2000)

Jameson, Storm. *Journey from the North* (autobiographical, including her time at Leeds University) (London: Collins, 1969)

Jeffreys, Sheila. *The Spinster and Her Enemies: Feminism and Sexuality 1880–1930* (London: Pandora, 1985)

Jones, Leta. *Coward's Custard* (London: Minerva, 1998)

Jordan, Jane. *Josephine Butler* (London: John Murray, 2001)

Kamm, Josephine. *Hope Deferred: Girls' Education in English History* (London: Methuen, 1965)

——*How Different from Us: A Biography of Miss Buss and Miss Beale* (London: Bodley Head, 1958)

Keene, Anne. 'Mothers of the House' (about principals of women's colleges), in *Oxford Today*, Hilary Term (January–March) 2003

Kelly, Thomas. *For Advancement of Learning: The University of Liverpool 1881–1981* (Liverpool: Liverpool University Press, 1981).

Lacey, Candida Ann (ed.). *Barbara Leigh Smith Bodichon and the Langham Place Group* (New York: Routledge and Kegan Paul, 1987)

'Lady Undergraduate'. 'A Day of Her Life at Oxford', *Murray's Magazine*, vol. 3 (May 1888)

Lawson, John, and Silver, Harold. *A Social History of Education in England* (London: Methuen, 1973)

Lehmann, Rosamund. *Dusty Answer* (London: Chatto and Windus, 1927)

Leonardi, S. *Dangerous by Degrees: Women at Oxford* (New Brunswick: Rutgers University Press, 1989)

Letters and Poems in Honour of . . . Margaret, Dutchess of Newcastle (London: Newcombe, 1676)

Levine, Philippa. *Feminist Lives in England: Private Roles and Public Commitment* (Oxford: Blackwell, 1990)

Lloyd, Anna. *A Memoir 1837–1925* (about Girton College) (London: Cayme Press, 1928)

Macaulay, Catherine. *Letters on Education* (London: Dilly, 1790)

Makin, Bathsua. *An Essay to Revive the Antient Education of Gentlewomen* (London: J. D., 1673)

Mallet, C. E. *A History of the University of Oxford,* 3 vols. (London: Methuen, 1924–7)

Marking, Stacey (ed.). *Oxford Originals: An Anthology of Writing from Lady Margaret Hall 1879–2001* (Oxford: Lady Margaret Hall, 2001)

Marshall, Mary Paley. *What I Remember* (Cambridge: Cambridge University Press, 1947)

Martin, Sir Theodore. *Queen Victoria As I Knew Her* (Edinburgh: Blackwood, 1901)

Mathers, Helen. *Steel City Scholars: A Centenary History of the University of Sheffield* (London: James and James, 2005)

Maudsley, Henry. 'Sex in Mind and Education', *Fortnightly Review*, vol. 15 (January–June 1874), 466–83

Maurice, F. D. *Queen's College, London* (London: John W. Parker, 1850)

Maynard, Constance Louisa. *Between College Terms* (autobiography) (London: Nisbet, 1910)

McWilliams-Tullberg, Rita. *Women at Cambridge: A Men's University – Though of a Mixed Type* (London: Gollancz, 1975)

Mill, John Stuart. *The Subjection of Women* (London: Longmans, Green et al., 1869)

More, Hannah. *Strictures on the Modern System of Female Education* (London: Cadell, 1799)

Morley, Edith. *Women Workers in Seven Professions* (London: Routledge, 1915)

Mountfield, Anne. *Women and Education* (Hove: Wayland, 1990)

Myers, Sylvia Harcstark. *The Bluestocking Circle* (Oxford: Clarendon Press, 1990)

Nethercott, Arthur. *The First Five Lives of Annie Besant* (London: Rupert Hart-Davis, 1961)

Neville, E. H. 'University of Reading', *Universities Review*, vol. 6(i) (1933), 5–8

'News and Views about Opportunities for Women', *Journal of Careers*, January 1928, 35

Nicholson, Virginia. *Singled Out: How Two Million Women Survived without Men After the First World War* (London: Viking, 2007)

Nightingale, Florence. *Suggestions for Thought to Searchers After Religious Truth*, 2 vols. (London: Eyre and Spottiswoode, 1860)

Oakley, Hilda. *My Adventure in Education* (London: Williams and Norgate, 1939)

Openshaw, Joyce. *All Change* (about St Anne's College) (privately printed, 2001)

Pascoe, Charles Eyre. *Schools for Girls and Colleges for Women: A Handbook of Middle Class Female Education* (London: Hardwicke and Bogue, 1879)

Pennington, Rev. Montagu. *Memoirs of the Life of Mrs Elizabeth Carter*, 2 vols. (London: F. C. & J. Rivington, 1807)

Peril, Lynn. *College Girls: Bluestockings, Sex-Kittens and Co-Eds Then and Now* (New York: Norton, 2006)

Phare, Elsie Elizabeth. 'From Devon to Cambridge, 1926: or, Mentioned with Derision', *Cambridge Review*, 26 February 1982, 144–50

Phillips, Ann (ed.). *A Newnham Anthology* (Cambridge: Cambridge University Press, 1979)

Phillips, M., and Tomkinson, W. S. *Englishwomen in Life and Letters* (Oxford: Oxford University Press, 1927)

Proctor, Mortimer R. *The English University Novel* (Berkeley: University of California Press, 1957)

Pym, Barbara. *A Very Private Eye* (about her time at Oxford University), ed. Hazel Holt and Hilary Pym (London: Macmillan, 1984)

Rathbone, Katie. *'The Dales': Growing Up in a Victorian Family* (Newnham College), ed. Bob and Harlan Walker (Birmingham: Northstep, 1989)

Rayner, Margaret. *The Centenary History of St Hilda's College, Oxford* (Oxford: St Hilda's College, 1993)

Reeves, Marjorie. *St Anne's College Oxford: An Informal History 1879–1979* (Oxford: St Anne's College, 1979)

Rogers, Annie M. A. H. *Degrees by Degrees* (Oxford: Oxford University Press, 1938)

Rothblatt, Sheldon. *Tradition and Change in English Liberal Education* (London: Faber and Faber, 1976)

Sanderson, Michael (ed.). *The Universities in the Nineteenth Century* (London: Routledge and Kegan Paul, 1975)

Sayers, Dorothy L. *Gaudy Night* (London: Gollancz, 1935)

Schneir, Miriam (ed.). *Vintage Book of Historical Feminism* (London: Vintage, 1996)

Sewell, Elizabeth Missing. *Principles of Education, Drawn from Nature and Revelation, and Applied to Female Education in the Upper Classes*, 2 vols. (London: Longmans, Green et al., 1865)

Shafe, Michael. *University Education in Dundee 1881–1981* (Dundee: Dundee University Press, 1982)

Sharp, Evelyn. *Hertha Ayrton 1854–1923: A Memoir* (about Cambridge) (London: Arnold, 1926)

Sherborne, J. W. *University College, Bristol, 1876–1909* (Bristol: Bristol Branch of the Historical Association, 1977)

Sidgwick, Mrs H. *Health Statistics of Women Students* (Cambridge: Cambridge University Press, 1890)

——*The Place of University Education in the Life of Women* (London: Women's Institute, 1897)

Silver, Harold, and Teague, S. John. *The History of British Universities 1806–1969: A Bibliography* (London: Society for Research into Higher Education, 1970)

Smith, Dr Sidney, and Bott, Michael. *100 Years of University Education in Reading* (Reading: University of Reading, 1992)

Spender, Dale (ed.). *The Education Papers: Women's Quest for Equality in Britain 1850–1912* (London: Routledge and Kegan Paul, 1987)

Stopes, Marie. *Sex and the Young* (London: Gill, 1926)

Strachey, Ray. *Careers and Openings for Women: A Study of Women's Employment and a Guide for Those Seeking Work* (London: Faber and Faber, 1935)

———*The Cause: A Short History of the Women's Movement in Great Britain* (Bath: Chivers, 1928)

Taylor, David. *The Godless Students of Gower Street* (London: UCL Union, 1968)

Teague, Frances. *Bathsua Makin, Woman of Learning* (Lewisburg: Bucknell University Press, 1998)

Thane, Pat. 'Girton Graduates: Earning a Living 1920s–1980s', *Women's History Review*, vol. 13 (2004), 347–50

Thomas, D. J. *Universities* (London: Batsford, 1973)

Tout, Mary. *Ashburne Hall: The First Fifty Years 1899–1949* (Manchester: Cloister Press, n.d.)

Turner, Barry. *Equality for Some: The Story of Girls' Education* (London: Ward Lock, 1974)

Tylecote, Mabel. *The Education of Women at Manchester University 1883–1933* (Manchester: Manchester University Press, 1941)

Van Schurman, Anna Maria. *Whether a Christian Woman Should be Educated*, ed. Joyce Irwin (Chicago: University of Chicago Press, 1998)

Vicinus, Martha. '"One Life to Stand Beside Me": Emotional Conflicts in First-Generation College Women in England', *Feminist Studies*, vol. 8, no. 3 (autumn 1982), 603–28

———*Independent Women: Work and Community for Single Women, 1850–1920* (London: Virago, 1985)

———*Intimate Friends: Women Who Loved Women 1778–1928* (Chicago: University of Chicago Press, 2004)

Vickery, Margaret Birney. *Buildings for Bluestockings: The Architecture and Social History of Women's Colleges in Late Victorian England* (Newark: University of Delaware Press, 1999)

Wallas, Ada. *Before the Bluestockings* (London: George Allen and Unwin, 1929)

Walsh, Beatrix (*née* Pearson). 'In Praise of Colleges', *Oxford Magazine*, vol. 119 (Trinity 1995), 6–7, 12

——'Women at Oxford, Now and Then', *Oxford Magazine*, vol. 98 (Michaelmas 1993), 7–14

Weeton, Ellen. *Miss Weeton: Journal of a Governess 1807–1811*, ed. Edward Hall (London: Oxford University Press, 1936)

Whiting, C. E. *The University of Durham 1832–1932* (London: Sheldon, 1932)

Within Sound of Great Tom (about Oxford; author unknown) (Oxford: Blackwell, 1897)

Wollstonecraft, Mary. *Vindication of the Rights of Woman* (1792) (London: Penguin, 1985)

Wood, A. C. *A History of the University College Nottingham 1881–1948* (Oxford: Blackwell, 1953)

Woolf, Virginia. *A Room of One's Own* (1929) (London: Penguin, 1945)

Woolley, Hannah. *The Gentlewoman's Companion* (1675) (Totnes: Prospect, 2001)

Wordsworth, Elizabeth. *Glimpses of the Past* (London: Mowbray, 1913)

Wortley Montagu, Mary. *The Works of the Right Honourable Lady Mary Wortley Montagu. Including Her Correspondence, Poems, and Essays*, 5 vols. (London: Phillips, 1803)

Index

Please note that page numbers in *italics* refer to illustrations in the text.